Three Wishes

Three Wishes

A True Story of Good Friends, Crushing Heartbreak, and Astonishing Luck on Our Way to Love and Motherhood

Carey Goldberg
Beth Jones
Pamela Ferdinand

LITTLE, BROWN AND COMPANY
NEW YORK • BOSTON • LONDON

Little, Brown and Company
Hachette Book Group
237 Park Avenue, New York, NY 10017
www.hachettebookgroup.com

First Edition: April 2010

The names and identifying characteristics of some individuals in this book have been changed.

Library of Congress Cataloging-in-Publication Data
Goldberg, Carey.
Three wishes : a true story of good friends, crushing heartbreak, and astonishing luck on our way to love and motherhood / Carey Goldberg, Beth Jones, Pamela Ferdinand.
p. cm.
ISBN 978-0-316-07906-8
1. Women—United States—Biography. 2. Goldberg, Carey. 3. Jones, Beth. 4. Ferdinand, Pamela. 5. Female friendship. 6. Self-realization in women. 7. Man-woman relationships. I. Jones, Beth. II. Ferdinand, Pamela. III. Title.
CT3260.G65 2010
920.720973—dc22 2009044730

10 9 8 7 6 5 4 3 2 1

RRD-IN

Printed in the United States of America

For our families

Contents

Three Wishes

The Decision

Carey: "Granted, six feet five is a little extreme."

Beth: "A blond southerner who likes terriers and Fontina cheese isn't what I was looking for either. But I trusted you."

Pam: "I trusted you, too. And that made my decision easier."

Carey

HELLO?"

The phone rang just as I happily settled into bed with a thick novel and a box of cereal. Once I freed myself from a day's deadline pressure, nothing restored me better than eating while I read, or reading while I ate. But the airy bedroom of my Cambridge town house was no real refuge. The *New York Times* copy desk could still call with urgent questions about an article I had written for the next day's paper, and I had to be available, always.

"Hello?" I said again. No answer. "Hello?"

Still no reply. Pressing the receiver harder against my ear, I made out the muffled voice of my boyfriend, a cosmopolitan scientist I'd been seeing for nearly a year.

It had been on and off, with a start so strong that I swore we were in love by the third date, then a crash followed by a long limping. I was usually rational to a fault, but with him I couldn't seem to let go.

It slowly dawned on me that I was listening to a conversation between my boyfriend and a female friend of his, a doctor I'd met and liked. I deduced that he must have accidentally pressed the Send button on his cell phone, and that it repeated the last number he called: mine.

"So what's up with you romantically?" I heard the doctor say.

"Oh," he said, "I'm back with Carey, and it's certainly not issue-free."

"Why don't you see other women, then?" she asked.

"I don't want to hurt Carey...I really don't want to hurt her."

"Well, what do you think you're looking for?"

"First of all," he said, "it would have to be somebody who really attracted me."

I felt my body start to shake, as it registered the depth of the rejection before my mind could absorb it. I would like to note here, in my own defense, that I am in fact generally considered attractive, and have occasionally even been called beautiful, but I am by no means to everyone's taste. I am tall and cello-shaped, with high cheekbones, a broad, even smile, and thick dark curls or frizz, depending on the weather. (He ended up marrying a buxom redhead so petite she could wear girls'-department clothes.)

I paged him—his cell phone was busy, obviously—and broke up with him, my limbs shivering so hard that it was difficult to talk.

★ ★ ★

There are more where that came from. Rejections of me. Rejections by me. All leading to the moment when, the night before I turned thirty-nine, on assignment in a remote town in northern Maine, I lay alone in an anonymous motel room bed, staring at the ceiling, and faced the biggest decision of my life.

It was biological midnight, at least as I had defined it for myself. I was a professional success, Boston bureau chief of the *New York Times,* and a romantic failure, dating doggedly into middle age and still incurably single. Now, my self-imposed deadline had struck. If I really wanted to have a baby before it was too late, I would have to do it on my own. It was time to give up on romantic love, and try to become a single mother.

It was a bad, but not all-bad, moment. What had seemed like such a depressing thought, such a failure, for so many years, suddenly started to seem like something that was hearteningly doable, unlike the endless frustrations of trying to make love work. It was a decoupling of the desire for a man and the desire for children, and it carried sudden, surprising relief.

It was also sad, sad, sad to plan to become a single mother. It was standing against the wall at the biggest dance of all. I had not been chosen. I was not desired. Not loved.

For nearly seven years, I lived out my long-standing dream of working as a Moscow correspondent, reporting mainly for the *Los Angeles Times* right through the climactic years when the Soviet Union was collapsing. I could have stayed longer, but when I was thirty-four I came home to work for the *New York Times* with the very explicit idea of Getting a Life.

I was aware of having an agenda, painfully aware. I knew that some of my failed relationships, if given more time and less pressure, might have turned into love. But there was no time. No time. I had always been a goal-getter. But now, having the goal got in the way of achieving it. I analyzed the problem to death. "What I want most in life now is to fall in love, marry, and have a family, but that is not the sort of thing you can make happen," I lamented to my best friend, Liz. "You can't go to school for it. You can't get on a waiting list for it. You can't directly apply. You can try to prepare for it, but what else?"

Time ran out before I could find an answer.

My own parents were separated before I was born. Their split was so rancorous that, family lore has it, my mother didn't want to allow my biological father into the hospital to meet me when I was born. He was a successful physician, professor, and author. He also had a violent temper, a two-pack-a-day habit, and the kind of superiority complex that led him to conclude, from personal experience, "Remember, Carey, a man never hits a woman unless she makes him feel totally powerless."

My mother, a supremely warm and hilarious woman, moved back into her parents' house and raised my brother and me on her own until I was two. Then, to our great good fortune, she married Charlie Ritz, the loving, wise, patient man who would become my stepfather—but who was really my dad, my father in every sense of the word except genetics. He always said that he could not possibly have loved us more if we had been his own biological children. When a car accident left my mother in a permanent coma in her midfifties, my dad spent hours with her shell of a body virtually every day for nearly two years, gently watching over her as the hope that she could recover slowly faded. He held her hand as she breathed her last breath. To this day, he wears his wedding ring.

Perhaps I would have my mother's luck in late-found love. At least I could think about having a child on my own as skipping the ugly divorce.

Two days after my birthday, I told my dad that I had decided to become a single mother.

"No matter what you do, I'll support you," he said firmly, sad-eyed. "I'm sure you'll make a great mother."

I could see the crumbling of a vision he'd had for me. On the other hand, I thought, my mother met him when she had a one-year-old and a two-year-old, so he couldn't think this was truly the end of all hope for love, could he?

I went to see the gynecologist at a women's clinic, the kind of inclusive, groovy place that would be accustomed to helping lesbian couples and single women get pregnant. We sat face to face in a tiny exam room. I wondered if he was single.

"Fertility varies tremendously from woman to woman," he said, "so the consequences of waiting longer in hopes of meeting the right man are hard to predict." But he had evolved a rule of thumb for cases like mine, he said: "If you think you could well end up heartbroken because you let your chance to have a child go by, you should do it now."

I went to see a wise older therapist who specialized in fertility issues, a fragile-looking woman revered by her clients. Another office the size of a walk-in closet.

"It's the morality of it that's troubling me," I said. "How can I knowingly bring a child into a situation that is less than optimal from the very get-go?"

"Well," she said, "what do you think a child needs?"

I had never tried to come up with a list.

"Love," I said. "A safe and stimulating environment. A circle of people who care, who can help her reach her potential, that kind of thing."

She was silent, smiling slightly, letting what I had just said sink in. Then she asked me, "Can you provide that?"

My mother, who would have been an ideal grandmother, all twinkle and fun and unconditional acceptance, was dead. But I had my dad, living just a few blocks away in Cambridge. He was in his midseventies, but still healthy, and would make a world-class grandfather. My brother and sister and best friend, Liz, lived in distant cities, but I had some close friends in Boston, a few dating back to my teen years. I had the money to hire excellent childcare, thanks to my late mother, my savings from Moscow, and the stock market. My job was demanding, but I was reaching the end of my stint as Boston bureau chief and was ready to ratchet down my career for the sake of a child. I had been blessed with a certain serenity all my life, and I thought it would morph easily into maternal stability.

"Yes," I finally said. "I can offer all of that."

I went to grill Sally, a single-mother friend with southern verve and inner strength, as she supervised her two-year-old son on a snowy playground.

"Carey, it's the best thing I ever did," she said.

As we pulled her blond son on a sled over the fast-melting snow, his cherub-cheeked face, rosy in the cold, shone with ecstasy.

I started to think about donors. I made lists of male friends and considered their pros and cons. I started dropping into conversations my plan to become a single mother, just to see if anybody nibbled.

A married couple with one beloved child offered the husband's sperm.

"As far as I can tell," he said, "having children is the highest thing we do."

The wife said that the child could be part of their extended family. But friends with children warned me that things could get terribly complicated that way.

Sperm banks started looking better and better.

"Would you like to be my labor coach?" I asked my sister, Morgan, on the phone one day.

She got a little choked up. "If we were normal, you would be asking me to be in your bridal party," she said. "But since we're abnormal, this is a great honor."

For something that was supposed to be somewhat secret, my baby plan was leaking out all over the place, and I was the main culprit. I told two older mothers at the *Times,* and they encouraged me but warned about the extent of the changes in store for me. One advised me to realize that children would be the front thing in my head for the next few years. Another said, approvingly, "Give yourself some joy!" and advised me to get on the stick about blood tests to check my hormone levels. I did not tell any of my editors. Bosses want your labor, and not the kind that ends in delivery.

I decided to slow down. Sally helped convince me that this was not a process to rush. I had to feel my way through each step, let each decision settle and make sure it still seemed right.

I also kept my profile active on Matchmaker.com, out of habit or momentum or the last vestiges of hope. I wrote a little note in my journal: "If you are a future child of mine reading this, I just want you to know that I really, really tried, in the weeks and months and years leading up to making you fatherless, to find you a dad."

I was doing a lot of online searching—sperm donors and potential dates and fertility information. I gave thanks to the inventors of all the technology that brought some of the deepest human needs right to my desktop.

"So what about this guy?" I asked Liz during one of a great

many phone calls so tedious that only a true best friend would ever tolerate them. "He's got an MD from Harvard, blond hair, blue eyes, he's five ten and one hundred sixty-five pounds, and he's interested in classical music and social events."

"Wait," she said. "Is this a potential donor or a potential date?"

"He's a donor, but there's even less information about him than you'd get on a dating website. How can stats this dry help you make the juiciest of human decisions? At least with online dating, you can quickly meet the guy for coffee and then go with your gut. With these sperm banks, all those mechanisms for mate selection that we evolved over millions of years have been disabled!"

She paused for thought. "You need to prioritize, given the little information you've got. What are you looking for most?"

"Good health, but I guess they all have that or they would have been screened out. And after that, let's face it, of things that a person can inherit—which seems to leave out character and virtue and the like—what I value most is intelligence."

"So do they give you IQs?"

"A few do, but most don't, not even the longer profiles I've ordered for extra money. They usually won't even tell you what college the guys are at. A few have SAT scores, or occupation, and years of education. But you're totally in the dark about what the person is really like. It makes a one-night stand with some guy you meet in a bar seem like lifelong intimacy by comparison..."

Liz was still single, too, despite her stunning Nordic beauty. She and I differed over one central value: if we couldn't have everything, I chose children over a man; she chose a man over children.

"What I don't want," she told me, "is for you to give up

your dream of having the supportive partner you want to make the family you want complete. You are a beautiful, loving, brilliant, warm, creative woman. And you are very open to people. I think it's just a question of timing. Your decision to seek a sperm donor doesn't doom your dream. I can understand your feeling of sadness, but I hope and believe that you won't let it keep you from seeking the partner you want."

After weeks of dithering, I settled on Donor 8282 of California Cryobank, the nation's largest sperm bank. His SAT scores were better than mine. He had six siblings and wanted to be a scientist who also wrote popular books. I was planning to become a science writer. If we ever met, I thought, what a nice conversation we might have.

California Cryobank provided the next best thing, an audio interview. In a deep voice that sounded intelligent and somehow clean-cut in a southern way, he said: "Hello. My donor number is 8282. I am six feet, five inches tall, and two hundred forty-five pounds. I have a medium build, my hair color is blond, and my eyes are blue. My skin color is fair, and I tan lightly. My mother's country of origin is Switzerland, and my father's country of origin is Belgium. My racial color code as established by California Cryobank is white."

The young woman interviewing him asked why he chose to study evolution, and he said, sounding confident and a touch professorial even as he hesitated, "Well, for me, evolution is... um... is a very basic sort of force that has shaped all of us, and I think understanding that is basic to understanding ourselves."

I ordered eight of his vials at $175 each, then bit my nails, hoping no one else would snatch them first.

The vials arrived from California Cryobank in late March, and went into the freezer at the touchy-feely clinic. The means to motherhood were in my hands—or under my name in a freezer, anyway. It was mine to make happen. But still I hesitated.

"So, Liz," I said, on perhaps our fiftieth phone call on the topic. "Listen to this e-mail from a Matchmaker.com guy.

"'Hi, Carey, I liked your essay answers, so I'm writing you. I would even venture to guess that we might have some overlap in our outlooks and sensibilities. For instance, I've loved reading Russian authors since I was a teenager. I don't know Platonov, but I find Mandelstam's poetry deeply moving. Doesn't it make you sad, though, to dwell on the desolation of that era in Russian history? Well, what do I know? I've never even been to Russia, much less worked there as a reporter. I do have a degree in anthropology, and I've published some travel writing, but Southeast Asia is more my area,' et cetera, et cetera, et cetera.... 'How about you, which reporters/writers do you admire? Take care—Sprax.'"

There was a long phone silence as she digested. She tended to temper my spurts of enthusiasm, bringing me back to my usual caution. "Sprax? What kind of name is that?"

"No idea. But he sounds an awful lot better than the usual 'Do you like to snowboard?' guys. And one thing's for sure. I'll never know how one of these donors feels about Mandelstam."

"Well, clearly it's a date and not a donor, right?"

"Yep, I'm meeting him tonight," I said, checking my makeup in the mirror for sufficient subtlety. "And the donor thing is over for now. The 8282 vials arrived today."

On our first date, Sprax and I sat next to each other in a downtown Boston auditorium, listening to a mountain climber describe his feats in Greenland, and I looked down and noticed how huge his knee was compared to mine.

He was wearing bulky army pants, but it was still clear that the knee was such a robust ball of strapping muscle and bone and ligament that I would want him and he would not want me. That is, he was too handsome and athletic, with mile-wide shoulders, tawny hair, and an open face of clean, straight, Scandinavian lines. He was intellectual as well, and worldly. So we could have some good times together, but the high school Renaissance man never dates the bookish girl for long, does he?

Somehow, the new power of having vials in the freezer lessened the sting of impending rejection. I did not need him. As we walked out, I said what I really thought: "The whole thing would have been so much more compelling if there had been some children on the top of the five-thousand-foot granite wall who needed saving, don't you think?"

On our second date, we sat in an intimate Persian restaurant eating velvety roasted eggplant and told each other intimate things. Sprax had been raised Mormon, but had long since rebelled and been excommunicated. His spirit seemed free, prone to wandering. He told stories from a wide variety of subcultures, from the geeks of MIT and his software jobs to the artists of Indonesia. I tried to match him with tales from Russia and the *Times*. We wandered around to my life plans.

"I'm hoping to have a baby soon," I blurted—and then added, "but you don't need to worry, because I'm going to do it on my own. I've already got the vials of sperm and all."

He took his head in his big hands, as if to say, Yes, this is a big, complex thing, then changed the subject without changing it.

"I tried to be a sperm donor once," he said, and moved into

an amusing story about the rigors of the testing that he hadn't quite passed.

Sprax was a write-off in my mind, a rejection waiting to happen. But for weeks we kept seeing each other, just because... just because it felt good.

"I really like being with you," he said, as we stood in a long but chaste hug in my kitchen, the air sweet with the wine and molasses of a simmering vegetable stew.

"It's nice, isn't it?" I replied. I had to lean back to meet his gentle blue eyes. He was a head taller than me—a rarity among men—and his height held a silly but undeniable appeal. Next to him, I was the right size.

"It's kind of scaring me," he said. "I don't want to just fall into another relationship."

"Go slow," I said, stepping away. "There's something here. Whatever it is, it's fine."

I told him that getting to know him reminded me of the pictures we made as kids by coloring all different rainbow colors on a piece of paper, then coloring over all of them with black, then scraping away a picture with a pin, and seeing all the colors emerge.

"It's there," he said.

"I know," I said, moving to the stove to ladle out the stew.

In May, we went north on a wilderness trip—a travel-section story for the *Times*—and hiked through the hyperbolically titled "Grand Canyon of Maine." At one point, we got to a little rock seat overlooking the rushing water of Gulf Hagas, and he put his arm around me, and said, "Thank you for bringing me here," and he kissed me lightly.

The next day, we kayaked out into Moosehead Lake to the

towering peninsula of Mount Kineo, and as we faced the great granite splendor of the massive rock face head-on, he leaned over and again kissed me, from his kayak.

It was a "when I die I won't be able to complain that I have not lived" moment.

There were little fights and pouts now and then, mainly when he was coaching me up rock faces, but mostly it got better and better. My new plan was to take the summer to play, and then start the baby making in September—either with him or without him. It made no sense to hope he would agree to help, of course, after we had known each other a mere few weeks and barely kissed. But he was a live, strapping, irresistible man right next to me, a man who had doffed his shirt and swung a sledgehammer on an old wall I needed to demolish. No abstract sperm donor could possibly compete.

Perhaps foolishly, I told Sprax my new schedule. We were planning a two-week climbing trip out west in late September, and I said I thought it might be too strenuous if I were pregnant. And also, I added with trepidation, I was sort of waiting to see what happened with him.

"It seems like we've known each other an awfully short period of time to face such a lifelong decision," he said.

"Well, I just want to tell you that I've come to understand that the baby is something I have to do on my own, and you should feel no pressure about it. It just would make no sense to have a child together when we're both feeling so tentative."

"Have you ever thought about how, no matter who you're with, it will always feel like something is missing?" he asked. "At some point, it just takes a leap of faith."

"I've always had trouble with that," I said. "I don't know how anyone does it..."

The romance fell apart. We had a painful kitchen-table

talk about how we had seemed to really fall for each other at first, but lately had been feeling less. He felt pressure for commitment, he said, even if I wasn't putting it on him directly. I told him that he was beautiful inside and out, but if this wasn't right, we needed to face it. We decided to break up, but remain friends.

"You're still my favorite person to be with," he said.

Whoop-de-do.

Just as I was adjusting to our new status and starting to orient myself toward an 8282 try, Sprax flip-flopped. We spent a memorable day on a monster hike in New Hampshire, and drove home at two a.m. in excruciating foot pain. On the way, he confessed, "I'm feeling all distracted again. Like I want to be more than friends."

"I don't trust how you're feeling," I said.

We went kayaking a ways out into Boston Harbor, and on Peddock's Island I gathered green sea glass and found an old shoe in the sand. We talked about the lyrics to "Stairway to Heaven." I gave him a piggyback ride, all 210 muscular pounds of him.

He took my hand as we were crossing a stream on the beach, and said: "However you want things to work out with the baby, I hope they do."

We got sort of back together, then instantly hit trouble again. He asked to cancel a rock-climbing day we'd planned in order to go on a bigger, harder climb with friends, including a gorgeous Dutchwoman. I agreed, then found myself sobbing in the car on my way home from work. My only coherent thought: I hope someday I'll find a man who really cares about me. When I saw Sprax that night, I told him I thought we should give up. He argued me out of it, his absolute unwillingness offering the very balm I needed.

Very sad, closer, much closer than before, we went to bed. Passion must be the feeling that somehow, over barriers of flesh and through blocks of intellect and boulders of emotion, you're trying desperately to join. It felt like that. I'd always kind of imagined that you had a night of passion and wham, you were joined. But no—morning comes again, with all the daylight problems.

The big trip came: Utah, Seattle, Mount Rainier, and then the climax, a week of climbing in the Bugaboo Mountains, high in the Canadian Rockies near Banff. It was a climbers' paradise, not far from touristy Lake Louise.

The Bugaboos were like nothing I had ever seen, mythical, jutting spires of granite. At the Conrad Kain hut, we stood eye to eye with glaciers, nestled in a tumble of boulders as big as houses and cars. Every now and then came the rumble of another little cascade of white snow off rock above us, briefly drowning out the constant rush of the glacial stream running through alpine flowers and mosses nearby. Thin, yellowing pines provided reminders of what a ninety-degree angle was; otherwise, there was nothing but slope.

It took from six in the morning until two the next morning to get up and down Bugaboo Spire. The slowness was mostly my fault. At one point, near the top, a wicked storm caught up with us, and we had to huddle in our guide's bivy sack. When we reached the summit at five p.m., another storm had started, and the rock buzzed with static electricity, making strands of my curly brown hair float upward in a Gorgon do. I was too ignorant to be scared, but Sprax yelled at me to get down quickly, and I did, annoyed at him for pulling me forward so roughly.

The descent was hellish. We short-roped downward, constantly pulling at each other, to the point that Sprax said days later that he still had phantom feelings that he was tied to me—and not in a good way.

I told Sprax later that even though we had reached the summit, the mountain had still won. Yet without knowing it, and with our relationship still in deep limbo, we laid down the first thin layer of what could become trust.

On September 27, two weeks after we got back, I went in for my first insemination.

The night before, Sprax stayed over for support, and admitted that the thought of having an "accident" that might leave me pregnant by him rather than an anonymous donor had crossed his mind. But that was as far as he went, and the next morning I called the clinic to say that I was coming in for my insemination.

"Wonderful!" the receptionist said.

It is? I thought. No one had ever reacted to my plan that way before.

I was so nervous as I drove that I missed the clinic entrance and had to make an illegal U-turn to get back to it. Inside, everyone was pleasantly matter-of-fact, and the procedure was surreally quick and simple.

I lay down in pelvic-exam position, my feet high in stirrups. The midwife, Ann, felt for my cervix with a gloved hand, inserted the speculum with a light, to see where the good cervical mucus was, and then shot the sperm up into it from a clear plastic "straw."

And that was that. She shook my hand when she was done.

The Plan

Beth: "I wanted to be married by the time I was thirty and have a baby by thirty-five. I married Russell when I was twenty-nine. Perfect timing. Or so I thought."

Carey: "Sometimes the harder you try to get things to fall into place, the more they go awry."

Pam: "Who *are* the people whose lives go according to plan?"

Carey: "Not us."

Beth

THE FIRST TIME WE MET, Russell took me canoeing on the Sudbury River. It was summer. We pushed off from the boat dock in Concord with a standard-issue first-date picnic: a bottle of Chardonnay, some Brie, a baguette, a couple of apples, and the hope that our blind date might actually turn out lucky.

He was wearing a loose white oxford shirt, jeans, and round gold-framed Armani sunglasses. I was tan, and my hair, curly from the coastal humidity and tinged auburn from the sun, was longer than it had been in years. I'd moved from Manhattan a year earlier, and started to shed any sign of New York hipness, trading in my black cowboy boots for sneakers, my miniskirts (most of them) for khaki shorts.

We paddled along, through weeds and past willow trees. We talked and laughed about nothing in particular. I paused up in the bow, and turned to him. "I like you," I said. "You're pretty funny." He lowered his sunglasses, looked over at me, put down his paddle, and uncorked the wine. He smiled.

"Here's to what might be," he said, pouring wine into plastic cups.

"And to hoping it is." I rested my paddle across the canoe as we floated along. It was very Victorian. He knew the river, where each branch would take us, and I thought he was eminently self-confident. Funny, smart, handsome in a kind of quirky, big-nosed way that had never appealed to me before. I liked him in the spicy way you take to someone immediately. He was an engineer, working on a project that involved submarine navigation and secrecy, complex and full of intrigue. I was a graduate student, working part-time teaching English as a second language, editing my master's thesis, and spending free time at the beach.

I saw a log covered with painted turtles. "Would you swing us over there?" I asked, pointing to the turtles. "Just watch out. It looks shallow." I thought I'd appear clever and environmentally engaged if I investigated. As we slid into the muck, I said, "Hold on. I see three turtles, but there might be more." I climbed out of the canoe and stood balanced on a rotted stump.

"Look at these." I picked one up, and it tried to run in place. "I think each painted turtle is born with an individual pattern, no two alike."

"Just like people," he said. It was as clichéd a conversation as on any first date.

I was placing the turtle back on a submerged tree limb

when Russell started to paddle away, off into the middle of the river. He smiled over his shoulder, and when he was too far for me to reach him, he put down the paddle, picked up his cup, and took a sip. "Cheers," he toasted, as I stood on the log.

It was minimally funny. Even the lousiest blind date wouldn't leave me in a swamp with no canoe, balanced on a wobbly stump. But as he started to turn back toward me, the canoe tilted, his smile disappeared, and he flipped sideways into the river. It was two feet deep but sufficient to soak his lower half, and splatter his white shirt in mud and silty river water.

It was the first time in our relationship that his attempt at a quick getaway was largely ineffective, but not the last.

"Am I allowed to laugh?" I asked him as he crawled back in and pulled the remains of our muddy picnic from the bottom of the river.

"No," he said. This time he wasn't joking. "If you laugh, I'm leaving you there."

He tried to wring out the soggy baguette, but ended up tossing it to the turtles. It took a while, but eventually he smiled. By the time we reached dry land, he was laughing, too.

Fast-forward to an icy Boston night, eight years later. The city was under a deep freeze when I arrived home from Jamaica. My plane was four hours late; the airport was nearly empty. I was just glad to be home, and the drive, usually twenty minutes, took an hour. The cab slid up to the front of our building on Beacon Street, and I looked up and saw Russell, a backlit shadow, watching down from the fourth-floor apartment. We'd been married for six and a half years, and those two weeks were the longest we'd ever been apart. I was away for his birthday, and I tried—over and over—to call him. Sometimes the call didn't go through, but mostly the answering machine didn't pick up. I figured it had broken, and he didn't have time to fix it. He didn't call until a day before I was leaving Montego Bay. "I'm really sorry," he said through the static. "I lost the number, and I turned the machine off by accident."

Before I reached the door Russell was down the stairs. I ran toward him along the icy path, dragging my bag behind me. Usually he'd wait upstairs, working on his computer in the office at the back of the apartment, not knowing I was home until he heard my key in the lock. I dropped my bag and moved to hug him, but he stepped back. "You have to come upstairs." His words came fast. No greeting. A push on the shoulder.

"Why, what is it?" I took his arm, turning him to face me, assuming someone was dead.

He pressed my back. "You just need to come upstairs. We need to go upstairs and talk."

In the apartment, the first thing I noticed was a bottle of Scotch on the living room floor next to the open futon couch. An old photo of his long-dead mother was propped next to his alarm clock. I'd never seen him drink Scotch. He'd been sleeping on the couch.

"Please sit down," he said.

"No, I don't want to sit down." I took a step backward and knocked into the futon. He didn't sit either. He looked at the picture of his mother and then turned to me. A long pause.

"I want a divorce and I don't want to talk about it." A pronouncement. A whack to the head.

I sat on the floor, missing the edge of the futon.

I hadn't taken my coat off.

He offered me Scotch, and I declined.

"I'm sorry," he said. "I really am. This seemed the easiest way. Just to tell you. Like pulling off a Band-Aid, I guess." He handed me a sheet of paper with two columns. "I made this," he continued, sitting next to me on the floor. "I hope it helps you understand. It's the positives and the negatives of our marriage. At least from my perspective."

An analytical brain if there ever was one.

He'd drawn a line down the middle of the page. Probably using a ruler.

Under the heading "Minuses of My Marriage," he'd listed "different personal interests," "sex not fully satisfying," and "incompatible spare-time activities." Under "Pluses of My Marriage" was "excellent senses of humor," "both physically and emotionally capable," and "we have interesting jobs."

Russell had made a reservation at the Holiday Inn up the street, but he offered to sleep on the couch that night if I didn't want to be alone. Even in my state of shock, I knew that was a ludicrous offer.

The best I could muster was, "If you're leaving, please leave now." Difficult words to say, but it would've been even more excruciating to lie in bed, trying to figure out what had just happened, with him sipping Scotch on the futon.

"Wait," he said. He took my arm and led me to the kitchen. He opened the refrigerator. Inside was an amazing array of food: bottles of tangerine juice, fine cheeses, ripe fruit, whole grain salads, jumbo shrimp cocktail. It was his idea of a trade-off. After nearly seven years of marriage he was leaving, but he stocked the fridge on the way out. "I got all the things you like, even the tangerine juice, and they don't always have that," he said. His hand moved across the shelves like a game show host displaying prizes.

"What am I going to do with all this?" I asked. "This isn't what I want."

"I thought it would help." It was absolution via shrimp cocktail.

After he left, I called my parents in Jamaica. They had two more weeks of vacation in a breezy rented house overlooking the Caribbean. "Mom," I said, crying through the static, realizing how easy it was to get a connection, "I'm alone."

"Where's Russell? He didn't pick you up at the airport?" Her response was almost quaint.

"No. He never picks me up at the airport. He left. He wants a divorce."

"He what? He wants a divorce? *He* wants a divorce from *you?*"

I nodded, didn't say anything.

"Artie!" she called my father, putting her hand over the receiver. I heard her tell him. "Oh, honey, I'm so sorry."

I heard my father say, "That son of a bitch."

"I'm so sorry," my mother repeated through the crackling line. "I wish there was something I could do."

"Like wring his neck!" my father shouted.

My mother ignored him. "I really am sorry."

I had the childish wish of wanting my mother to be there. But she couldn't fix it.

It was a long night, and I never felt warm.

When Russell was gone, I kept thinking, again and again, of the previous summer, and my positive pregnancy test.

After examining the two test sticks from all angles, I climbed into bed where Russell was reading.

"I'm pregnant," I told him. It was a hot, sticky night.

"You're pregnant? Are you sure?"

"Pretty sure."

"You need to make sure." He put his book down. "You need to be certain. Because this will change things."

I stared at him, then said: "I'd considered happiness as a possible response from you." My hurt turned to sarcasm. "But fortunately that passed quickly."

He exhaled. "This isn't the most convenient time. And there's no point in being happy, or anything else, until you're sure one way or the other." He picked up his book. I miscarried two weeks later.

I went to the doctor alone. "I'm certain," I told Russell. "I'm no longer pregnant." I was hoping he'd touch me, say something thoughtful.

He nodded. "Okay," he said. "That's fine. It's better to plan for these things."

It would be a lie to say there was nothing memorable or fun in our time together. More than once, we took our bikes to Italy. With very little money, and nothing more than a guidebook and what we could carry in our panniers, we rode past fields of sunflowers in Tuscany and crisscrossed the Swiss border in the Lake District. Once, when I wanted to paint, he bought an artist's box for me. It was filled with watercolors, pastels, tubes of oils, brushes, a palette, and small canvases. For years, we made each other laugh.

One night, just before Thanksgiving, Russell came home while I was cooking sweet potatoes, and said that, once again, he'd be working all weekend. The kitchen was small and I held a paring knife in one hand and a carrot peeler in the other. I had no intention of stabbing or shredding him, but when I turned toward him, he stepped back and banged into the door. If the only way to get your husband's attention is to have him think you're about to kill him, the marriage is probably in deep trouble.

On Christmas Eve, Russell told me he wanted to wait to have children, that his work—a start-up Internet business—required all his energy and time. He couldn't control everything that was happening professionally, and he wanted to make sure that something in his life was controllable. Children would be the equivalent of a management nightmare.

"When?" I asked. "When do you think you'll be ready?"

"Six months. At least."

We were walking to his business partner's house for dinner. Arguing was pointless; I couldn't force him to have kids. I had a splitting headache. I wanted to turn around, go home, get in bed, have sex, get pregnant, and start the life we'd agreed to have. I was so chronically angry with him at that point, so lonely and sad in my marriage, that I simultaneously wanted to strangle him on the street and have him hold me. "So much for holiday cheer," I muttered, bundled against the cold, marching down the sidewalk behind him. "I guess I shouldn't expect anything from Santa, either."

He let out a snort.

He kept walking fast in front of me and didn't look back. "You're Jewish," he said. "What difference does it make what day it is?"

"Why is this so hard for you?" I asked him.

He didn't answer until the therapy session he'd arranged for twelve hours after I came home from Jamaica.

* * *

While I was dealing with an infected jellyfish sting in Montego Bay, Russell was putting his ducks in a row. He set up a counseling session for the two of us—at eight a.m. on the morning after I'd arrived—with a petite, pashmina-draped therapist named Deedee, who kept two drooling sheepdogs in her office. The dogs were larger than she was. "When we had that pregnancy scare," he revealed at the meeting, "I realized I didn't want to have children with you. I want to have them someday. But not with you."

Deedee already knew this; of course she did. He'd seen her while I was gone. Yet I naively believed we were seeing her to help salvage our marriage. I eventually called the sessions "dissolution therapy."

By week three of my separation from Russell, one of my brothers, a New York attorney, found Benjamin Grossman, my stocky, bearded gorilla of a divorce lawyer. Big Benny, as we called him, told us he occasionally wore bulletproof vests to depositions, that he'd represented Boston's highest-profile divorcées, and that he would get me whatever I deserved. According to Big Benny, he was my avenging angel in a flak jacket.

He told me to write a narrative about my marriage, depicting "the good, the bad, and the ugly." My thirteen pages include revealing facts: Russell not returning my calls from Jamaica for a week; Russell having sessions three times a week at six a.m. with his twenty-year-old female personal trainer; Russell and I not eating dinner together for more than a month before he left; and Russell's denial when I asked if he was having an affair with the trainer.

"I know this is very difficult," Big Benny acknowledged. "But you have to realize, no man goes to see his female personal trainer three times a week, at six a.m., unless he's having an affair with her. It just doesn't happen. I'm sorry, but I've seen this a hundred times. And the sooner you understand that, the quicker we can help you."

Russell's excuse for having no time (and the need to de-stress at the gym) was his company, Conine ("cash only, no inventory, no employees"). Russell and his partner created Gametown, the first real-time multiuser game on the Web. After three years of development and beta testing in an old olive oil warehouse in Boston, they put bingo online for the masses. It was addictive, mind-numbing, and popular.

Venture capitalists made their way to Boston. Like a pack of fairy godmothers dripping with cash, they provided an infusion of funding to Conine and arranged a sale of Gametown to Lycos for $52 million. This coincided, conveniently, with my divorce. As my father said once the numbers were on the table, "Russell must be kicking himself for not leaving you a year earlier."

Around the same time the offer was made by Lycos, Big Benny and I met with Russell and his lawyer. Russell offered a *very* lowball settlement. Big Benny laughed, and asked, "You're kidding, right?"

Russell looked at me, smiled in a manner that seemed half-desperate and half-solicitous, and said, "It's enough to buy one of those brownstones in Brookline you like and still have something left over."

Big Benny turned to opposing counsel and said, "He's kidding, right?" Russell's attorney shook his head. Big Benny sighed, closed his legal binder, and said, "Thank you both for your time. We have no further business here today." He pulled my chair out and said, "We're leaving now. We'll wait for your next offer."

The kicker was a restraining order we put on Russell's finances. He couldn't do anything with his proceeds from the sale until we'd settled or gone to court.

One huge saving grace was my job. I loved my work. In urban classrooms across the country, I found my greatest satisfaction and distraction.

By teaching stress resiliency in graffiti-scrawled public schools in Newark, East and South Central LA, and Roxbury, Massachusetts, at Head Start centers, and in the hallowed halls of Harvard (my employer, the Mind/Body Medical Institute, was an affiliate of Harvard Medical School), I was able to remember how strong our wills can be, how powerful something as basic as breathing is, and how to relax, if only for a minute.

At Central High School in Newark, where I saw one student stab another in the eye, where a third of the girls were pregnant by the eleventh grade, where drug dealers pulled fire alarms so they could get through the emergency exits and avoid the metal detectors, I found the best job of my life. The kids learned that by using little more than their breath and their creative energy, they could find a quiet that wasn't available on the streets.

"You have everything you need to calm yourself, even when the world around you is nuts," I told a class in Newark.

"Yeah, right," a tenth grader scoffed at me. "I just breathe, and that makes everything better. You the one who's nuts."

Maybe I was, but while I couldn't eliminate the violence that surrounded them, once those kids learned some basic stress resiliency skills—how to use diaphragmatic breathing to let go, how to put their heads on their desks and follow a guided visualization—their breathing slowed, and so did their minds and bodies. Violent incidents decreased in the school while attention and classwork improved.

Teachers arrived for lunch in an abandoned lab room to lay their heads on the dusty slate tables, close their eyes, and spend a rare, quiet fifteen minutes. I brought a modicum of peace to those broken classrooms, while saving a little for myself.

But later, when I was stuck in my office in Boston, writing grant proposals and receiving big bills from Big Benny, I'd resort to magical thinking. "What next?" I asked my banged-up Magic 8 Ball. "Will I be able to pay the rent? Will Russell wake up bald one day?" Like so many people under duress, I wanted to believe in fate. I watched the sidewalk cracks when I walked. I looked for signs in the clouds.

When the time came to prepare for Russell's deposition, Big Benny showed me a video of various strategies a client might use when confronted by opposing counsel. I sat in a small conference room, watching a TV monitor. Big Benny closed the door, then stood behind me. He slowly rubbed my arms from shoulder to elbow. "You'll need to relax," he told me, leaning down to my ear and speaking softly. "Depositions are stressful. I can help you relax." I didn't relax. Deep breathing didn't help.

Russell's deposition took four hours. I found out things I didn't really want to know about his sex life with his personal trainer, and some of it was so patently unpleasant that I didn't know what sort of expression to keep on my face.

I sat across the table from him, knowing that it's impossible to remain blank and impassive when you hear your former spouse talking about your own life in a manner that's distant and removed. Or when he reports for the stenographer that he moved in with his personal trainer to celebrate Valentine's Day, a day on which I had never even received a card.

He refused to admit that he'd started sleeping with her before he left me. When asked, he said, "I don't remember the day. Or the date." This from a guy who had a Rain Man's ability to recall strings of numbers.

I dressed nicely, looked sexy. I wanted it to be clear to Russell that I had a fine, fine life without him and that I was in charge from my side of the table.

And in many ways I was. But no woman wants to hear about her former love's current love from across a conference table with lawyers as witnesses and a stenographer tapping her life into documentation.

I found peace where I kept it—in my quiet apartment. I eradicated every last one of Russell's belongings, had sage-burning ceremonies with girlfriends, painted the walls, tossed any sheet he'd slept on, any fork he'd eaten with, any furniture he'd contributed, and brought color back into my world. One wall in the living room I painted red. The dining room became green, the kitchen, yellow. It's amazing what a new coat of paint can do. I took classes and went to movies. I think we all call upon hidden reserves when necessary, and we soldier on, using whatever tools necessary—paint, trash bags, new silverware, friends to help clean out the linen closet—and we keep marching forward.

I'd spent a lot of time trying to keep Russell interested in our marriage. When he was gone, I took some of that energy and made new friends. Once I stopped working so hard to have him want me, I found that the world was full of intriguing people.

I met Pam at a cemetery tour of New England Spiritualists

given by a mutual friend. I loved being busy and was ready to investigate or do anything, including tour a cemetery on a weekend morning to learn about people who believed their lives were as rich after death as during life. When I was busy, I was thinking about what I was doing, not about the implosion of my marriage, my divorce, or the future.

Forest Hills Cemetery is beautiful, and as much an arboretum as a burial ground. A Goth couple snapped hundreds of photos of each other lurking behind the elaborate tombstones and mausoleums. A silent slip of a girl floated along with us. Pam, slim and doe-eyed, raised her eyebrows. She was a little taller than me, with light brown hair in a long bob. She looked casual, but as if she'd put herself together with care. Not the kind of care that indicated she was hoping to meet a living male heir to a dead Spiritualist, but as if she thought the world was worth looking good for. She was on the tour alone, and so was I.

"You look remarkably normal for this group," she said.

"Remarkably," I agreed. "But if you factor in that we're touring a cemetery on a Saturday morning, it's not such a surprise."

We started walking together, and though I didn't even notice at first, it was pleasant to be with someone, however unplanned. We fell into step and spent the rest of the tour together. I think she enjoyed it, too.

All the romantic tombstones—beloved wife, devoted husband—brought us to talking about our own love lives. We were in a similar spot: reluctantly single, but determined to do more than chase after unsatisfactory men, in cemeteries or elsewhere.

"I'd like to be somebody's beloved something." Pam sighed.

"Before I'm dead," I told her.

"True, not just for posterity."

The Goth couple scurried around. We learned that e. e. cummings's aunt had paid for his headstone and used uppercase letters against his wishes. "I'm a journalist," she told me, when I asked what she did. I felt a thrill, as if I was on a blind date with someone I'd like to see again. Journalism was my road not taken. I'd written a few travel articles for the *New York Times* but had stopped short of pursuing newswriting, thinking that without a journalism degree I'd never be able to break into a field populated by writers who started in their twenties.

"I'm envious," I told her. "That's where I'd like to be."

"It's great, but not all it's cracked up to be. A lot of driving. A lot of phone calls about murders in the middle of the night."

"Still, you get to tell all of us about what happens in the middle of the night. We just read about it over coffee."

"There's a lot of mornings I'd prefer to drink coffee, especially if I could find someone to drink it with."

By the end of the tour, it might have seemed as if we'd arrived together. We walked to our cars and exchanged phone numbers.

"This is better than meeting in a bar," Pam joked, ripping a page out of a steno pad and writing her number.

"I don't know if most people would agree with that." I wrote my number on her pad, and except for the fact that we were standing in the crematorium parking lot, it felt just like the end of a good first date: I was reluctant to leave, thinking I might not see her again.

From the get-go, it was clear that Pam was an incorrigible romantic. She got a faraway look when she talked hopefully about her dream of having a "soul mate."

"A soul mate?" I asked, the first time I heard her utter the term. "How would you define that?" Cynic that I am, it was a challenge from the outset not to roll my eyes every time she said it.

"I guess someone I think of as my destiny. I don't believe in supernatural intervention, but I believe there's someone out there, and we're intended for each other."

"How very Victorian of you."

"Yeah, I know, I know. I can't help it. I've always been kind of sappy that way."

Our relationship was cemented after we agreed to spend an evening at a local Spiritualist church—a modern-day séance—in an old, paint-peeling Colonial house in a leafy, residential neighborhood. A quirky first outing with a new friend. My mother was visiting, and she came too.

A séance was about as far as we could get from a singles' event.

I knew I really liked Pam when the medium for the evening, a small, thin, middle-aged man, turned his attention to her. "I see the specter of a gentleman behind you," he told her. "He's wearing a fedora hat. Does that sound like a person familiar to you? He appears to be carrying a tray of cookies, and they're for you." Pam had those big brown eyes, and, although tall, she appeared petite. She might have seemed an easy target, but from what little I knew of her, she wasn't going to be convinced that the ghost of a dead uncle was hovering behind her. Our visit was sociological, not spectral.

"No," she replied without hesitation. "That's not anyone I know. I'm allergic to wheat."

When we were leaving, she asked, "Can you believe that

guy? What a sham. And that old woman in front of me. He said he saw her husband, Frank. Can you imagine how much money she's given him over the years just to believe that Frank's lurking around in that dusty old room? What a fraud."

On our way home, my mother said, "I like that Pam. She's feisty."

The divorce proceeded, and the deal with Lycos moved toward closing. I'd been living off a reserve from my savings account, borrowing money from my parents, and trying not to spend beyond my means. My nonprofit salary was minimal, and Russell took his larger salary with him, so my finances were bleak.

Eventually I extricated myself from the tag-team therapy with Russell and Deedee. It occurred to me in early spring that by continuing to show up, I was helping Russell prepare for his next relationship, providing a lab for him to learn and improve his interpersonal skills. After Russell made some remark about how I didn't wax my legs often enough, and that in itself was grounds to move toward divorce, Deedee had no choice but to tell him he was being judgmental, and perhaps over the years he too had displayed imperfections. He puzzled over that, and concluded that it was unlikely he possessed any habits I could disapprove of, but maybe he'd been *a little* too judgmental, and perhaps his judgments hadn't benefited our relationship, and in the future he'd be more careful of others' feelings.

During one of our sessions, he looked at Deedee with a serious gaze. Then he turned to me and nodded with insight. "Therapy *is* really helpful," he told us. "I'm learning a lot about myself. I've been thinking about it, about what we're accomplishing here and how I can use these new skills to avoid hurting other people." He turned to me, smiled, and said, "Thanks for that."

I should have packed up immediately. But I was still feeling broken and ensnared by the past and by the mistaken belief that it was meant to also be the future.

When we were leaving Deedee's one warm morning, he stopped me outside her front door. He removed his copy of our shared credit card from his wallet, bent it back and forth until it cracked, then ripped it down the center.

"Is that meant to be symbolic?" I asked, as he offered the pieces to me, saw I wasn't going to take them, and put them back in his pocket.

"No." He shrugged. "I thought you'd just want to know I wasn't using it anymore."

At what turned out to be our final session together, Russell arrived first, and he was already in the office with Deedee.

After she greeted me, and Russell gave me his typical neutral nod, she took a breath. "I'd like you both to imagine your ideal divorce settlement."

When Russell stared straight ahead, not glancing toward me, I became suspicious. "What I'm really talking about," Deedee continued, "is the legal, financial settlement, not your emotional settling." She leaned toward me. "What do you feel is reasonable? What will allow you to say good-bye without anger or resentment?"

"Equitable distribution," I told her. "If it's come down to money. Fifty percent."

Russell nearly jumped off his couch, unsettling one of Deedee's sheepdogs. "Fifty percent of what? *My* company? You want half of *my* company? What have you ever done to help with the business? Do you want to start coming to the office every day? What the hell gives you the right to think about getting any part of *my* company?"

This didn't seem much like therapy to me.

When I picked up my bag and stood to leave, halfway through the session but done with Deedee forever, she reached toward me and said, "Wait, before you go..." so I stood there, hand on the doorknob. Then she took out a legal pad and asked me, in all earnestness, with pen poised, "Based on your contributions to your marriage, and the fact that you never actually worked in Conine's offices, do you realistically feel that you earned the right to benefit financially from the company's holdings or any future sale of the company?"

I looked down at her, and she and Russell and the sheepdogs were all looking intently up at me. "How is that a relevant question for a therapy session?" I asked. "You can talk to my lawyer." And then I left.

I was at work when Big Benny called. My office mate was behind me on her phone. It was sunny through our windows.

"Are you sitting down? Because..." He laughed. "Because... and here's the drumroll." He tapped on the phone. "You, my dear client, are a very rich woman."

My divorce settlement was more than $10 million in stock.

I spent the next week in shock. One more day in court, and I would no longer be a married woman. I would be a really rich divorcée with no children but a lot of money. I could pay off my debts, I could quit my job. I could travel. I could start a foundation. I could recover in style. I could buy a black-market baby. I could buy two black-market babies. And hire two nannies. I'd never have to see Russell again. Or Big Benny. I was nearly done.

And that was it. We went to court early in the morning, the day before my thirty-seventh birthday, and sat in a room full of couples separated by benches and attorneys and the rest of their lives. Everyone was quiet, and I suspect most of us were sleep-deprived and relieved that we'd be able to stop spending our time and money with and on these lawyers. I was wearing a short blue silk dress. Big Benny leaned over and said he liked it.

We were the first to be called to the bench that morning. The judge asked if either of us wanted to rescind, if we wanted to remain married, if we were making this decision voluntarily. We nodded. We shook our heads. We did whatever we had to do to answer the questions, avoid looking at each other, and get the hell out of there.

The gavel fell and the judge declared us divorced. For a moment, I didn't know what to do. Do you kiss your ex-husband good-bye when your divorce is final? Let loose a joyful noise? Tell him what you really think about him? I blinked and stood there until Big Benny said, "Let's go," and led me by the elbow out the door.

In the hall, Russell and I nodded at each other as if we'd both survived a duel. We shook hands, and then stepped back. "Good luck," I said. He nodded and said, "You too." No big crescendo. Just footsteps echoing on the marble courthouse floor as we walked in opposite directions.

The Romance

Pam: "I can't help it. I do believe in soul mates."

Beth: "Oh, sweet, deluded Pam."

Carey: "What are we going to do with you?"

Pam

I WAS SCREWED. Half an hour to deadline, and the Internet connection in my Vermont hotel room had crashed. I desperately removed, then reinserted, the computer cable. I called the front desk. Sorry. Too late to do anything, and all the other rooms were booked.

"This can't be happening," I muttered to myself, staring at the brightly lit words on my laptop screen. In all likelihood, I would have to read them aloud to some unlucky copy editor hundreds of miles away at the *Washington Post* news desk.

The story was important: A state that had been the first to abolish slavery was now on its way to reinventing marriage with "civil unions" for gay and lesbian couples. I had followed the controversy for months, listening to fiery debates and personal recriminations that pitted neighbor against neighbor and religious conservatives against gay couples nationwide.

"By a vote of 79 to 68, legislators here did more than solidify

Vermont's independent pedigree in creating an institution parallel to marriage—called civil union—that legally recognizes the lifelong commitment of a man to a man and a woman to a woman," I wrote that night. "They also gave birth to a new verb: civil unionize."

A historic moment, but my story would see print only if I could file it. I picked up the phone and called Carey, my *New York Times* counterpart working a few doors away.

"Carey, I'm in a total bind. Can I send my story from your room?"

"Sure," she said. "I'm just filing myself. Give me a minute and head on over."

I padded down in my socks to her room. Friendly competitors, we each tracked breaking news across New England. We shared directions to crime scenes and double-checked press conference quotes—not giving too much away—and slowly we were becoming friends.

After setting up the cable connection on her desk, I glanced outside. A small crowd was spilling out of a vintage movie theater across the street. Several couples, their smiling faces illuminated by the antique marquee, held hands as they strolled home past brick-and-granite storefronts. A harsh winter was refusing to surrender to spring, and the trees were barren, the sidewalks patchy with ice. And here we were, two single women in our thirties, having spent the evening hunched over our laptops, fingers tapping and faces tense.

Carey and I were both stirred by the romance of this story, the desire of gay and lesbian couples to be joined until death, in sickness and in health, just like everyone else. I hadn't had any luck finding someone who wanted to broach the subject of forever. Much less fight a state supreme court for it.

We sat on the edges of two double beds, waiting for my

story to go through and for editors to call. An empty coffee mug and the remnants of a club sandwich from room service sat on a tray next to the minibar. I eyed a half-eaten pickle and realized I had forgotten about dinner.

"I met someone," Carey said, breaking my hunger trance. She had a full head of luscious black curls. When she drew them back from her face, I could see there was a slight glow despite her fatigue. "His name is Sprax, and we really get along."

"Sprax?" I asked.

"It's kind of an unusual name, but he's smart, good-looking," she said. "He went to MIT and climbs mountains. I don't know. We'll see where it goes."

There was more, I could tell. Her voice was calm, but she had a sly smile.

"He knows I'm going to try to have a baby, and he's okay with it." She broke out in a wide grin.

"You are? He is?"

Carey had tried online dating before most people I knew. Now here she was on the front line of something else altogether.

"What do you mean, try to have a baby? With him?"

"No, Pam," Carey said, as if it was a silly question. "I bought some sperm, and I'm planning to use it. In fact, I got the vials the same day I met Sprax."

She explained the technicalities: the sperm banks, the expense, the procedure. So this was a new world, after all. A universe where gays and lesbians (at least in one state) could recite lifelong vows. Where single straight women could multitask career, companionship, and conception. A place where so many of us yearned for the traditional—love, commitment, family—and the ways of acquiring it had suddenly become anything but.

I sensed relief and purpose in Carey. She had in essence met two men, each with their own promise. The urgency that so many of us experienced in our desire to make a new relationship work so we could have children was largely absent in her now. It seemed brave, even radical, to me.

"I can just enjoy getting to know Sprax and not postpone having a baby," she said.

Optimistic, and perhaps idealistic, I hadn't given up on finding love and a father for my children, all wrapped into one. I wondered if Sprax really would go along with the plan and stay with her in the long run, especially if she got pregnant with the donor sperm. I figured it wasn't my business to ask.

Instead, I said, "You know, it seems like Sprax and Donor 8282 are oddly similar: tall, fair, intellectual science and technology guys."

"You're right!" She gasped.

"So," I ventured, "you'll see which one takes first?"

We both laughed. "Yes, I guess it comes down to that," she said.

In my early twenties, I had imagined myself in the future as a married mother with five children living on a farm in Vermont. Just how I was supposed to achieve that rural reverie was not clear after almost a decade and a half in newspapers, covering blood-splattered double-murder scenes, neighborhoods flattened by hurricanes, and terrorists on trial for bomb plots. I knew I wanted a mate and wouldn't be able to have children forever, yet I hadn't made it a top priority.

My whole life, I was what you'd call a late bloomer, slow to flirt, slow to date, and slow to discover sex. A shy, bookish child others called "The Brain." I had deep brown eyes and curly auburn hair, thin arms and long legs, and a small chest that, frankly, didn't grow much larger with age. My nose was crooked and, until I had it fixed after college, held me back from ever feeling I was anything more than "kind of pretty," as a childhood friend once said to my face, not realizing the sting.

I was boy crazy despite never managing to get the boy. In junior high school, Danny, with a raspy voice and long, gossamer eyelashes, captured my heart even as we competed against each other for top scores on math quizzes and spelling tests. Would he go out with me?

"He says you're too smart for him," a friend told me. "He likes Laura."

Crisp bows in her hair. Dimples. I wore zippered one-piece pantsuits my mom ordered from Sears.

Mom tried to reassure me that the right guy would come along when I was older. She was twenty-one when she married my dad.

"Oh, honey, they're just intimidated by you," she said, stroking my hair. "A lot of boys have trouble with smart girls. Besides," she'd added, "he's too short for you." Another time, she said the boy was too tall. Whatever it took to make me feel better.

I believed her and her promise that an admirer was waiting for me in the "real world," and I tried not to worry too much when I moved through high school and college without a steady boyfriend. I clung to the hope that the right man for me would suddenly appear one day, an unconditionally loving prince, as if from nothingness. As if Mom and I had conjured him ourselves.

After I became a journalist, most of the men I met were editors and criminals, and even if I had been desperate or crazy enough to date them, my travel and long work hours left little time for a private life.

First London, where my job for a daily commodities newspaper required me to cultivate sources who resembled the metals they traded. I met lead dealers in France with ashen faces and dull suits, gold traders with manicures and designer ties, and platinum sellers with flashy rings and luxury cars who showcased novelty bridal gowns spun of silk and glinting metal. I did my best trying to decipher the goings-on of financial markets, but I was barely twenty-four, unable to balance my own checkbook.

Next Miami, where I drove more than two hours back and forth every day from South Beach to a nearly windowless news bureau on the fringe of the Everglades with the charm of an FBI safe house. Then Boston, where breaking news forced me to cancel dinners with friends at night and miss rowing classes on the Charles River in the morning. Mail stacked up on my counter. Laundry went undone.

"I'm so sorry to do this again," became my rescheduling refrain.

When the mail got too high, the dinner invitations too few, and the skipped classes too expensive, I quit the *Boston Globe* newsroom. I didn't fall out of love with journalism, but I looked up from my notepad and knew it was time to figure out if it wasn't too late to have it all. I felt the tug. I wanted love, an intellectual life, children. I wanted it to happen, and I worried it would not. So did many of my single working women friends.

"I'm like a plane in a holding pattern, flying in circles, waiting for clearance to land," said Clare, my British former housemate. She was successfully climbing the corporate ladder of an international accounting firm and spending vacations on the beach in Tanzania or biking across Lebanon. She was brilliant and stylish and, to my mind, inexplicably single.

"You know what they say, don't you?" I replied. "You can't have a job, a car, a home, and a man at the same time. One always has to give."

I wondered how I could pay the bills, find a man, have a baby, and do rewarding work all at once. Should I take an easy and lucrative public relations job that gave me time to look for a mate and have a child, compromising my journalism career and, perhaps, my sanity? Should I move somewhere more affordable so I could keep writing and concentrate more on dating? I cut back on coffee but still lost sleep as I tried to work all this out in my head, my stomach in knots.

Boston felt like home, so I stayed put and freelanced until the *Washington Post* called with one assignment, and another, and I was on my way. The paper made it easy to do my job. Editors were smart, professional, and courteous, and I was given a retainer and a contract that provided a regular flow of work and money. I was miles away from office politics and gossip, talking to Maria von Trapp from *The Sound of Music* in Vermont one week, covering a Kennedy family funeral on Cape Cod the next. I could wrap up interviews and be home in time for dinner. I could work and find a partner and have a family.

Finally, at thirty-one years old, with room to breathe, I could write that part of my life.

Carey helped. At her urging ("You have to, *have to,* let them see what you look like," she nudged), I posted a photo of myself at Walden Pond on two singles websites: JDate.com, for Jewish singles, and Match.com, for just about everyone else. In the photo, I wore a T-shirt, carried a water bottle, and smiled brightly: "Here is an easygoing girl who loves the outdoors." Low-maintenance, cheerful.

I had immediate second thoughts, picturing colleagues and neighbors witnessing my desperation, but left the ad up because it was worth the risk. Chaste no more, I had experienced first love, a few short-term relationships, and even a couple of one-night stands, yet no lasting intimacy.

I met an arrogant inventor who put me down over sushi, and I had cocktails with a man whose eyes shook in their sockets for an hour. (He never said why; I never asked.) There was a stand-up comic who loved to gamble and hated to joke offstage. A manic-depressive who played the drums and worshipped Guns N' Roses. A doctor with strange body odor who spoke so softly I couldn't hear what he was saying. A roster of others who preferred corresponding by anonymous e-mail to going on actual dates.

I took up pottery and Jewish studies, joined a gym and traveled to Europe and the Middle East, attended cocktail parties and barbecues. All this, even though I believed in my sappy, things-work-out-for-the-best way that I would meet my mate spontaneously and seemed to receive signs that this would be so.

"Wait for love and children," a female stranger told me one evening as I sat at the bar of a neighborhood restaurant waiting for friends. Unsolicited. Was it the way I nursed my drink? A scent of loneliness that gave me away?

The woman's words echoed in my ears for days: "It will come when it's ready."

A few months later, a Jewish philanthropy in Boston threw its annual celebration for young leaders at the timeworn Park Plaza Hotel. It was the kind of place where my parents and their parents might have met, with its sparkling crystal chandeliers and gilded balconies. A grand hotel of the 1920s, and that, of course, was fitting. Young leadership, schmeadership. Even I, not the most observant of Jews, knew enough to decrypt the ancient matchmaking code: this was a singles event, like the "Matzo Ball," an extravaganza where young Jewish professionals met other young Jewish professionals to marry and have lots and lots of Jewish babies and make our *mamalehs* proud.

No one, of course, wanted to admit that. We wouldn't be caught dead at a singles event, but there we were. I got a glass of red wine and tottered around the room in high heels a half size too small until I saw some familiar faces. My friend Philip taught computer science at a local university; another friend worked as a community organizer. They were discussing politics, and a man to my right who had been introduced as Adam said he admired a certain South Boston politician whom I disliked.

Adam had green eyes flecked with gold. Unruly, curly brown hair grazed the back of his neck and seemed to defy his starched business shirt. I liked the look of it.

While I dated Jewish men, among others, I often found it hard going because there seemed to be an instant familiarity that bred friction instead of romance. We made assumptions about each other and leapt into each other's personal space, debating and interrupting as if we were related. While it could be satisfying and fun sharing a cultural shorthand, being Jewish did not mean we viewed faith in the same way or had much else in common.

Adam and I tangled, yet our physical chemistry was undeniable. The next week, when I read about a film of New York intellectuals called *Arguing the World,* I tracked down his phone number and asked him if he wanted to go.

We met at Zaftig's, an upscale deli whose buxom and

thick-ankled maternal mascot decorated murals and menus offering Chardonnay along with blintzes. Adam spread some cream cheese on a bagel chip and leaned back against the vinyl booth. We started in on the basics: hometown (a suburb north of Chicago for me, one outside Pittsburgh for him); siblings (a younger brother for me; a younger brother and sister for him). It seemed we were both close to our families.

"You know, I thought after our last conversation you'd be . . . ," he said, pausing. "How do I put this politely?"

"Just say it. It's okay."

"A bitch."

I raised my eyebrows.

He laughed. "But you're not."

"Why, thank you."

An afternoon Rollerblading along the Charles River a few weeks later ended at his condo. We dumped our skates by the front door, and he sank into a wide armchair in the living room. As I walked past him to the couch, he grabbed me by my waist and pulled me onto his lap. I straddled him, we squirmed in the chair, temperatures rising. It would be several weeks before any clothes came off.

Adam was a nice Jewish boy, a thirty-seven-year-old sales representative who wrote me love notes in a slanted, childlike handwriting. He watched Pittsburgh Steelers football games and read books that weren't really books, more self-help guides like *Don't Sweat the Small Stuff.* I wondered if the cultural gap—or my lack of interest in sports—would leave us with anything to talk about in our old age.

Still, I was ready to compromise for sweetness and the long haul, including children. Adam taped photos of himself with friends' babies on his refrigerator. He told me he wanted a boy and a girl, and that sounded good to me.

★ ★ ★

That November, I turned thirty-three.

"Life is one big adventure with you and what an exhilarating journey it has been!" Adam wrote in a birthday card with a lone kayaker plummeting over a waterfall, a rainbow in the background. "My Angel Love, there is a connection that exists between us like two silent angels floating, side by side, flying to God's rhythm just beyond our world."

Earlier that autumn, he had taken me to a nineteenth-century bed-and-breakfast with a three-thousand-bottle wine cellar, Jacuzzis, and king-sized beds—"a perfect choice for honeymooners, romantics, and those seeking adult sanctuary," the brochure promised. We hiked by day and in the late afternoon sat in Adirondack chairs looking out at a spectacular vista of blazing red-and-orange foliage. Adam pulled me onto his lap.

"I have something to tell you." His unshaven jaw brushed my cheek. "I love you."

"I love you, too," I said. We must have looked like a *Yankee* magazine travel ad, with plaid blankets tossed over our khaki shorts and Irish wool sweaters. Adam must mean it, I thought; he was too deliberate to say something like that on impulse.

Everything seemed great, and that made me worry. My college friend Kevin told me to relax. It was a warm night for the time of year, and we sat drinking beer on my front stoop. My second-floor apartment overlooked a garden running the length of the street, lined by historic brownstones with bay windows and wrought-iron railings.

"Adam's great, but I'm happy and anxious all at once," I said. "I feel like something bad is just around the corner."

Kevin shrugged. A former model and actor with pretty-boy

looks, he possessed the down-to-earth directness of a midwestern upbringing.

"It is," he said.

"What do you mean?"

"Something bad is just around the corner," he said.

"What?" Not what I wanted to hear.

"All I'm saying is don't worry about the good times in your life coming to an end because they will. They always do." Kevin began to smile. "Then they come around again." He had been a college swim team captain and clearly knew how to motivate.

I relaxed into Adam, his family, hobbies, friends, how life might endlessly be. Between assignments for the *Post,* I spent Thanksgiving with his parents and cheered him on during weekend basketball tournaments. We socialized with his married friends who had starter homes and toddlers. They told me they adored him. They also told me they hoped he hung onto me, and I took that as a compliment rather than a warning.

Even his ninety-year-old grandmother, frail but feisty, framed a photo of the two of us. "This is Pam," she said, introducing me to a friend. "She's new."

So this is how it feels, I thought, approaching what had always been the elusive door of commitment. My family approved.

"Wow," said my dad's girlfriend. "He's quite a catch."

A year passed, and ditching the newsroom had made all the difference. I had time to hang out with my boyfriend on evenings and weekends and regularly saw friends, took classes, and rarely spent more than a night or two on the road for stories that were interesting and sometimes challenging.

Carey and I often ran into each other, and over the summer we covered the fatal offshore plane crash of John F. Kennedy,

Jr., his wife, and her sister. Like other reporters, we were either camping outside the Kennedys' Cape Cod compound with celebrity journalists shaded by tents, or tromping down the beach on Martha's Vineyard to write about driftwood memorials below striped clay cliffs. Reeking of sweat, sunscreen, and sea salt at the end of the workday, we never saw the splash site or the remains of Kennedy's plane; we could only imagine the wreckage, and away from our own loved ones, Carey and I both were struck by the fragility of family.

"You know, all I think about these days is having a child, not usually the risks and fears that come with it," she said, as we waited to catch the ferry across Vineyard Sound one day. It was a relief to share our feelings privately after reining them in on the job.

"Me, neither. That rarely occurs to me."

"Let's talk about something happier. Tell me Adam has been showering you with so many flowers and bonbons you're sick to death of them!"

I was touched by how hopeful Carey could be about my love life, especially when hers was shaky.

"I don't know about that, but things are okay," I replied.

Adam and I were still close. Status quo close in a way that made me wonder if I was wrong in picturing a wedding at his parents' house. Maybe this was just the way he liked it: together in the present, no thought to the future. I wasn't so sure it was the way I liked it. But I didn't want to pressure him. I didn't want to be *that* girl.

He gave me a call at home after work one night. I was cooking pasta for dinner, rinsing off some tomatoes and a bunch of basil in the sink. My galley kitchen opened onto the living room, whose high ceiling and white pine floor lent it a bright, sunny air in the daytime. The bedroom and small office down the hall led through French doors to a large wooden deck, where I grew a ragtag profusion of flowers and spent mornings reading the paper.

"My aunt is having a barbecue Friday," Adam said.

"Sounds great. I don't think we have any other plans."

"Actually, you might want to stay home. It'll take me about forty minutes to get there, and I'm only going to stay for a little while," he said. "Why don't you have a normal Friday night?"

"Because I'd like to see you. That's my normal Friday night." Sarcasm seeped into my voice. Nestling the phone between my shoulder and ear, I took the boiling pot off the stove.

"I know, but it really isn't worth it. I'll see you over the weekend."

"Uh, okay. I'll miss you."

"Me, too."

I was puzzled, but I let it go. Another week, he joined a pottery studio. Not my pottery studio—another one, in another town. He talked about trying out for a baseball league that required he lie and shave ten years off his age to be eligible. He bought a king-size bed. "We can sleep in it and not even know the other person is there!" he crowed.

He had yet to make it to my hometown of Chicago or go on an extended holiday with me or give me a key to his apartment, even though I regularly spent the night there. Adam told me he had been looking at new condos with a real estate agent, and that he was thinking about buying a convertible.

"One day, I'll have a family, and then it won't be the most practical car," he said.

I'll have, he said. *One day*. The little alarm bell in my head began ringing more loudly, and finally it became deafening when we discussed our summer plans. Adam rented a house every year on Martha's Vineyard, and I was excited at the prospect of our first extended vacation together. It got me thinking about the sexy lingerie I could bring and the talks we might have about our future.

A few weeks before our departure, Adam came over after work. Tossing his jacket and overnight bag on my bedroom dresser, he sat down on the bed. I gave him a quick peck on the lips. He smiled, and, as he loosened his tie and took off his shoes, said we should talk about the trip.

"Sure, sweetie." I assumed he meant ferry reservations and what to pack.

He said his brother wanted to come, and his best friend, Carl. Fine by me.

"I thought what you could do is come over with me and spend the first five days there. Then the guys would come." He undid his belt, slipped off his socks.

"You mean, I'd leave? After five days?" I wasn't sure I heard right. Adam rented the house for ten days.

"All right?" he said, with no idea that anything was wrong with his plan. I would stay five days, then go home, alone. He didn't ask what I'd do with the rest of the time, which I'd already arranged to take off from work.

I might be his girlfriend. But clearly I was not the rest of his life.

"No, actually, not all right." I stood and stormed into the hallway, fighting back tears. Adam looked stunned. His recent signs of withdrawal, pushed to the back of my mind, couldn't be ignored anymore. "I feel like I don't really matter to you."

"You do," he said. He moved closer to me. I started to cry.

"You compartmentalize me. It's always, 'I'm going to do this' or 'I'm going to do that.' It's never 'us.' Us." I sat down on the floor. Pulled my knees up to my forehead. "Go to the Vineyard without me," I said.

And he did.

The arms of sisterhood were all around me.

Kathy, one of my college roommates, was one of the most beautiful women I knew. She had alabaster skin and black hair, like a contemporary Snow White, and a sweet smile that belied her bawdy sense of humor. At school, she loved men and promised to make her millions writing bodice rippers. Now, years later, she had found happiness with a woman and a graphic design business, and she did not waver as a friend.

"Sweetie, you have never been half-assed in anything you've done, and that includes relationships," she said. "If he can't commit, he needs to understand the consequences."

She was visiting from Maryland, and we were on our way to Filene's Basement as part of my retail therapy while Adam was away. Strolling through the Public Garden, we passed cascading flowers and exotic plants. Tourists waited in a long line for Swan Boat rides, and a grinning wedding party posed for portraits. We noticed a pair of swans gliding under the bridge, craning their necks toward each other. I couldn't help it; I started to cry. People stared.

"I know you're right. It's just hard to think of letting him go, of being alone again." I'd put so much time into the relationship, and Adam was basically a good man, even if he needed to grow up.

Then there was Anna and her opinion, which I had to respect given her good luck in love. She was another one of my best friends from college, a sensual Greek who lived a high-volume life with a low bullshit threshold. She married a younger man who painted a carton of eggs with scenes from each of their first dates. He bought her a piano for her birthday and followed her from Maine to San Francisco, where they now lived and worked. He knew the way to her heart, and he knew better than to let go.

"I know it sucks, but you deserve more," she said, during one of our long-distance phone calls.

I told Carey what they said, and she agreed. It was early on an overcast weekday morning, and we waited behind the police cordon for a press conference at a crime scene north of Boston. Television crews set up cameras and attached microphones to a makeshift lectern. I had missed a button on my shirt, which Carey pointed out. She too had rushed out the door, and her hair was still damp after a quick shower.

"Pam, I don't think you should have to struggle so much, to try to wrangle commitment from a man who won't even take a proper vacation with you," Carey said.

I knew what she was going through with Sprax, whom I had encountered only briefly on his way in or out of her home. A tall man with a head of bountiful blond curls to Carey's dark ones, and a shy smile. She had met Adam and liked him well enough, but felt protective of me.

"Imagine trying to make bigger decisions with him down the line," she said, looking me in the eye. "The really *important* ones."

Adam came home from his time on the Vineyard and called to say he spent most of it missing me. Looking at the stars from the beach at night and thinking how romantic it would have been to be by my side and realizing that his brother could be a real pain in the ass.

He invited me over. It sounded like a turning point, that I might finally have what I wanted all along. He greeted me with a bear hug and a lingering kiss, took my hand and led me to his couch. A small bouquet of red roses leaned against one of the cushions.

"I know now that I want to get engaged and marry you. I want to have children with you, and, in the meantime, I'll even adopt your cat," he said, laughing. He also said he would see a therapist.

It wasn't a marriage proposal, exactly. More like a proposal to make a proposal.

"Here, this is for you," he said. He pulled a duplicate condo key out of his pocket. A tiny white ribbon was wrapped around it. "I hope it's not too late."

"It's not if it works," I said. He laughed.

He placed the key in my palm and squeezed my hand closed. I felt my stomach relax, my shoulders un-tense. I might be a wife and a mother one day soon. He handed me a sheet of paper to read aloud. A Top 10 list of "What Makes You Special to Me" that included: Number 1: You understand me. Number 2: Great listener. Number 6: Close to family. And Number 10: Forgiving.

I appreciated his honesty. This was progress.

Months later, as I moved aside some papers on a glass coffee table in his living room, I found a memo with my name on it. Under his company's blue-and-gold motto "Reach for the Best," Adam had written a note to himself: "Pam may not be the most beautiful girl, but she has a good heart and loves me." A good heart. Kind of pretty. Maybe this was his private therapy exercise. I knew I shouldn't have read anything without his permission, even if it was there in plain view, yet I couldn't help myself. Who could? I kept quiet, but the cold assessment seeped into my heart.

I thought about the times Adam questioned my commitment to health and fitness, despite my 130-pound, five-foot, eight-inch frame, and my love of hiking and swimming. Carey and other friends were constantly saying I could stand to gain a little more weight; my parents told me they couldn't believe how much energy I always had. Still, to Adam, I knew on some level I couldn't possibly measure up.

He was so devoted to working out at the gym that my stepfather, Patrick, a philosophy professor and Latin scholar, gave him the nickname "Mr. Upper Body Strength."

"I ordered a turkey sandwich, potato chips, and a Diet Coke for lunch the other day, and Adam called me a 'junk food junkie,'" I told Patrick. He groaned.

I didn't tell him about my recent appointment with Adam and his therapist. We sat facing him in separate armchairs in an office with industrial carpeting and a fake ivy plant.

"Health is important to me," Adam said. "What if Pam doesn't take care of herself and weighs three hundred pounds one day?"

The therapist glanced at me. "Do you take care of yourself?" he asked.

"Yes," I replied.

"Have you ever been overweight?"

"No." I wore a size six or eight.

"Do you have any serious health issues?"

"No."

He looked back at Adam. Brow creased, Adam still looked worried.

"Let's say," the therapist continued, "for the sake of argument, that she does gain a lot of weight. You'll still love her . . . ," he said. Silence. "Right?"

Another afternoon Adam and I drove to his parents' house. We took separate cars because I needed to be home early. As he approached the turnpike tollbooth ahead of me, I performed a bit of magical thinking: if Adam really is the man for me, he'll pay my toll.

"He didn't," I told Carey afterward. My disappointment was silly, but there it was.

Carey overflowed with tenderness for anyone suffering hurt or disappointment, but she was much more of a pragmatist than I'd ever be. A gentle demeanor belied the strength of her opinions, and she didn't let me off the hook.

"Pam, you're such a smart woman. Why are you thinking at the level of a remote rain-forest tribe? Why in the world would you play that game with yourself, and with your relationship?" Carey said, aghast. "I don't understand."

"I know it seems nuts. But my family always pays both tolls if one of us is driving behind the other; they're thoughtful about each other that way," I said.

I wondered if Adam would ever commit. I also worried he would commit, and not really be in love with me. Maybe the differences I accepted early in our relationship wouldn't make me happy, either. I liked Russian movies and backpacking; he liked football and Club Med. I found myself thinking more and more about putting myself first, ahead even of the family-making fantasy I envisioned for the two of us.

Something else stirred in me when I went to Vermont to write about the first civil union ceremony for the *Washington Post*. Seemingly against the odds in a nation built on one man–one woman, the law had taken effect, and it came down to this: Two men, under a gazebo in a Brattleboro park at midnight, declaring their love and commitment to each other. They had fashioned a life together, and this was a final acknowledgment and public embrace.

Early the next morning, I attended another ceremony, this

one in a white clapboard church where two other men, Declan and Kevin, recited their vows. Pink, yellow, and violet roses perfumed the air as a justice of the peace spoke of sacred unity, friendship, and the expanse and limits of love.

"Declan, do you take this man to be your lawfully wedded partner in civil union?" he asked.

"I do," Declan said. To which Kevin added, "Boy, do I."

Church bells pealed minutes later as Declan lifted his partner for a piggyback ride to their truck. Heart-shaped "Just Married" balloons flapped from the roof.

"It's more than I ever expected," Kevin told me before they drove off, as giddy as any newlyweds. "I feel like the king of the world."

That was what I wanted. To be loved by someone who would shout it out loud, with joy and without hesitation—or who made it obvious to me in myriad, quieter ways that there was no question of his devotion. These couples fought the law, society, and prejudice to forge commitments. It wasn't easy. Still, when they were together, that's how they made it look. It was what I imagined for myself.

I rushed home to Adam. He had come to his own conclusions, and I had barely stepped in the door when he blurted out, "I'm not ready for marriage. I'm not sure about us."

I thought I was going to throw up. I felt as if I had no choice: I told him I could still see him but needed to start dating other people.

One day not long after that, a stranger ran up to Adam and me as we stopped for a red light at a downtown intersection. Breathless and shouting, the stranger looked at Adam and asked, "So, are you going to marry this woman?" He paused. "No, wait, it's already been decided. Congratulations! Have a beautiful life."

He didn't look crazy, this exuberant man in a windbreaker with a clean-shaven face and broad smile. He extended his hand to Adam, who shook it.

The man looked deeply into my eyes. "You know this is what you want."

He turned to Adam. "You know this is what she wants."

I shook his hand, and he walked away, shouting back at us, "Have a beautiful life."

Adam still didn't know what he wanted, but I knew I had had enough. Three of my closest friends married the next weekend. At thirty-five, I opted for the singles tables. Adam and I split up.

The Trying

Pam: "For someone so rational, you seemed obsessed."

Carey: "I felt as if I was trying to will a baby into existence, and the world kept getting in my way."

Beth: "Obviously, the world just didn't know who it was dealing with."

Carey

THE NIGHT AFTER MY DONOR INSEMINATION, Sprax changed his mind and offered to help me get pregnant. Our relationship was wobbling along as tentatively as ever, but he said he had decided not to be so "shy" about it.

We talked a bit further, and then he said he thought we had exhausted the topic. I had to agree. Talking did not seem to illuminate it much. There seemed to be bigger forces than ourselves at work, and we could just shut up.

That September try didn't take. I breathed a sigh of relief. It was disappointing, but at least there would be no need for DNA tests to determine whether the baby was Sprax's or the donor's.

The next month, as my ovulation time approached, I let Sprax know that his next "mission" would come in a few days, and he said, gallantly, "My mission will be with you."

But his work demands at a software start-up weighed heavily and he had been seeming distant, and I worried that he might change his mind. If he did, would I go to the clinic again?

Not this month, I decided; I'd need to nurse my disappointment first. Often, when we kissed good-bye, I felt such heart surges that one kiss turned into four or five, and it seemed to be mutual.

I must be feeling so insecure because I'm in need, I thought. I'm in the unaccustomed position of needing something from him, something very specific, and that makes me feel weak, that dependence. If I knew he really wanted to do it, that would equal out the balance. I must—this refrain again—talk to him about it.

After I got my period that month, I did. I leaned back against my pillow, turned toward him but without meeting his eyes, and said, "If you want to back out, you know, you can, but now is the time to say so."

He misunderstood at first: "Back out? I thought we'd decided I'd be only as involved as I choose . . . ?"

"No, I mean back out of baby making altogether, if you're troubled by it. You haven't been saying much about it lately . . ."

He was silent for a moment, then turned to face me fully. Our eyes met. I tried to keep my face neutral, accepting of whatever he would say. "No," he said finally, "I'm not backing out. I mostly see it as helping you."

"And I'm so grateful for it. And I know there's a giant inconsistency in this, because our emotions are otherwise nowhere near ready to do something this serious."

"Uh-huh," he said. "It's about the most serious thing a couple can ever do together. Well, maybe, in this capitalist culture, buying a house together is more serious. But as I understand it, it will be your baby, and I'll be only as involved as I feel comfortable. Though of course I could always contribute if it meant the child could go to a better school..."

I politely declined. I could do nothing about my own time pressure, but I could try to lift any other possible pressure on him. The ace-in-the-hole feeling of having the donor sperm was fading quickly. More and more these days, I was hoping that Sprax and I would stay together, and that he, not an anonymous donor, would be the father of my child.

In mid-November, I noticed just a bit of blood on my toilet paper. And there was just a bit more later that same morning. My period wasn't due for another week, so it was either early menopause or implantation spotting—a bit of bleeding sometimes caused by the embryo burrowing into the womb. That seemed by far the likeliest possibility.

I walked around Home Depot with Sprax in a daze, wondering if it could be true, suddenly seeing a long road into the future—the growing up of a child. I would be so grateful if it were so. I told Sprax about the blood and at first he started to commiserate, thinking blood must be bad. Then he got it, and met my happy gaze with one of his own. But it could be nothing, I told him, even though I somehow felt sure it was significant.

Nine days later, the pregnancy tests were driving me crazy. My period was a couple of days late, but the lines on the tests were so faint I couldn't tell if they counted as positive or not.

I resorted to a different brand, and it did seem to show a very, very faint line. But again, who could be sure? And to top it all off, I began foolishly reading on the Web about how low levels of the pregnancy hormone HCG bode ill for an embryo. It also tormented me that I didn't really feel anything different. No nausea, no breast tenderness, nothing.

I told Sprax: "This is a little like how I imagine it is to have cancer. There's all kinds of stuff going on in your body, and you're powerless to affect it, even though there's a particular outcome you desperately want to achieve. But you can't do a thing toward achieving it."

He gave me a tight, long hug. "Remember that the usual outcome is a normal, healthy child, despite all the things they tell you can go wrong."

But I was right to worry. My levels of HCG failed to rise the way they should have, and when I was nine weeks into the pregnancy, I began to bleed in earnest.

It was a week after my fortieth birthday. Knowing that I was pregnant had helped me through that daunting date, and the day itself had been filled with pleasure. We spent it skiing in New Hampshire with Liz and her new boyfriend, Jeff, a considerate and affectionate outdoorsman who actually seemed to love her more for her extraordinary goodness than her extraordinary blue-eyed beauty—a rarity among men. Liz and I glowed with happiness for each other; we each seemed to be getting what we wanted most.

I spent the next Friday night at Sprax's house, and in the morning there was a quarter-sized dollop of red blood on my toilet paper.

"I really think this is it," I told him, not crying yet. "I think I'm miscarrying."

He looked crestfallen, then visibly pulled it together. "We'll just have to try again," he said.

I called the hospital. An obstetric nurse called back and, in trying to offer hope, only sowed confusion: it might not be anything, she said in barely comprehensible English. In any case, there was nothing we could do until the ultrasound unit opened on Monday.

In the early evening, the spotting turned into flowing, and Sprax, though exhausted, drove me to the hospital.

"You don't need to stay. I'll really be fine on my own," I told him.

"I'll just be thinking about it anyway," he said.

There was little they could do at the hospital; tests were inconclusive. The bleeding abated, but I spent the weekend afraid to move.

Things felt strangely tenuous with Sprax, even as he was being so supportive. I worried that losing the fetus would send him further away. His friends had told him he was crazy to agree to my baby plan. Maybe my having his baby would alienate him, too. It was all unfathomable. Maybe that was why all I seemed to want to do was spend the weekend sitting in my blue living room chair and staring into space, willing the pregnancy to be all right and trying to accept that so many of the really important things in life were largely out of my control.

On Monday, the ultrasound showed that the embryo had stopped growing at five or six weeks. I found Sprax in the waiting room and told him, "It's bad." In an exam room, waiting for the doctor to come speak with us, he held me as I cried.

"Well, it's all a learning experience," he said.

"One thing I've learned is that you're wonderful to be with in a crisis," I said.

Bob, the obstetrician, was sympathetic and empathetic and encouraging and everything you could wish for at the bedside while you try not to sob.

"Miscarriages are amazingly common," he said. "In sensitivity training, we're taught not to pat women on the shoulder and say they can just get pregnant again, but I do hope to see you soon in happier circumstances."

He didn't mention anything about my advanced age, which was nice, considering that the older you get, the more common miscarriages are. But when I brought it up, he said he'd be willing to be a bit more aggressive about testing for things that might be wrong, like a hormone imbalance, since I felt as if I had little time.

I went to work, but I couldn't fake it. When an editor called to ask me to write a daily story, I wimped out for purely personal reasons, a first in my *Times* career.

"I can't," I said. "I'm kind of a wreck."

And I went home to cry in bed.

The next morning, Sprax asked how I was feeling.

I wrapped my sheet tighter. "A little sad."

"I'm feeling a little empty," he said. "When there was a baby coming, I felt like I was doing something, creating something, even though I was only hanging out."

"Maybe you weren't building a baby," I said. "But maybe you were building a love."

He looked away. "I wish I could figure out all this stuff faster," he said.

I fell silent. I worried that he'd been giving so much lately that he'd need to pull away—maybe all the way away. In which case, I decided, I'd just be grateful that I'd had him while I did. It had been a long time since I'd had to lean on anybody so hard, and he'd been beautifully there.

The next morning, Sprax and I drove up to the Balsams, a sprawling and creaky old New Hampshire resort famous for its historic role as the venue where the first vote in the nation is cast during presidential elections. I was working on another *Times* travel piece, and we were planning to enjoy as many distracting winter sports as we could squeeze into a weekend.

With the downhill and cross-country skiing and the skating

and Ping-Pong, we did a pretty creditable job of having fun until Saturday evening, when I made the mistake of bringing up talk of us over dinner. Jackets and ties were required in the noble old dining room, and his nubbly gray sports coat brought out the gray-blue of his eyes. But his good looks only made me feel worse, more doomed to lose him.

"I feel like such a failure right now," I confessed to him. "I'm just expecting further catastrophe: that you'll tell me you don't want to be with me anymore."

He reassured me, but he never could slather on the mushy talk. He did not say he loved me, which would have been the greatest comfort of all. He must not be able to, I thought, and that is not something to ignore.

We tried playing Ping-Pong, but I told him there was a hole in my heart, and I ended up going to bed and leaking tears. He tried to comfort me and soften what he'd said, but I told him that I must just be in some hypervulnerable state. Sleep was what I loved best in the world, those days.

We met out in Utah a week later, for some hiking and skiing in Bryce Canyon and Zion National Park. He was sick, and I was so depressed that I wanted to sleep more than I wanted to live, but by the end of the trip, all that western red-cliff beauty was working its magic, and a faint dilution of happiness was starting to course back into my veins.

Life is as good as it has always been, I told myself. It's just minus that extra-good thing that I had been hoping for. And there is still more hope to be had.

I toyed with the idea of naming the lost embryo and planting a tree in its memory, but the truth was that I thought of it as a bunch of cells that had failed to realize their potential, not as a lost baby. I read online postings by women who felt as if they would never get over the loss of their "angels." That was not me. But I had an inkling now of how the parents of stillborn babies felt, or even worse, of babies who died after being born. It was too painful to contemplate. There was a whole new world of potential sadness out there for parents, dwarfing any other possible loss.

A couple of weeks later, Sprax was laid off from the unstable start-up where he wrote high-level software. Well, we said to each other, at least he didn't have to worry that there was a baby coming. Not that he would have had to support it anyway, but still, it was somehow a relief that his job status affected only him.

It seemed exorbitant: nearly $200 for a mysterious little machine that purported to be able to tell you far more about your ovulation cycle than the typical drugstore sticks I had been using to determine my most fertile time of month. But I had a good salary, and there was nothing I cared about more than getting pregnant. So I bought a Clearblue Easy Fertility Monitor. In April, the first month I tried it, it told me that I ovulated not on Day 15 after my period began, as I had come to expect, but on Day 17. Suddenly it felt lucky that Sprax was on a hiatus from work and had plenty of time between rock-climbing expeditions. We were each headed west on separate trips soon, but we could try before we left.

On my third day in Arizona, it was time to check whether I was pregnant, but I didn't have a pregnancy test and I didn't have a car at my motel. So I set out along roaring lanes of traffic, marching along a strip where walking was so unthinkable that it not only had no sidewalks, it had no crosswalks even at intersections with traffic lights. Through my head went my most recent mantra, a chunk of an Emily Dickinson poem:

"Hope" is the thing with feathers—
That perches in the soul—
And sings the tune without the words—
And never stops—at all—

I made it to a drugstore and made it back to the hotel room bathroom, and this time there was no doubt. There was a bright blue "yes!" line right where it was supposed to be.

Sprax was unreachable, up on a cliff somewhere, so I called my best friend, Liz, who was mildly excited, as I was. That is what miscarriage does to you; a positive pregnancy test means nothing more than a promising start. It is better than nothing, but too far from a baby for real elation.

That night, I had a portentous dream. I was climbing among a complex of rickety staircases, almost like fire escapes, high up in the clouds. It was perilous, but my hand was being firmly held by the trunk of a baby elephant, which was climbing with me. The trunk fitted neatly inside my fist, reminding me of how, when my little sister, Morgan, was barely toddling, I would help her walk by letting her hold my index fingers inside her small fists as she moved along. The baby elephant gave me a comforting feeling of not being alone, even though she—and it was definitely a she—was just a baby, and could not really do anything to help me.

In the months that followed, that dream helped me believe that everything would be all right with this pregnancy, and I would be joined by a robust little friend.

With his duty to me done, Sprax was freer than ever to live the life of a climbing bum, stopping at the best cliffs around the West and picking up belay partners. He encountered hard-core types who had done virtually nothing but climb for the last twenty years, and happily shared campfires and tales with them. His muscles swelled; his hair grew almost to his shoulders and he bleached it blond-white. His looks started to remind me of one of those tan, brawny types on the covers of romance novels, with a slightly spooky, dissipated twist—a stoner Fabio.

But his money was starting to run out. A friend of a friend offered him a job in a local start-up, and the end of his climbing spree loomed. He chafed at the prospect of being leashed to a desk again, and I suspected that, though his monthly obligation at my ovulation time was done, I was looking more and more like a captor as well, one of the forces conspiring against his freedom.

Meanwhile, I was scheduled for my twelve-week checkup in mid-June. All seemed to be going well. An ultrasound at six weeks had shown the embryo's pulsating heart. But I was very nervous, had heard too many tales of women going in at twelve weeks, expecting to get out of the woods of miscarriage anxiety and announce the pregnancy to the world, only to find that the heartbeat had disappeared.

Sprax decided to take off on a last impromptu climbing trip to New Hampshire instead of going to the checkup with me. I told him I was kind of surprised that he would choose the trip over the once-in-a-lifetime experience of hearing his first child's heartbeat.

"Do you think I'm running away?" he asked.

Of course I did.

"If you are, I understand," I said.

The appointment went very well. Bob could hear the heartbeat right away with his stethoscope, and he said my uterus was nice and big. It was a gigantic relief.

Sprax called that afternoon to ask how it had gone.

Then he didn't call again for six days.

Finally, I left him a message on his cell phone, asking if he was all right. He didn't call back until the morning he was planning to return.

I was trying to feel understanding, and failing.

"I've been spending long days on the cliffs, and camping out at night," he said.

This was not the Himalayas. It was New Hampshire.

I knew my time constraints had put him in a completely unfair position. I knew he felt hideous pressure to commit. But the point was how he was treating me right now. I was pregnant with his child and he had not seen fit to call me for a week.

By the time he came over that night, the words that came out of my mouth were: "If you want to go, why don't you just go?"

"I can't separate how I treat you right now from the pressure I feel from you for a commitment," he said. "It's all of a piece." His feelings had swung far away from the desire to settle down, he said; he was confused, but right now he wasn't sure he would ever settle down.

He thought I'd already decided we should break up. I hadn't, but now felt myself inexorably falling toward the decision.

"I need a stand-up guy," I found myself telling him. "This is a scary period. I need people I can count on. I need you to, a little bit, take care of me. I'm with you, but I don't feel loved by you, and that makes me unhappy. It would be easier for me to be on my own than to be with someone who doesn't love me."

"If you need me to beam love straight at you, I can't do that, given the other things I'm feeling, and I don't have a switch I can turn off and on," he said.

"Does being with me block your fulfillment in some way?"

He thought a bit. "Life with you is good and easy," he said. "And maybe I'm not so hungry because of it."

I laughed. "And that's bad? I feel damned if I do and damned if I don't. If life had been bad with me, that would be cause for complaint, too."

It went on and on. We sat on the couch, me with my legs pulled protectively to my chest, and never raised our voices. I asked what he really wanted out of life. He said: to do something semicreative, get rich, and move out west. I pressed him. Why didn't he just move out west now? He got a little defensive: It's one thing to go play out there, he said, and another to move out there for real, to work. But if he had known we were going to break up, he would have made plans a couple of months ago to move back out there. Now he wanted to be here for the baby's birth.

We officially broke up. My tears came and went. He packed all the gear he'd been keeping at my house. We ate some baked potatoes. I hugged him, my heart aching, and went upstairs to sleep it off. The next morning, his size thirteen shoes were no longer in front of the fireplace. Mine were back in an orderly array.

"I feel like calling him and telling him I made a terrible mistake," I told Liz. "I also feel like the only hope is for him to get a good taste of life without me, and decide it's better with me. One thing is for sure: I miss him. I've never felt as much love for him as I do right now."

We stayed broken up. I wasn't sure if it was the right thing, but it did ease the tensions between us a great deal. We saw each other once or twice a week when he was around, as friends, and gave each other big hugs but no more.

He broke his ankle in a climbing fall that also left a gash in his thigh big enough to need twenty stitches. When he came in for my amniocentesis, I had to wheel him around the obstetrics offices in a borrowed hospital wheelchair. He held my hand while the amnio needle went in, and we watched together on the ultrasound as the baby wiggled wildly in the womb.

In terms of measurements, Bob said, it looked "perfect." The yummiest word, "perfect." You would never expect it of a child later in life, but at this moment, it was the best of all possible words.

Two weeks later, the genetic counselor called my office at the *Times* bureau with the results. My skin froze when she identified herself, but she said instantly that everything was all right, and that I would be having a girl. It was uncontainable news: I staggered out of my little office to the anteroom, where Julie Flaherty, my young assistant, was sitting.

"It's a girl! And she's all right!"

Julie jumped up and down. "It's a girl! It's a girl! It's a girl!"

I had hoped for a girl. Not only because I imagined I would be more naturally attuned to her, but because the father situation was so unclear. Somehow, I imagined, if Sprax ended up largely absent, that would be less likely to mess up a girl than a boy. She would have me as a primary parental model, and my dad as a frequent male presence in her life, and that might do it. A boy might need more maleness than I could provide.

At the end of July, I officially went on leave from the *New York Times*. To my great good fortune, I had been chosen for a Knight Science Journalism Fellowship, a Massachusetts Institute of Technology program that allows midcareer journalists to take a blissful year off and audit any courses they choose at MIT and Harvard. For me, it was a ticket to make the change from the endless cycles of crime and politics I covered to what I imagined would be the more lofty and uplifting news of health and science.

The *Times* bureau threw me a farewell party, complete with a mock page of the paper—"Carey Hanging Up Babushka to Put Her Sass in Science" was the lead headline—that is the traditional parting gift. It was a heady affair, made headier by the stifling night and the poor air circulation in my stuffy living room. The two grand old men who shared the bureau with me attended: the preternaturally erudite book reviewer Richard Eder and the übermensch columnist Tony Lewis; Sprax was there, along with a couple of dozen friends and colleagues. They read the mock paper aloud, and I laughed until my smile muscles hurt. But the best fun of the party was quietly dropping the bomb into conversation after conversation: "And also, I'm four months pregnant..."

Still, I was having some pangs of "What have I gotten myself into?" The more I read about taking care of babies, the more I struggled to accept that I would basically lose the second half of the fellowship, unable to do much more than care for my daughter and catch up on sleep.

I missed Sprax, but I also saw no reason to believe that, if we got back together, things would be any better than they had been. I hoped against hope that he wouldn't start going out with anyone else for a long, long time.

One day I ran into Sprax's old live-in girlfriend, his longest love, and we compared notes.

"He's not dependable," she cautioned me. "You should figure on doing whatever is needed for the baby on your own."

"Oh, I will," I said. "I'm not scared of him letting me down. I'm only a bit scared that he might fall so in love with the baby that he'll fight for custody or something."

"No, no," she assured me. "He's really a decent person at heart, and he wouldn't do something like that."

The fellowship began, and I wore loose clothing to the first couple of informal meetings with the nine other fellows, not quite ready to come out as a pregnant single mother.

Finally, at a seafood lunch with the fellowship's distinguished director, Boyce Rensberger, I told him.

He had just taken a big bite of roll, and almost choked on it.

I apologized that I wouldn't be able to give the second half of the fellowship as much time as I'd like, but swore that I'd do my very best to squeeze the most out of the whole experience, and miss as little as possible. He was supremely gracious; mainly, he wondered if there might not be some way I could get back together with the baby's father.

"I don't think so," I said. "But I'll be fine on my own—really."

As my pregnancy progressed, it got me down sometimes, the single-mother thing. Other women had loving men who stuck with them through the birth and beyond, but I was somehow Not Good Enough for that. The only worse state from an evolutionary point of view was to be unable to get anyone to impregnate you at all, I thought, and it sure came close to that for me. For all my modern woman's strength and independence, it still hurt at some very basic level.

Though Sprax was willing to attend the hospital's daylong prenatal class with me, it occurred to me that I might actually get stood up in the delivery room. I was on a river and the only way out was through Class 5 rapids, possibly alone. I thought about inviting Morgan and Liz—or would it be too crowded if they all came?

"You don't understand. I really am afraid of the delivery," said Sprax, the man who climbed two-hundred-foot cliffs. "When I was growing up, there was a lot of talk of fathers passing out. I guess in some ways I'm a fifties man. My dad was never present at our births... and it looks so painful, so extreme..."

I placed an ad in Boston's Russian newspaper for a nanny and fielded a deluge of responses. Finally I met Leeza Titova. A former aeronautical engineer from Ukraine, she was about my age and had two nearly grown children of her own. There was something solid about her and the spotless apartment where she lived with her husband and children, a good counterweight to the flimsier situation at my house. Hiring her was one of the best decisions I ever made.

I was growing and growing, up thirty pounds with two months still to go. My hair grew longer too, more luxuriant than ever before, and my skin glowed. I was spared diabetes and gum disease, and had only a moderate case of hemorrhoids.

I had a nightmare that I looked in the mirror and saw that I was thin and couldn't remember how I had lost the pregnancy. Somehow it made me focus on how important it was to me to prove to Sprax that I could bear a healthy child.

He and I went out to a movie one night, and in my kitchen afterward, he put his hand on my swelling belly in hopes of feeling a kick. Nothing, of course. He took his hand away.

"I feel shy about it," he said.

"No need to."

"I'll really be coming around more now."

Sprax and I did the paperwork. I borrowed the text of a no-strings fatherhood agreement from my single-mother friend Sally, and I saw a lawyer for a $200 hour to talk it through. She kept bringing up far-fetched possibilities that would work out better if I could get Sprax to sign away all his paternal rights.

"What if," she said, "you marry another man whose social security benefits could accrue to your daughter only if he could legally adopt her?"

But I would have none of it. "Sprax found the courage to father this child with me," I said. "He is her father unless he decides otherwise. I am not going to ask him to sign that away."

In the end, Sprax and I both read the document and agreed to it, but we never got around to signing it in front of a notary, which would have made it legally binding.

Sprax and I met before dawn one morning to see the Leonids meteor shower from a dark peninsula. Without touching, we lay back in a beached boat high on a little hill and scanned the skies. It was wondrous, streaks of light across the black sky every second or so, then a stealthy dawn over the rocks and water. I tried wishing on the shooting stars—health and joy for the baby—but it didn't seem like a wishing situation. There were too many of them.

Sprax swore he could remember seeing the elephants on a trip to the zoo that happened while he was still in his mother's womb, and he said we should ask the baby when she was old enough whether she remembered this.

Later, as we drank steaming tea at my kitchen table, I brought up the climbing trip in Mexico he had planned for two weeks before my due date. It was unlikely that he would miss my delivery, I told him, but I still couldn't understand his willingness to take that chance.

There was a long pause.

"I know this will sound crazy," he said, "but it's bothering me that I don't feel very needed."

I quashed an impulse to shout in outrage. Instead I folded my hands on the table and leaned forward, carefully calm. I'd built a structure of twenty-four-hour care for the baby, I told him, and all I wanted was to know how much he planned to participate.

"I really do want to be around a lot, and to support you," he said. "I still have such guilt feelings, that I agreed to have a child with you, but then couldn't commit. I feel like a heel."

The last thing I wanted him to feel was guilt. Guilt could lead to avoidance.

"Don't. Really don't. You've done me a greater favor than anyone else has ever done me."

As we hugged good-bye, I wanted to say I loved him. Instead, I just gave him an extra kiss on the cheek.

I chose the name Liliana, after my grandmother Lillian, and Isa after my mother. Sprax agreed easily to both.

Days before my due date, deep under the spell of all the science I was learning at MIT and Harvard, I went a little crazy and wrote an essay about the cosmic significance of the baby I was about to bear.

It linked her to the great chain of living that went back a couple of billion years to the first eukaryotic cells and a few billion years further back to the formation of the stars in which the carbon of her body had been formed.

"This is the chain she joins," I wrote,

> *and with her birth, Life has triumphed once again, marching forward one being at a time into the future. Life has triumphed over all kinds of physical forces—the high odds against a sperm reaching an egg, and the increased odds against a woman my age being able to have a baby, and the astronomical odds against a single cell developing correctly into a beautifully formed little being of several trillion cells, all of them in just the right place and serving just the right function . . .*
>
> *The future is what a baby carries. On a planet already crowded with six billion people, it sometimes strikes me as strange that everyone views a birth as such a joyous event. The world, you could argue, doesn't need another person. But the thing is, maybe it needs this person. This little person comes bearing hope, plump with promise. And she is cause for*

cheer, too, because she is a tiny traveler embarking on a great adventure, and we know a little of how wondrous that adventure is likely to be. We know a lot of what she'll find out: the beauty of the trees and waters and skies of this planet, and the joys of the mind and the body and the soul, of the love of fellow beings, and sometimes pain and sorrow.

But we also don't know anything about how her young life will intersect with the roiling life of the world at large; we know only that for all our failings, all our laziness, all our aimlessness, all our procrastination, we're getting some kind of second chance. Maybe what we didn't do, or what we didn't get right, the next generation will, and maybe we can raise them to be better than we are—at least there is that hope. At least this child will march forward, and maybe she'll get someplace.

All of which is not to say that the main purpose of a child is to fix our mistakes and turn out better than we are. The purpose of a child is simply to be, and to be loved and cherished and taught. My only real hope for Liliana is that she love the world, and love her own life within it.

Sprax called twice from Mexico, walking an hour each way from the cliff campsite to the phone booth.

"I think," Liz said, "that you and Sprax really do love each other."

"That may be true," I said, "but that doesn't necessarily mean we should be together. It's true, though: I have a terribly tender spot for him."

Liz was in the midst of agonizing over her own relationship with Jeff, the outdoorsman, loving him deeply but also seeing flaws in the relationship that she wasn't sure she could accept.

I couldn't advise her.

My due date came and went. Then another day. And another. My feet puffed up, so full of fluid I could no longer see any veins or bones in them. When I looked down on them, they reminded me of dog or cat paws. People kept calling, to the point that I put a message on my voicemail saying that the day's baby forecast was "Nothing imminent."

Sprax, back from Mexico in plenty of time, stopped by often, and took to carrying my old *Times* pager so he could be reached as soon as labor began.

We had meandering kitchen-table talks in the evenings. He told me that when he was little, he would wander off and get lost so often that his parents put an ID bracelet on his wrist so that the people who found him could call them to come get him.

"What a benign world it was then!" I said. And what a little character, always climbing out of his crib, wandering away, making rambunctious mischief. Maybe some people, I thought, shy away from commitments because of a pure wandering temperament, a footloose nature bred deep in the bone. His mother had told me that he climbed out of his crib at a mere nine months. At MIT, he had transferred from physics to computers to neuroscience, unable to stay fenced in by a single discipline. The Mormon Church, for all its potent culture, could not keep him in. He seemed to hold no grudges against the institutions or people he escaped. He just needed to go.

Finally, we decided to induce. I spent my last day as a non-mother reading a *New Yorker,* napping, and eating pizza with grape soda. Liz flew in from Washington, DC. Sprax came over. So did Morgan. With her hair dyed deep black, setting off her pale blue eyes and pale, perfect skin, she had fit in well for years in the tattooed slacker culture of Seattle, but this birth was enough to help bring her back to the hidebound East. She had just moved home to Boston, in part to be an involved aunt.

We were all nonplussed. None of us had been where I was going. We didn't really even know what to say about it, except that it was going to be big and very different.

The Birth Team—Sprax, Liz, and Morgan—drove me to the hospital at six a.m. The IV line went in, the pitocin drip started to get labor going. My belly ballooned out the hospital johnny to almost the size of the huge exercise ball we'd brought to help with labor. The fetal monitor showed I had been having contractions; I just hadn't been feeling them. In midafternoon, my water broke, gushing as I was walking to the bathroom, but nothing much else happened. By evening, the pain picked up and I asked for my epidural. It didn't seem to last very long, and I kept asking for another bolus. Bolus: I imagined it as a great white ball of painlessness that swept down my spine. But the relief lasted only an hour or so, and then I'd be moaning, "Ow, ow, ow!" again.

Liz and Morgan each held a leg as I pushed, and Sprax massaged my shoulders and back in various places and seemed to be trying to will the birth to happen as he watched the pushing. I'd thought I wouldn't want him down there staring at my shaved labia, but all modesty was moot now.

By morning, the doctors said that if I didn't make much progress in another half hour or so, they thought I should consider a cesarean section. The baby's head seemed stuck, and though there was no sign that she was in distress, the labor was getting long. I pushed and pushed and pushed, and then assented, sad to surrender but not sad that this would all soon be over.

They cranked up my epidural for the C-section, but I could still feel violent pushing and tugging, as if they were pulling out all my organs and laying them along my body on display. I had the shakes, powerfully. My chattering teeth entertained me. Sprax held my hand through the whole thing, and, watching over the drape across my torso, saw Liliana first when she came out.

"She's perfect," a doctor said as soon as she emerged, and when I heard her mewling cry, I broke into tears myself, my heart flooding with welcome, the feeling of "You're here. You're here!"

It had been a long, long road, this, and it hadn't been clear until now that we would ever get here, she and I.

Liz said later that "perfect" was the word that occurred to her as well, when she first saw Liliana. True, this little girl had a very unorthodox start, Liz thought, but she was whole and beautiful, and she would be surrounded by love and have everything she needed. Life did not need to be conventional to be wonderful.

"She's a big one," someone said. The scale read nine pounds, four ounces.

Sprax was the first to hold her, his huge hands cradling her gently. Then they laid her near me as they wheeled me out of the room, and at the sight of her unfamiliar and beloved face, I felt my tears dripping onto the gurney. How funny, not to know her but to love her so. Oh! was my thought. So it was you in there all this time!

She looked nothing like me, everything like Sprax, and she was so *ours*.

The Transfer

Beth: "I guess I was ready. The transfer of those vials was an act of hope."

Pam: "Not ideal."

Beth: "No."

Carey: "But hopeful. And I was ready to let them go."

Beth

WITH THE DIVORCE BARELY BEHIND ME, I arrived at my friend Marie's house for a bike ride. She and her husband, Jake, lived just north of Boston, across from the Middlesex Fells, an urban mountain biker's paradise. Jake had cashed out of his software business a year earlier, and their financial status had gone from comfortable to wealthy. He offered me coffee and asked if I'd seen *Boston* magazine, the city's biggest glossy monthly.

"No," I told him.

He handed it to me and pointed to the headline. "Take a deep breath first," he warned.

"First Came Love, Then Came Money: Beantown's Power Divorces" was splashed across the cover.

And there I was, on page 124, stuck between the divorces

of Sumner Redstone and the guy who started Staples. Suddenly my divorce was high profile.

The article portrayed me as the injured party, the jilted spouse. But that was a lean upside.

"Jesus," I said, looking up at Jake. "How did I get in here?"

"Keep reading."

I'd kept the details of my settlement private; I didn't want to deal with my boss's and my colleagues' reactions.

The gossip hound at my office greeted me the next morning demanding more than asking, "Did you see *Boston* magazine?" He nearly drooled the question, hoping to spring the news. Other people in my office just raised their eyebrows, nodded at me, and rubbed their thumbs and forefingers together. I closed my door, and my office mate swiveled her chair toward me. "You get 'em, tiger," she growled.

"I did my best," I told her, dropping into my seat. "It's ten a.m., and I need a drink."

"The best I can offer is chocolate pretzels, but I'm willing to drink whatever you provide. We can keep the door closed all day." Aside from going to the bathroom, that's what I did. I avoided everyone, feeling totally exposed. I was the girl down the hall who won the lottery.

And how did *Boston* get the saucy details?

I never found out. Nobody interviewed me or asked my permission. But I have my theories about who talked.

I thought about suing. But I just wanted to live my life, or find out what my life was at that point, and learn to live it.

It could be anywhere. So I went to Paris. And California. I could be anyone. So I got my navel pierced. I got a tattoo. I had some random flings.

* * *

I spent a week with my grandmother that summer. She was an artist, a women's rights activist, a former client of Margaret Sanger's, a resident of Santa Cruz and Laguna. We planted flowers, talked about the importance of being independent. "Gran," I said, as I pulled weeds and didn't look at her. "I'm thinking that if I don't meet somebody, *and* I don't really think I will, at least not soon enough, I'll have a baby on my own."

She was arthritic and had diabetes. She'd survived three battles with cancer, confronted plenty in life that might have broken her, but she wore Hawaiian print shirts and had an optimism that couldn't be shaken. She put down her spade, sat on the stone steps of her bungalow, and rested her hands on her knees. "Honey, I don't wish for you the work of raising a child alone, but I wish for you what you wish for yourself, and you're strong enough to do it. I was a child when I had your mother, and I'm not sorry I did it, but I still remember driving home from the hospital, with her lying across my lap, and wondering, What am I supposed to do with this tiny fragile thing?"

"You seem to have done okay," I said, trimming one of her rose bushes and handing her a yellow bud. She tucked it behind her ear.

"You will too."

There with my gran in her garden planted with roses and a palm tree she'd grown from a coconut, I stated my decision to have a baby. And while opening my mouth didn't make it real, it was progress.

I continued searching for ways to redefine myself. And I found them. Beyond the tattoo and the piercing, I meditated, I ran miles along the Charles River, I went dogsledding and to the symphony. I smoked pot and went to an all-girls surf camp. I got happy. I felt like Venus rising in Boston, lifting to enter the light. I became someone I liked, but who still made mistakes. And who, at some point, would have a baby.

There were altruistic things I wanted for that baby: love, a world without war, a mother who did a decent job of picking romantic partners, but I also wanted that baby to have financial security. I figured that even if I couldn't prevent war, I could rely on a healthy bank account. Or so I thought.

Then the bottom fell out of the stock market and Lycos completely collapsed. I'd hired lousy advisors and held onto the stock for too long. I'm fortunate that I came out with about a third of the money I'd started with. It was a hard break, but bearable.

I was still wealthy. But had I changed? And if I had, what had changed me? The divorce? The money? I lent and gifted money, but that didn't make the beneficiaries millionaires. It helped them pay off debts. I was no longer another working girl who had to watch her checking account. I felt relieved, and thrilled to still be more than solvent, but I also felt a strange shift. All my adult life I'd worked, I'd had bosses, or I'd lived on the edge as a temp or a freelancer, and now I could drop out of the working world.

Marie and Jake had been here, too. Jake had nothing but a Ford van when he started his first company, and he'd sold his third business for a fortune. They'd been financially comfortable for years, but suddenly their bank accounts had skyrocketed. Marie was a good friend. I figured she had some insight.

"Do I get people more extravagant gifts now?" I asked her as we bumped along a mountain bike trail through the Winchester Fells. We spent hours, in sun and rain, cycling through the reservation, careening down dirt trails. It felt more like

Vermont than suburbia. "What percentage do you guys give to philanthropy?" I turned a corner and rode up a difficult rocky incline. "I'm confused. I only know myself as a working woman, checking my bank account every time I take something out or put something in to make sure I don't overdraft or bounce the electric bill. How is a wealthy divorcée supposed to act? Should I feel different? Do I start paying for everyone's dinners? It's making me feel off-kilter."

"Pay attention to the trail or you're going to break your neck," she shouted from behind me. "And then you'll end up using all your money on disability payments. Think of it this way. Your friends are happy for your good fortune, but they don't want it pushed in their faces."

Pam and I stayed friends. We were an unlikely duo: the romantic and the cynic, the sylph and the jock. But we were both curious about the world and had flexible schedules. On a trip to northern Maine we spent an evening at a strip club, doing research for a potential story on the local economy. The place reeked of smoke, beer, and sweat. Men spun into the parking lot on snowmobiles, and motors revved louder than the deafening music from inside. The dancers were young, very young. Some not yet out of their teens. Peaches, a sweet brunette in a bleached-blond bob wig, told us their pay and tips barely covered food and rent. Most were mothers, and they ended up talking about their kids. "I'm all my daughter has," Peaches shouted over the pulsing music and through the smoke. "This"—she gestured with her lipstick at the men who waited to watch her dance—"this means nothing."

A drunk guy fell into the tiny dressing room, knocking down the beaded curtain. The bouncer, Peaches's boyfriend, shoved him back toward the bar. Peaches stepped over him. "You do what you have to do," she told us as she grabbed a pink boa off the vanity. She straightened her wig and walked through the curtain toward her next lap dance.

When we stepped outside the bar, the world was suddenly silent. Only snow and ice crunching under our boots and a black, black sky. We both breathed deeply, the biting air a complete shock after the overheated, stale bar.

"You do what you have to do," Pam repeated, looking over at me.

"I think you'd do anything," I said, unlocking the car. "When you have kids."

Pam was always heading off somewhere, then racing to meet a deadline.

"I'd like to go back to journalism," I told her when we were home from Maine. I'd stopped writing after graduate school, and felt like a student approaching her professor.

"Here, write this down," she said, with no hesitation. I was driving, juggling my cell phone and a pen. "I'll give you my old editor's name."

I pulled over. That was Pam. She didn't know anything about my writing, but she knew how to share, even in a highly competitive profession. "And I'll call to let her know you'll be contacting her."

I phoned the editor immediately. She took a risk and, based on Pam's recommendation, gave me my first assignment. Many followed. I found a new career. I wrote mostly for the *Boston Globe*'s city section, about offbeat topics: a cache of Paul Revere's silver that was found in the dusty basement of a Unitarian church; Boston's sewage being converted into fertilizer for Florida orange groves; fish processing; abandoned Nike missile silos on the Harbor Islands.

And I was living an offbeat life. I left my job at the Mind/Body Medical Institute and became a self-employed divorcée, a statistic, but I was okay with that. On a fine morning in April I dug through my jewelry box and found my wedding ring. Russell didn't believe in the merchandising of marriage, so we'd bought inexpensive rings at a discount jeweler. As I left the house for a run, I shoved the thin gold band into my pocket. I jogged to a park along the Charles River, slowed my pace, and took it out. I looked at it briefly, thinking, Good riddance, then threw the ring as far into the muddy river as possible. It caught the sun and glinted as it sailed away from me. Then it was gone, below the surface. A rower in a single scull watched me and glided past. I smiled, and kept running.

Russell had done me a favor by insisting on cheap bands. The elemental pleasure of watching the ring disappear below the murky water far outweighed its value.

While there were moments when I wanted someone to be with me, for the most part, I was fine, fine, fine.

Then the holidays. There were so many people staying at my parents' house for Thanksgiving that, no longer part of a couple, I was relegated to sleeping on the couch. That didn't make me feel fine. I ate a lot of stuffing, hid behind the barn to smoke cigarettes, and tried not to roll onto the floor in the middle of the night.

"What are you doing for Christmas?" Pam asked me.

I laughed. Or scoffed. "My nails. The manicurists are Buddhists. Maybe I'll start a new trend for single Jews."

"Sign me up," she said.

* * *

Christmas Eve is an odd night for Jews. With no plans for the evening, we decided to go to Brookline: Jewish speed dating at a Kabbalah Centre.

"Hey," I said to her, "at least we won't be eating Chinese and watching a Woody Allen movie."

"That might be preferable." She sighed as we walked in the Kabbalah Centre door, faced with a large crowd of twenty- and thirty-somethings sizing one another up. There was wine and cheese. Some mini bagels. Lots of darting eyes. Eight potential Jewish dates, eight minutes to converse with each. Conversations ended abruptly, and we were sent along to our next partner. It felt distressingly like middle school square dancing.

While we were moving around the room, between possible dates four and five, I stopped Pam. "I think I'm done," I told her. "You were right. It only takes three minutes to figure this out. Three minutes to decide if you ever want to see a person again. Three minutes for a political debate to start. Three minutes to get bored beyond belief. Three minutes to want to run."

We skipped out on the dating and had dinner at a Thai restaurant. It wasn't exactly Chinese, but it wasn't ideal either.

There were moments during that dinner when our loneliness felt as enduring as the chilly New England night. I remember looking out the plate glass, and in the same way that it seems as if the whole world's smoking when you're trying to quit, everyone walking along the street seemed to be partnered. Christmas lights glittered in the clear night.

I pulled my scarf tight as we left the restaurant. "I'm almost thinking we should've grabbed a couple of Kabbalah boys."

"Bad idea," Pam said. "Someone's out there. Waiting. Just

not at the Kabbalah Centre." An unrelenting believer. Me, I was willing to settle for a warm body and some mistletoe.

We hugged, then moved toward home, walking our separate ways.

I set out to find love. Jewish speed dating, bars, friends' former boyfriends, and a foray into online dating had failed, so I paid a matchmaker named Zelda $2,000 to find me the right man. I fired her after the first two setups and demanded a refund. One guy was a right-wing banker who rarely stepped foot outside his office except to drive his Miata around Wellesley, the other a divorced back surgeon who was so tired on our three dates that I had to resist snapping my fingers in his face.

But I wasn't fully committed. I balanced my quest with some exciting and shallow flings: The twenty-one-year-old sexy-as-hell parking valet from my garage. A colleague's friend who invited me to Chicago and took me to a Cubs game. A slick PR guy who kept a Hooters calendar next to his bed. A plumber. A television news anchor. I turned down my college professor, who was on a book tour and told me he'd wanted me since I was nineteen.

I was being shallow and knew it. But, I reasoned, it was a phase. A fun phase. I wanted a hiatus from the heavy stuff. No legal wrangling, no one else's emotions as my responsibility. Pretty clothes, a hot bod, and a tan. Sex about sex, not about love, romance, or a future. A tasty cocktail and a nice dinner. A hot dog at a baseball game.

But that wasn't the whole story. I was willing to forgo all of it on one condition. I was willing to grow up yet again, to go deeper into my motives and acknowledge that there could be, in fact, more to my life. If I could have the most elemental experience allowed to a person, I would take it and run happily headlong into the future. Without digging too deeply, I knew I still wanted the least shallow, most simultaneously selfish and unselfish thing in the world. Far more than I realized, and to a degree that startled me, I wanted—and hoped I hadn't waited too long for—a child.

I'd missed my projected motherhood deadline and, at thirty-nine, was barreling toward that scary marker for women: forty. I'd become careless with birth control, even with completely inappropriate partners. And that was a wake-up call, a milestone, a clear indication that I should stop being dismissive of my motives. I needed to be proactive, and that meant not using contraceptive failure as the means for constructing a future.

If I'm honest, I have to admit that every one of the men I slept with I considered as a possible sperm donor. There were drawbacks to all of them. The one I considered the most seriously was the sexy wanna-be fighter-pilot parking valet, who I figured I'd never tell. As an experiment, every now and then I asked a male friend if he'd be interested in parenting my child. All said they were pleased to be asked. None accepted.

And this is where I entered the wide world of sperm donorship. Its myriad possibilities and infinite choices.

Freelance journalism offers unlimited opportunities for procrastination; if your story is filed by deadline, nobody cares what else you're doing in front of your computer. So I spent hours online looking up donors on sperm bank sites and considering who of the multitudes might be the biological father of my future child. Listed before me were thousands upon thousands of men. All were young and (claimed to be) healthy. Some were strapping rugby players, others slim aesthetes. They were athletic, brainy, dog lovers, ornithologists, horse trainers, Olympic swimmers. A rainbow coalition of Jews, Muslims, vegetarians, and cowboys. It was like French pastry: everything was appealing, but it couldn't all be as good as it looked.

In late August, Pam performed an amazing feat of matchmaking. One afternoon, we sat on her little urban terrace overlooking trees and parking spaces. It was muggy, everyone in the city was sticky from the heat, and we tried unsuccessfully to mediate the humidity by drinking frozen lemonade and occasionally dipping our faces into a bowl full of ice water. I complained that it was difficult to select a father for your child out of the thousands of sperm donors available. "Ethnomusicologist with a love for Rottweilers and part ownership in a tent hotel in Fiji?" I asked her. "Or the sensitive kindergarten teacher who babysits for his nephews and is a trained Cordon Bleu chef? Football or hacky sack? Glaciology PhD and 780 math SATs or Peace Corps volunteer with functional Zulu? Do I want dimples? Long eyelashes? "

"I like the idea of Fiji and dimples. Any of them have a villa in Tuscany?" She brought her laptop outside with more lemonade. "Let's take a peek, shall we?" I gave her my password to Xytex, and she logged on. "Amazing," she agreed. "The choices are infinite. Overwhelming, almost."

I sighed. Then sighed again. "Not that I'm averse to the sperm having a villa anywhere, but chances are my child and the father would probably never meet. *Mi casa no es su casa.* Kind of a postmodern arranged marriage. You pick who you want, but you never meet him, just have his kid."

"Not the perfect arrangement."

"No. Not perfect. But what marriage is? It's all about compromise, right?" The searching inspired a blend of exhilaration and depression. I could have what I wanted, but the price was having less than I desired.

"I might know someone who can help," she told me. "I think my friend Carey has some extra vials of sperm."

Not the answer everyone's looking for, but it worked for me.

Carey was in her living room, with blond baby Liliana asleep in a porta-crib on the torrentially rainy night we met. There were tumbling mats on the floor, and the room was in a general state of disarray. This can be me, I thought, looking around at the tipped bottles, scattered toys, and piles of picture books. This woman looks happy.

"I know this is a strange way to meet," she said as she welcomed me in and we sat on the floor. "But you're a friend of Pam's, and that's enough of an endorsement for me. And I'd really love to have somebody use the vials." No small talk with Carey. "Also, selfishly, it'd be great to know someone who makes the same decision as me."

I was comfortable in Carey's house, sitting on the floor in a place that was all about a family of two. We made tea. Then she took waking Liliana out of her crib, and held her baby's sleepy body against her chest. Outside, rain was falling hard. The weather had cooled; late summer was moving toward autumn. We spent a few minutes quietly watching Liliana breathe.

"She's amazing, isn't she?" Carey asked me, truly a question, not a statement, as if she were startled by her daughter's existence. "I don't know how much you know about how Liliana got here," she added. "But Sprax and I aren't involved anymore. Except through her." She kissed the baby's head, then her palm. Pam had told me a little, but I chose to look blank. Then Carey told me about Sprax, about how he'd ultimately agreed to be a father, and how she still owned the seven remaining vials of 8282. They were in deep freeze in Arlington. While we were talking, Sprax arrived, drenched, having ridden his bike over after work. He and Carey greeted each other coolly, and after Carey kissed Liliana's head, Sprax quickly went upstairs with the baby.

"He's a big outdoorsman," Carey told me. "You hike too, right? Maybe you and Sprax would make a better match than we did."

I noticed a photo of a smiling, curly-haired woman on the mantel, and Carey said it was her mother. "One thing I'm really sorry about," she told me, "is that my mother isn't here for this."

Carey needed to run errands during the few hours Sprax would be at the house, so we drank the tea, then cleared it away. She loaded me up with books about single motherhood before I left.

"It feels like a juggernaut," I told her when I was getting ready to go. "It's weird, making this decision this way." I held up the books. "With supplemental reading material and some deep-freeze sperm. Not quite what I had in mind. I thought there'd be a bed if nothing else."

Carey shrugged. "I got a bed, but that part didn't last. It's the baby that matters, not how she got here."

Her kitchen was messy, her daughter's father wasn't all she'd hoped for, but she had this nearly perfect little family, a great job, an incredible Russian nanny, a doting grandpa. I'd just met this woman, but she had what I wanted, down to the sperm to make it happen. Carey and I agreed that if I made a donation to a children's organization, the sperm could be mine. Easy as that.

Donor 8282 didn't meet my criteria. I wanted dark hair and blue eyes. He was blond. I wanted tall, but not six feet five. I wanted funny, and from his profile 8282 didn't sound very funny. He liked small dogs, football, and Italian cheese. That was about as exciting as it got. But I liked Carey immediately, and she liked 8282.

I gratefully accepted the vials.

The Verge

Carey: "Did you ever stop dreaming of romantic love?"

Pam: "I stopped believing that love would happen in time for a baby. But I never stopped believing that love would happen."

Beth: "Despite all evidence to the contrary?"

Pam

I FOUND MYSELF CHANNELING my late Jewish grandmother Ruth, a birdlike woman with impeccable 1950s style and a way with chopped liver. She signaled that I was sorely mistaken if I thought I was going to meet Mr. Right by working at home, living in a gay male neighborhood, exercising at an all-female gym, and throwing clay at a pottery studio with still more women.

"This," she intoned in my head, "is how you expect to meet a boy, get married, and have babies?" Pause, for dramatic effect. "I think not."

I ditched the girls' gym and joined a coed health club. I signed up for evening guitar classes and scanned apartments for rent across the river in Cambridge, where universities and coffeehouses brimmed with new possibilities. I wanted to feel truly known by someone, to grow old with him, travel the world, and create a family. I wanted love for all the clichéd and overwrought reasons so many people believe love can make life together more satisfying than life apart.

Only how to get there stumped me: Do you make love happen or does love happen to you? How much was beyond my control, no matter how many blind dates I went on or wine tastings I signed up for? Was it possible to meet my true love on a speed date, at a clothing-optional encounter group, or in a swing dancing class?

In our down moments, my girlfriends and I reached into the Hat of Hopeful Stories—the coworker who met her husband on the commuter train, the neighbor who had her first child at forty-four. We pep-talked one another into blind dates on which we were not supposed to mention the two Cs: commitment or (God forbid) children. Stick to quality, not quantity, some said. Others disagreed.

We weren't necessarily desperate, but we were determined.

Her own hopes shaken by a vicious divorce that somehow spared her wit and warmth, Beth became the surprise close friend I thought I could or would no longer make at the ripe old age of thirty-three. I always had an immediate and singular connection with the most important people in my life—men and women—from the very start, the minute we met. Beth and I clicked that way. Two girls who had bad luck with men, but good luck with friends.

Right off the bat, she seemed sporty and energetic, with cropped hair that set off sparkling green eyes. She mixed references to writers and local history with Yiddish slang, and her dry wisecracks made me laugh out loud. Even better, she laughed at my jokes.

When it seemed so many people our age had settled into their social circles and routines, with little time to spare for making new friends or interests, Beth was a flurry of activity, simultaneously trying to outrun her grief over a failed marriage and establish a new life. She was free-spirited enough to take surfing lessons one week, fly to Paris the next, and, soon after we met, accompany me to northern Maine at the last minute for an article I was writing on snowmobiling.

After driving more than five hours through a blizzard—spinning out at one point, skidding into a parked car at another—we wound up at a crowded bar at the end of the Appalachian Trail, where we had stale popcorn and flat beer for dinner. The next day, the sun over Moosehead Lake shone sunny and bright, and our good-looking guide kitted us out in fluorescent jumpsuits, boots, and helmets. He taught us hand signals for our day on the trails and, hopping on his snowmobile, waved for us to follow.

We started out slow and nervous, city chicks on big machines, accelerating a bit, panicking, slowing down, pretending we wanted to look at something. It wasn't long, though, before we were flying at eighty miles an hour through remote forests and past frozen lakes, sometimes literally flying as the snowmobiles hit hidden bumps.

"Wooooohoooooo!" we screamed, unable to hear each other over the roar of our engines. If Beth remembered her hand signals, I never saw them. She was a blur; the trees were a blur. Our noggins shook like bobblehead dolls. Exhilarating, fun, noisy, and stupid.

We dismounted eight hours and 120 miles later, our snowsuits damp, our butts numb, and inner thighs paralyzed.

"Here's hoping we can still have children," I whispered under my breath as we waddled away, wincing with each bow-legged step.

Minutes later, we found that the hot tub we had looked forward to all day was in fact cold so we set off for our cabin.

Beth paused at the front door and smiled. "This was really fun. Thanks for inviting me," she said. Her teeth chattered, but I could tell she meant it. "Especially since you don't even really know me."

"I thought we'd have fun."

"And we did," she said.

Whenever I considered it, single motherhood scared me a little bit and appealed to me a lot. It was a prospect both alien and desirable. I'd yet to meet a woman in her late thirties or forties who chose to be a single mother and told me not to do it. I was sure they existed, yet the handful of women I knew could not imagine life without their children and said it was the best thing they had ever done. Carey was no exception, and now Beth seemed poised to follow suit.

I had been accepted by MIT for a Knight Science Journalism Fellowship in the fall, the same one Carey had two years earlier. We were no longer competitors on the New England beat, and it was a relief. We didn't have to censor ourselves discussing work, and we let our guard down even more talking about our private lives. I looked to her not only as a journalist who shared some of my interests, but also as a single woman a few years older and a couple of steps ahead of me in trying to find ways to balance work and create a satisfying personal life.

I had introduced Beth to Carey when she was interested in the donor sperm, and now I wanted to find out myself what

Carey had to say about single motherhood. When I stopped by to see her one afternoon, Liliana's stroller was parked by the front door, toys scattered around it, with a pair of miniature Mary Jane shoes nearby. Totally adorable, I thought. I also thought that choosing to make that happen seemed like a gigantic leap. A leap she encouraged me to make sooner rather than later.

"I just felt like my time had run out," she told me as we sat on her porch drinking iced tea. The air was pungent with the summer scents of freshly mown grass and sweet honeysuckle. "If I could have put it off until I was fifty, I probably would have because life was fun, and, like you, I wanted to meet the right man. But I wanted a baby, and knowing what I know now about motherhood, I wish I had done it four or five years earlier. It's just the best love I've ever experienced. And it feels like such a meaningful mission."

This, from a woman who had covered the fall of communism.

"Not that it's easy," she said. I noticed the shadows under her eyes from lack of sleep. Sitting next to us, Liliana hugged a baby doll. She had Carey's round face and Sprax's fair complexion. "The hardest part is that even though no individual task is especially hard, it's just relentless. I mean, how hard is it to change a diaper?"

"I don't know yet!" We laughed. "How hard?"

"It's just 24/7. I've signed over every minute of my life to taking care of Liliana, and if I want time to myself, I need to either pay someone for it or negotiate it with Sprax or my dad or someone else."

That sounded...manageable. I wasn't there when Carey was fixing a baby bottle, trying to write a story on deadline, arranging a sitter. Sometimes, probably, all at once. This was the first time we were really talking about the details of her life as a single mom. I wanted to understand what it was like for her sake, to be a better friend to her, and for mine.

Carey said it was unrealistic to expect both work and mothering to go well at the same time. They rarely did, and it was tight financially. (It reminded me of the admonition that we could not have a man, job, car, and home all at once.) I wondered, too, if I could pull it off without family nearby. Carey's father was a warm, lively man who clearly adored his granddaughter and played an important role in their lives. I knew my own dad would be thrilled to be a grandfather, but he lived in Chicago, not down the street.

"For me, family's been incredibly important," Carey said. Liliana crawled onto her lap, and Carey stroked her pale plump cheek. Carey's face softened, and she looked at me. "But you have so many friends who love you that maybe that could be like your family here."

"That's sweet of you to say," I said. Even so, the thought of raising a child away from my parents and brother made me sad. Carey nodded and scooched closer to me, as if she knew what I was thinking.

"Do you think I'd be a good mother?" I asked her.

She reached out and grabbed my hand, squeezing it tightly.

"Oh, Pam, you would be an amazing mom. You are one of the kindest, most loving people I know."

From time to time, I had mulled having a child with a friend, including a few married men whose wives might have been amenable. Carey and Beth told me they'd had similar prospects who had fallen through for one reason or another. For me, a longtime British friend, Simon, seemed a possibility. We met in college and had never hooked up romantically, though I sometimes sensed attraction on his part.

A flirtatious forty-something who was divorced and now lived in northern California, Simon was still a kid himself—taking bartending lessons by day, swing dancing by night. We once joked that we should get together if we were still single at forty, an age that seemed at the time as distant a reality as intergalactic travel. I tested the waters once by making a casual pitch for parenthood when Simon visited Boston.

"So," I ventured as we dug into a lunch of spicy peanut noodles and iced tea at a local café. "It seems like everyone around us is having kids."

"I know. Jennifer is pregnant, and Nicole and Peter are expecting their second," he said.

"Wow. I didn't know that, Si," I said, wondering where to go with this. "I was thinking it might be fun to do."

"What's that?"

I thought maybe the clatter of dishes and conversation around us may have drowned me out. I cleared my throat, and tried again.

"Have a baby."

"Really?" He concentrated on twirling pasta around his fork with one hand while holding back his luxurious mop of hair with the other. Would our child have hair like that? I wondered. Mouth full, he mumbled something that sounded like "Interesting."

"Yeah, it's just something that I've always wanted, and I'm getting older," I said. Simon shrugged and looked sideways at the next table. A young woman with a pierced nose and dreadlocks was describing a previous night's concert to her companion. "Don't you think it would be fun?" I pressed.

I saw him squirm in his seat, so I changed the subject. I

realized with disappointment that part of me had assumed he would jump at the chance to do something so unconventional, this freewheeling friend of mine. Bicoastal baby! Why not?

I didn't expect to be asking an old friend to have a baby with me. Nor did I view single motherhood as a zero-sum game where, by having a baby on my own, I was forever giving up my chance to fall in love and have a mate. I saw happy single mothers and married miserable ones, so there didn't seem to be any path that came with guarantees.

I didn't rule out adoption, but I knew it was an expensive and often complicated process. Policies governing single-parent adoptions seemed to change all the time, from country to country. Selfish or not, I also wanted to try to experience pregnancy and childbirth firsthand before my body failed me.

Egg freezing was not yet a viable or reliable option, though there had been sporadic reports of success around the world. But donor sperm could work. When I discussed single motherhood with Carey and Beth, each mentioned Donor 8282 and the remaining seven vials sitting in a clinic freezer, now under Beth's name.

Theirs was a straightforward transaction, they both told me. Startling in its simplicity given what was potentially at stake: a child, a new life. But I had felt confident in my matchmaking. I knew Carey possessed a deep well of generosity and wouldn't hesitate to help another single woman she liked, one I had recommended; and I knew Beth, having met Carey, would trust her intellect and proven capability as a single mother enough to accept Carey's choice of donor sperm from the anonymous multitudes. I also suspected they would become friends.

"I didn't always know if I wanted a child. I waffled for a

long time," Beth told me. "But when I did, I realized I really did. It's kind of amazing now with the sperm to be able to do it if I want to, when I want to."

Carey said, "Think about going the donor sperm route before it's too late." I began to seriously consider going it alone with a stranger. Or, rather, with a total stranger's sperm.

I had floated the idea of single motherhood to my family with mixed results. My parents divorced after twenty-five years of marriage and two children conceived in their early twenties. They didn't much remember a time before us kids and, long after my younger brother and I grew up and left home, my dad said he still wondered where we were every time he left the house. My parents never pressured us for grandchildren and, watching my brother and me fall in and out of love with alarming regularity, might have given up for all we knew.

Once, between boyfriends, I had asked Mom what she thought of my becoming a mother on my own if a relationship never worked out. We were walking along the Lake Michigan beach near her house one summer day, holding hands as we usually did. She was barefoot, wearing beige capris and a baggy T-shirt, her long hair pinned up with barrettes. She looked so young that people often mistook us for sisters.

"Go for it!" She beamed. "These guys can't get it together, and you'd be a terrific mom, better than I ever was. I was so young; I didn't know what the heck I was doing."

"Yes, you did. You were wonderful, loving. That's all that counts."

"You'll be so much better. You have all this wisdom I never had." Mom had stayed at home full-time until my brother and I were in high school.

"Not really. I'll just find new and interesting ways to mess up my kid."

She shook her head. "Honey, you can do it. I just want you to be happy, and I'll do whatever I need to do to support you."

I thought, okay, maybe she hadn't given up on grandchildren after all.

My younger brother, Ben, looked concerned, if not downright confused, when I explained donor sperm to him one day at a neighborhood pub.

"That's a little weird," he said. I could see from his expression that he also thought it was a bad idea. More seriously, he told me, "My married friends with kids have a hard time. Doing it alone has got to be really, really hard. I wouldn't want to do it." In other words, he wouldn't want me to do it.

We loved each other and were close friends and backpacking buddies, and had traveled through the Middle East and Southeast Asia together. I knew he had my best interests at heart, but Ben and his thirty-five-year-old sperm could likely hang out another three decades and still find a woman in her twenties or thirties—at the peak of her fertility—to bear his children. I had no such luxury, and I also knew it was unfair to expect that he would understand.

Dad surprised me in a different way. Given his sixty-one years and traditional outlook, I thought he would be the biggest opponent of his daughter having a baby on her own. He was part of a generation that grew up on the cusp of radicalism, yet only the cusp. The college class after his listened to the Rolling Stones and smoked pot and experimented with free love. Not my dad, who rarely drank and played Jelly Roll Morton on the piano.

I gave him too little credit. The first time I mentioned the possibility of my going it alone, we were sitting on a short wooden pier by the pond behind his house. Willow trees swayed in the breeze, and a duck glided by, algae dangling from its bill. Peaceful.

Dad sat next to me, his hands gripping the edge of the pier and his legs dangling over the side. He didn't say much. Just nodded. I took it as a good sign that he didn't dismiss or criticize the idea. He was the parent who, for better or worse, pushed me to excel and didn't settle for a B when he thought I could have gotten an A. Some months later, I mentioned again that I was thinking more seriously about single motherhood.

"In that case, I strongly suggest that you live in Chicago," he said.

"Very funny, Dad!" I was touched by his not-so-subtle "suggestions" that I move back home. He sent me fruit every month from a gourmet delivery service, and the card always said the same thing: "Tastes better in Chicago."

"I'm serious. There's nothing like family." A former lawyer, he spoke with conviction.

I recalled how his parents had spent so much time with us, bringing lox and bagels over on Sundays, babysitting my brother and me on weekends, taking us to Six Flags and Colonial Williamsburg. It occurred to me for the first time that they were not only wonderful grandparents, but also a tremendous source of support and relief for my young and inexperienced parents.

The next time I brought up the subject, Dad seemed to have taken into account my community of friends in Boston or realized how much I valued my work there. Maybe he just figured I wasn't going to change my mind and knew how much it meant to me to have his support.

"Whatever you want to do is fine with me. I'm here for you," he said, putting his hand over mine. My eyes welled up with tears.

"Thanks, Dad."

Finally, at thirty-seven years old, I confronted myself. I considered what I could not live without and immediately knew it was a child. That for me, life would have a far lesser purpose if I could not be a mother. I once read that the ancient Egyptians described childless women as "mothers of the missing ones," and that imagery wrenched me to the core. I could almost feel an ache in my bones for the child who would be missing to me.

The Question

Beth: "The question is, 'Once you have the baby, do you still need the man?' "

Pam: "Need or want?"

Carey: "It depends on the man."

Carey

WE TOOK LILIANA HOME when she was six days old, a bit late because my blood pressure had jumped to worrisome levels after she was born. I imagined that the fluids in my body had swelled to such oceanic levels that my poor, aging vascular system was simply overwhelmed. Finally, I was put on blood pressure pills, asked to demonstrate that I could strap Liliana into her car seat correctly, and allowed to go home.

Sprax drove me, and when we got into the house and placed Liliana, sleeping in her car seat, carefully on the couch, I found myself crying in relief and disbelief. What a ride, what a harrowing ride. But oh, the prize! The prize!

In those first days home, Liliana proved to be a joy of a baby, a long, heavy sleeper bothered by nothing and an excellent eater who helped me over the awkward first trials of breastfeeding. The exhaustion I'd expected failed to materialize. She slept six and seven hours at a stretch, which I assumed was one of the great advantages of bearing an infant the size of a typical three-month-old.

As it turned out, she slept a little too well. When I brought her in for her first pediatrician's appointment at two weeks, she had dropped from her birth weight of nine pounds, four ounces, to a mere eight pounds. The pediatrician was concerned, and I was devastated. So much for thinking I knew what I was doing. So much for all my good maternal intentions. The pediatrician said I would need to start supplementing my breast milk with formula, and I felt like a breastfeeding failure, not to mention a mothering failure for not having realized that something was wrong.

My postpartum hormones were bottoming out, I was such a pathetic rookie at motherhood that I had endangered my child, and Sprax had once again turned into an iceman. I told him as much, saying that I felt frozen out, even though he was being a wonderful and loving father to Liliana. He would come by and hold her and play with her, even change her dirtiest diapers, but he was as distant with me as I could remember. Of course, no one could ever fall in love with a puffy, exhausted, weepy postpartum woman, but still, somehow, I found myself longing for him again, hoping against hope that we would raise this baby together—as a couple. We had just been through so much together, just borne a child together. Didn't it seem only right?

When Liliana was six weeks old, Sprax and I took her cross-country skiing in Vermont, where she happily tolerated her ride in the baby litter Sprax pulled behind him across the snow. But, sleep-deprived novices, we both flunked parenting school: he forgot to bring her formula, and I realized only after we arrived in Vermont that I had failed to strap her car seat into the seat belt.

Once such a long sleeper, now she was going down for only about three hours at a time, and life was cloaked in haze. But I was back at the biweekly fellowship seminars (I never missed a single one, thanks to MIT's long winter break) and had lost forty pounds, with only about twenty more to go. Sprax would take night duty at least a couple of times a week, and he would sometimes lie next to me in bed, but not with me. If he spent the night, he slept in the guest room on the third floor.

As my body deflated, my spirit, too, seemed to deflate. I had once been such a chirpy little eager beaver, always ready for the next adventure. Now my buoyancy was gone, and I wanted it back.

I talked to Sprax about it.

"Is it because of us not getting along?" he asked.

I supposed so, but it was also that the very tenor of life had changed. I no longer had the exciting feeling that the future was open before me, sure to be a twist-filled story starring moi. Now, when I woke up in the morning, I knew pretty well what I would be doing for the next twenty years, or at least a good chunk of it: raising Liliana. I would also be pursuing a career as a science journalist. And, I supposed, I'd be looking for love.

I felt grateful to Sprax for all his nighttime help, and the gratitude mixed with warmth, but I didn't dare express warmth toward him for fear he'd once again worry that I was expecting a commitment from him, and feel forced to turn cold again. It was a crazy situation. And yet, in many ways, it was not bad: he helped out with Liliana much more than many men would, and, as Leeza pointed out, he made no demands. If only I hadn't believed there was a love for me somewhere out there, it would have been just fine for the long term.

One day, he asked: "Doesn't having Liliana make you really want other children?"

"Well... now that I'm aware of the price—the great ordeal and health risks of pregnancy and the first few weeks—I wouldn't say I was eager to rush into it again. I feel no need right now. But if I were with a guy who really wanted a child, I'd be willing to have another one."

"Ah."

"I figure Liliana is the child I'm entitled to have under zero population growth principles. And you'll probably have a passel of kids with someone else. So she counts as my reproductive unit." I paused. "Does she make you want to have more kids?"

He nodded emphatically.

Sure, why not? I thought with a splash of bitterness. Come and go as you please, no pregnancy, no labor, no childcare expenses. Have a dozen, why don't you?

Spring arrived, and with it Liliana's first tree buds, her first daffodils, her first time lying in grass. As I took her walking in her stroller, I sang a little ditty:

I love Lily and she loves me;
we're as happy as we can be;
she's my sweetie and I'm her mom,
and we're so happy all day long because...

And repeat!

She started sleeping through the night, more or less. Her skin was a translucent alabaster, and her eyes had stayed blue.

I announced a hundred-day party for Liliana, a Korean tradition, and Sprax asked me if I really wanted him to come.

"Of course I do!"

"These events are really for the adults, anyway, and it's bad that it's in the middle of the weekend, so it cuts into climbing."

I was appalled, as appalled as I was when he occasionally failed to spend any weekend time with her. "It's so strange to me," I said. "I can see how much you love her and love being with her, so I don't understand how you choose to spend your time."

"It's just that climbing gives me the fix I need after the stress of the workweek... though when I think about it, I would probably feel better after being with Lily than after climbing."

He came, but the party got me down. I didn't have enough help setting up, though my dad came through heroically with all the errands I assigned him. I got too much food. Sprax held and fed Liliana, but he also spent a long time out on the porch with his friend Suzanne, a tall, pencil-thin climber and Buddhist whose body language seemed to suggest flirtation. There was no point in feeling jealous, but her presence was somehow openly humiliating, inviting people to speculate on whether this was the woman Sprax preferred to me. And I felt fat, very fat.

In May, my fellowship was ending and it was time to face my work future. I ordered large-scale copies of some of my front-page stories and made an appointment to meet with Howell Raines, then the new editor in chief of the *Times*.

When I arrived in New York, his secretary told me that my clips had somehow been lost.

Howell greeted me without particular warmth, though he did ask how "the baby" was doing. I cursed myself. For my own good, I should have cultivated a friendly relationship with him in years past, before he ascended to the throne. But he always scared me somehow; I imagined that his drawling charm served as a mask for icy ruthlessness. When our paths crossed, I quietly avoided him, and now I had no personal connection with him at all: I was just one more old reporter in a staff that he was determined to shake up.

I proposed that I give up my staff position and all benefits, but be given a stable contract for a certain number of stories written or a quantity of time worked. No, Howell said. No contract. If I wanted to stay in Boston and go part-time, I would have to work on a purely freelance basis, paid per story I wrote.

I thought, but did not say, And how am I supposed to support my daughter on a freelance salary?

For the six years that I worked for the *New York Times,* the newspaper owned my life. I had a blast, it is true, but at the price of that ownership. I could be called or paged at any moment and sent anywhere, and I often had been. I'd lived out of a suitcase for months at a time. But the moral I take from this story is: So what? Your institution owes you nothing. It is not your family. It does not care if you help create humanity's next generation; in fact, it might well prefer you didn't. Beyond a brief maternity leave, it has no obligation to support you. In fact, you become less valuable if your new responsibilities limit your ability to go anywhere at any time. As a new mother, I asked for an accommodation. Let me be more honest: I hoped for kindness. But institutions, of course, are not about kindness, though individual managers may try.

I kept it together while I was in Howell's office, but when I walked out and a friend asked, "How'd it go?" I could get out only a few words before my voice broke and tears of utter shame and insult started to spill. She dragged me into an empty office, away from the newsroom's rows of desks and faces, and handed me tissues and chocolates until I could slip abjectly out of the building.

I was determined never to cry again over my departure from the *Times,* and I never did. I readily admit that leaving would have hurt under any circumstances. It is a heady elixir, the power and the camaraderie and the potential to do good in the world. But it particularly angered me that the refusal to bend came from Howell and his administration chief—both older men who'd had wives to deal with the babies during their own reporting days. On the train ride home to Boston, wounded and fuming, I kept imagining a nomadic tribe in which the women who bear children are, for a time, slower than the rest and unusually dependent on others because they are caring for the babies. If the male leaders care only about speed—or budget—they leave the mothers behind. I would run the world very differently, I thought, if I were in charge.

When I got home that night and told Sprax what had happened, I barely teared up.

He was silent for a long moment, his eyes full of empathy.

"I have some money," he offered finally.

"Thanks," I said, touched. "But I mentioned to Marty Baron, the editor in chief of the *Globe,* that I might be applying to him, and he seemed receptive, so I may not be unemployed for too long. It's good to know, though. Thanks."

Sprax and I took off on a swing through the West. We stopped at the Grand Canyon; in Utah, to let his parents meet Liliana; and in Arizona, for Sprax to show her off to his ninety-year-old grandparents. In pictures from that trip, we sometimes stand together, one of us holding Liliana, but we are never touching.

At the Grand Canyon, we lucked into the last little cabin available nearby and found that there was only one small bed. Liliana slept in her Pack'n Play, and Sprax and I crammed ourselves into the bed. In a novel, I thought, this would be the climactic moment: the hero and heroine, forced into tight proximity, suddenly find their enmity overcome by passion, and they fall into a fiery embrace. In real life, our legs touched, and there was some tossing and turning, but that was all.

That clinches it, I thought. I will now finally reach the acceptance I've been seeking for so long: Sprax does not love me, did not love me, will not love me. End of story. Nor do I love him. If I did, I would surely reach out to him now.

This time, the attempt at acceptance finally took. It was greatly helped along by the emotional revolution that I found stirring in me in the months after Liliana's birth. It went something like this:

For twenty-five-odd years, romance had been the central focus of my life. Though of course I had pursued learning and work and doing good and friendship and personal growth, the deep-down top priority (especially in the last ten years) had been men. Now, to my own shock and gigantic relief, those days were over. And they were not over because I had thought my way out of them, because I had finally managed to convince myself that life without a man could be just as good as life with one. It was nothing so conscious. It was simply that in my postpartum state, my sex drive had dwindled to less than zero, and I had suddenly discovered a new kind of love that was infinitely more fulfilling than any romantic experience—or at least, any romantic experience of mine I could call to mind. To a few friends who were parents, I expressed my dismay: Why didn't you tell me that my love for a child could be so amazing and satisfying? Why didn't anyone push me any harder to do this, and tell me more emphatically that really, Carey, if you possibly can, you should make sure to become a mother? It seemed no accident that "fulfilled" has the word "filled" in it. My life felt full, rich, centered.

It was only the beginning of Liliana's life, but I felt as if, whatever happened now, I had my happy ending.

I also felt lucky to finally be out of the game. The ups and downs of dating had become tedious, and the painful blows fell on parts of me already too well bruised. I knew that—if only for Liliana's sake—I would need to keep seeking a mate, but for now I felt no inclination whatsoever to do so. I had quit. It felt subversive and liberating, like a bra burning. Enormous swaths of our culture concerned self-improvement for the purposes of romance, movies and books whose only real arc followed romance, endless girl talk revolving only around romance. I would henceforth be happily immune. The shift was tectonic, and the geological metaphor struck me as apt: at last, this change was welling up from deep inside me, instead of being a tactical maneuver I was consciously imposing on myself to spare my own feelings. I had really, truly quit. And I delighted in proclaiming as much whenever the opportunity arose.

It's so predictable, isn't it? But true. Just a few weeks after the Grand Canyon trip, a dear friend, Neil, invited me out to dinner to tell me that he was getting a divorce.

It was a hair-raising story. Neil had gone out with Mary, a willowy blonde, for several years. I'd met him near the beginning of their courtship, introduced by a mutual friend, and had liked him immensely. But he had never done more than flirt, and he eventually explained that he was involved with Mary and, much as he'd like to get closer to me, his hands were tied. Still, he said, I was, shall we say, "on deck." And there I stayed for years. Every few weeks or months, we would go out for friendly dinners and have scintillating conversations about current events and our personal lives, but no more.

Neil was a journalist manqué, and he had picture-perfect academic credentials. He was a verbal whiz and a high-energy interlocutor, likely to pepper you with questions faster than you could answer them. He was also tall and gallant, though not conventionally handsome; a fine and decent person; a caring and generous friend.

If he had a fatal flaw, in my unvoiced opinion, it was that his rational side so totally ruled him that he had not fallen in love since his early twenties, and now he was in his late forties. Though he was all but living with her, he did not seem to have fallen in love with Mary, either. He tended to avoid speaking about her, but when he did, he would say—without much enthusiasm—that he did love her, that she adored and worshipped him, and that she had many fine qualities. No one's perfect, he would say. True, I would think, but it would help if you had less of a tendency to focus automatically on a person's imperfections.

Finally, Neil married Mary in a tiny ceremony at his house, and was palpably relieved to stop being a talked-about bachelor. (Is he gay? Are you sure? What's with him, then?) The two of them visited me and brought a gift when Liliana was still tiny, and they'd seemed so at ease with each other that I'd wondered whether perhaps I should have tried at some point to fight for Neil. But no, I decided, he apparently liked the worshipping type, and that was not in my repertoire.

Just a few days after their first anniversary, Mary abruptly left. That would have been bad enough, but there was a financial twist: Neil was very rich, and Mary was penniless and constantly running up debt, and in their prenuptial agreement, one divorce clause specified that as of their first anniversary, Mary was entitled to a lump sum payment of $100,000, in addition to the alimony that had been guaranteed from their wedding day.

We sat long at dinner at an empty Brazilian restaurant as he, reluctantly but obsessively, reeled out the whole sorry tale. I felt washes of sympathy for him, and also a strange bemusement. At long last, after all these years, Neil was available, and though he'd need time to heal, his subtext was clearly that with time, he would now want to pursue me.

Marty Baron agreed to hire me as a three-day-a-week science and health reporter at the *Boston Globe* for a decent staff salary and the reduced benefits of a part-timer. The *Globe* had a civilized tradition of allowing some mothers to work three days a week, without relegating them all the way to the margins of the news. It struck me as miles ahead of the *Times* in that.

I needed to work for money, and I needed to work for sanity, but I was surprised to discover inside myself a total resistance to working full-time while Liliana was small. It felt as if it would be wrong to delegate so much of her care, even though I by no means criticized other mothers who worked full-time. But for me, it was some personal line in the sand that I hadn't known would exist.

In the coming months, I gauged my progress on letting go by counting how long it took me, when I met someone new, to get around to mentioning that I had formerly worked at the *New York Times*. It started out at about five minutes, max, but with time that grew to ten, fifteen, and then to infinity. I met new people without a professional trump card that might instantly impress them. It was harder, and healthier.

Neil began asking me out to dinner on nights when Sprax could stay with Liliana. There was a definite babysitting advantage to being a single mother with a father in the picture.

The dinners got frequent enough that Sprax finally asked, "You're not going out with him, are you?"

"Not now," I said, "but it's headed that way."

"Because I don't think—" Sprax said, and then cut himself off.

"You don't think what?"

"Never mind."

Liliana crawled, then pulled herself up and cruised around the furniture. She had a mischievous little urchin face, and Leeza plied her with a delicious homemade "soupik" of chicken and vegetables and "kasha" of oatmeal or rice.

Neil's divorce progressed, and our dinners eventually turned into overnights and even whole weekends. One small second-floor room of his house was designated as Liliana's room and held a large playpen and some toys and books. She was at a difficult age for bonding, preverbal and tightly attached to me, but he tried, playing nose-snatching games and peekaboo.

When she was about nine months old, I spent a weekend away from her for the first time, going off with Neil to meet his parents. It was intoxicating to be away again, unencumbered and on the road. We held hands as we walked along the street, and his father proclaimed me prettier than Mary—a definite sign of failing eyesight. Maria, my old therapist, was with us as well (I had gone to see her in the first place because she was friendly with Neil), and I found myself exulting to her about how wonderful all this was, that I had Liliana and Neil as well, and how lucky we all were.

"I hope it works out," she said, not darkly, but with a loving sadness that splashed cold water on the moment.

She had picked up on a looming problem. I loved and admired Neil, and felt eternally grateful that he wanted me in all my single-mother imperfection. But for now, the center was missing from our relationship: neither one of us was in love with the other. For Neil, this was typical, but for me, it was not, and now Liliana was competing for my time and affection.

Neil was not used to seeing somebody else get 95 percent of his girlfriend's attention while he was present, and I was not used to having to take into account a man's needs in addition to my baby's, modest as his were.

When I went to bed at night, having been up since six a.m. or earlier with Liliana, all I wanted to do was sleep. My sex drive remained dormant, and there was something a little frantic in our embraces that reminded me of teenagers imitating the passions of movie scenes. I was holding and lifting and snuggling Liliana all day, so I didn't really want even cuddling. And Neil, with his verbal energy, liked to talk talk talk talk talk, while I had never been in more contact with another human being in my adult life and needed desperately to retreat into silence or a book. The going-to-bed moment was often the hardest: he would put on big, owlish glasses and a nightshirt that somehow made him look like an old man, and I would wish that we really were an ancient couple and could just drift off to sleep, instead of going through the motions of a younger pair.

Neil also made a few verbal missteps that made my heart drop. As we were discussing the future one day, months after we'd started going out, he said of Liliana, "I don't love her yet, but I'm sure I will love her."

I was dumbfounded. How could he not love her? Okay, she wasn't much of a conversationalist, but she was a delightful and easy baby.

I ran a reality check with friends, and they did not like the sound of it.

Another night, talking again about our future together, Neil said that it would need to be clear that he would be playing the primary role of father in Liliana's life, not Sprax.

"What do you mean?"

"For example, if there are teacher-parent meetings at school, I'd be the one who goes, not Sprax."

That might have been easier to envision if he already loved Liliana. But so far, he was not very convincing father material. And in any case, that was not the point:

"But Sprax is her father," I protested. "I owe her existence partly to him. I can't imagine closing him out of roles he wants to take on."

I grant you that American parents drown their children in stuff. But it was also disturbing when Neil asked whether I wasn't "spoiling" Liliana with too many toys. This from a man whose wealthy father was so cheap that he had refused to buy Neil a second walkie-talkie, saying one was enough.

Still, we tottered along, starting even to idly house-hunt. In my generally exhausted and unromantic state, it was the old-couple feel of our relationship that I liked best. That, and Neil's willingness to take care of things, to book restaurants and planes, to—a little—take care of me. He paid for dinners, and even, when I brought Leeza with us to visit his parents in a resort community, chipped in for her overtime.

He also agreed to come with me to the wedding I had so long awaited. Liz, my best friend in all the world, had agreed to marry Jeff, the mellow outdoorsman, and asked me to be her maid of honor. On the plane to Washington, Neil clearly enjoyed other travelers' obvious assumption that he was the father of the little blond moppet we handed back and forth.

I all but flunked my maid-of-honor role, though. Juggling Liliana's care with my own dressing made me so late for the prewedding preparations that Liz was already camera-ready, glorious in a long cream gown, by the time I got to the farmhouse where the ceremony would be held. Another close friend had helped her, and ended up helping me as well, stitching up the central seam of my vintage dress to keep it from giving way to my unlost weight. Liz forgave me, but I could not forgive myself.

At the outdoor ceremony, Neil held Liliana while I stood beside Liz near the minister. Liliana, already unhappy to be away from me, was so bothered by the strong autumn wind that she cried and would not be consoled. I kept expecting Neil to do the logical thing and walk away with her so she would stop disturbing the ceremony, but it didn't seem to dawn on him as he jiggled her desperately up and down. Liz and Jeff looked into each other's tear-filled eyes and proclaimed their love and loyalty, and my heart swelled for them even as I counted the seconds until I could get Liliana inside and quiet her down.

The next morning, I asked Liz what a wedding night was like, and she said, "It was the most beautiful night of my life." I told her how happy I was for her, and I was, but deep down, for myself, I felt an ugly surge of cynicism and disbelief. Brides follow a script and so do their emotions, I thought; you have to drink the Kool-Aid to hit those highs, and I don't anymore.

Sprax remained loyal, regularly spending time with Liliana, and sometimes with me as well. He was amazingly attuned to Liliana, a born father, and he was a warm, gentle presence in my life too. But Neil loomed and, for me, Sprax faded. He was dating openly too now, infatuated with a beautiful thirtyish blonde named Nicole.

One day, he had me bring Liliana over to his condo for brunch so Nicole could meet both of us. He provided an array of muffins and fruit—the first time I'd ever seen him make an effort to feed people. He must have it bad, I thought.

I felt strangely un-jealous, totally outclassed lookswise and not really caring, happy to be where I was in life and not back where Nicole was.

The growing closeness between Neil and me, and the growing distance between Sprax and me, reached the point that when it came time for Liliana's first birthday party, Leeza and my dad asked whether I would invite Sprax, assuming that Neil would come instead.

It was awkward. I sounded Sprax out about whether he wanted to come, and he said he did, sounding taken aback that there was any question about it. So they were both invited. And we took a group photo of Team Liliana: Sprax, me holding her as she leaned toward Sprax, Neil, Leeza, my sister, Morgan, and my dad.

Some of the smiles look a bit forced.

Nicole and Sprax called it quits, and he moved on to an artsy woman with a former drug problem and many tattoos. I never saw her myself, but Leeza did, and her eyes widened as she described the body art to me. I got a better taste of what Sprax must have been feeling about Neil: his daughter was in close contact with this other person; would she be safe and cherished? I had visions of Sprax's girlfriend relapsing into addiction while Liliana was left in her care.

"I'm not trying to dictate who you go out with," I said. "But I think we should agree that we won't leave Liliana in the care of our boyfriends or girlfriends without the other parent's agreement."

"I agree," he said instantly.

A new colleague at the *Globe* commented that I seemed

incredibly happy. Overall, I was: I felt supremely lucky to have my job and enjoyed it deeply. Liliana was walking and starting to talk and was generally healthy, fed on Leeza's kasha and homemade soups. Sprax and I got along fine, and so did Neil and I. Life was good.

Most nights, I would ask Liliana, "Do you want a story?" And she would instantly answer "Otay!" and would flip onto her left side and spoon herself against me, in story position. And I would begin.

"Once upon a time, there was a little girl named Liliana. And she lived in a house with her mommy in Cambridge, Massachusetts, 02138, in the United States of America, on the continent of North America, on the planet Earth, in the solar system Sol, in the Milky Way galaxy, in the universe. And she loved lots of people: her mommy and her daddy and her grandfather and her aunties and her Leeza . . ."

Most of the stories ended up as cautionary tales, and many involved rides on the backs of friendly animals. I yawned as much as she did through most of them.

Sometimes Sprax and I would sit on either side of her on the bed and talk. He was frustrated with his love life, he said one night, and the eternal search for "the one." He went on, "You know, at times, I thought you were the one. Maybe you were."

"Could have fooled me."

I was not interested. I was completely oriented toward Neil, and Sprax seemed young and flighty by comparison. Mainly, I had been there, done that. I changed the subject.

Sprax started going out with a woman I couldn't help but like. Lucy was forty, a six-foot-two African American do-good lawyer with hair plaited high into tiny black braids. She was very pretty but had a gummy, endearingly childlike smile. She was sweet with Liliana, but didn't try too hard.

"I hope you can bring Sprax some happiness," I said.

As Liliana's second spring gave way to summer, I found myself inexplicably stricken with cabin fever. That is, though Leeza was costing me two-thirds of my salary, I was suddenly obsessed with the idea of buying a tiny cabin up north somewhere, so that Liliana would be able to run free in nature. The trouble was, real estate was booming and the money I could invest would buy only a shack or a trailer.

A friend who was reading a book of Chinese philosophy found an interesting passage about how, as we get older, we need to watch out for an overweening passion to acquire.

"I do think there may be some of that going on with me," I said. "It's a passion that rises as the passion of sex and romance declines."

It didn't feel like sublimation, though. That would have implied that there was sexual energy there in the first place.

I pestered a *Globe* colleague who was the mother of three about whether her sex drive dwindled—like, dwindled to less than zero—after her children were born.

"Well," she said, reaching back in her memory. "I can remember that when the kids were really, really little, I tended to be so exhausted that I didn't care whether my husband and I made love or not."

"Yes, but did you actively prefer cuddling with your child to lying with your husband?"

She looked dubious and a touch concerned.

"Oh, now..." Long pause. "No. But there's that known phenomenon of getting 'touched out.' Like, if you touch your children all day, you may not want to be touched at night."

"No, what I'm feeling is more than that. It's so baffling. Here I am with this great boyfriend, incredibly lucky, and if I were a guy I'd say that I just can't get it up."

"Well, maybe he's the wrong guy."

"No, no . . . it must be the hormones."

Sometimes a person is only mildly allergic to a food like peanut butter, and then one day, out of the blue, a trace of the stuff triggers a full-blown reaction, anaphylactic shock, the works. The immune system suddenly blows its gaskets and overreacts, for no obvious reason.

One weekend in June, something like that happened with Neil. Liliana and I were spending the day at his house, and as always I felt the strain of fitting in to his well-established ways, polite as he was about trying to adapt. He was an older man in his bathrobe, doing a bit of work in his office, and for some unclear reason, Liliana and I were marooned in his house, when it would have been far more comfortable to be at home.

After Liz's wedding, I recalled, her mother had opined that Neil was too old for me, and I had pooh-poohed her, saying that she was deceived by his appearance. And Mary had told him that life was simply no fun with him. It was not that he was dour in any way, I thought; it was perhaps that his personality was just so strong, it seemed to suck up all the air around him.

On that gray Saturday, I found myself dreading, deeply dreading, the prospect of going to bed that night. I popped Liliana into her jogging stroller and went for a run, thinking that I might be premenstrual and simply need a pick-me-up. It did no good. Finally, I told him that I was just in a bitchy mood and thought the best thing would be to go home. A bit baffled, he agreed.

And then, as if I had picked up Sprax's worst habits, I avoided Neil's calls and did not call him back for several days. It was inexcusably cruel, and he upbraided me gently when we finally spoke.

"I know," I said. "I just couldn't face you, to tell you what I need to tell you."

He was, I think, shocked but not surprised.

"Could this really be happening to us?" he asked. "I can't believe it."

I told him I was more than willing to talk anything out with him, if it would help him. But it would not change anything. "You're a wonderful man in every way," I said, and meant it. "I wouldn't choose to feel this way, but I do."

He preferred to have no contact, he said, and from then on, we had none.

I felt terrible about the pain I'd caused him but liked to think that I had served a valuable function as the "transitional woman" who helped him over the worst of his divorce. And I was wondrously relieved that it was over. The future looked more uncertain again, financially and romantically, but it felt easier to live with uncertainty than its opposite, the squeezing sense of lacking room.

Within days, the burning question in my mind was whether to try to have a second child on my own now. I was forty-two and a half, and forty-three somehow seemed like even more of a fertility cliff than forty.

"I go back and forth," I told Liz. "I want one, but I'm frightened by how much harder it will be. But only for a couple of years, I tell myself. And anyway, who even knows if I can get pregnant at this late date? I know I'm not willing to go through major fertility treatment. I'm too happy with the status quo. And yet, it does seem worth trying. There's something about having two children that makes it a family."

"So you would ask Sprax?"

"Uh-huh," I said. "We've been through a lot together and never done anything to lose each other's respect. That means a lot."

Sprax was still going out with Lucy that summer, but a few times he spent a weekend day with Lily and me, going up to see potential vacation cabins I'd found on the Internet. One day, we checked out a barn in southwestern Maine that I thought I might be able to convert into living space, and combined the visit with a swim in a lake perfect for toddlers, shallow and sandy and shaded. Sprax threw Liliana high up into the air and caught her again and again, her giggles ringing out across the pond.

On the way home, he talked about how, though Lucy was a great person, he wasn't sure about her. "She particularly scares me with this kind of barely suppressed insistence that I be with her," he said. "She tends to call at around midnight, as if to check up on me. And she made some crack about how she thinks she's been very restrained, because she could have tried to get to me through Liliana, by making Liliana really crazy about her, but she has refrained. It makes me really uneasy."

To me, it sounded as if she had fallen for him but not vice versa. How deadly it can be to show too much emotion in those merciless dating dances, I thought.

It seemed an opportune moment.

"So I've been thinking...," I said. "I'm forty-two and a half, and I don't even know if I can do it anymore, but if I'm ever going to have a sibling for Liliana, it probably has to be now."

I was driving and didn't look at him. He was sitting in back with Liliana, holding her hand as she slept.

"So I've been wondering," I went on, "whether you might like to try to have a second child with me. Same deal as before. I know you're going out with Lucy, and she's pretty sure not to like the idea, but we wouldn't have to do it the fun way. We could use a turkey baster or something. And you don't need to answer right away. I just wanted to ask, to let you start thinking about it." I paused. "I think you're a truly gifted father, and I think it would be great for Liliana to have a full sibling. But I'll totally understand if you say no."

He was silent for several beats. "I'll think about it," he said finally.

A couple of days later, he said yes. Lucy was not happy about the idea, he said, but she was much more unhappy about his cooling interest in her.

"Well, I don't want to mess anything up for you."

"No," he said firmly. "Don't worry about it. The truth is, there's no way this thing with Lucy is going to last anyway. I can read my own signs. And another thing: If we have a second child, I think my contribution in terms of time and money should be greater. I'm working steadily and earning good money, and I think I should."

That would get no argument from me.

We both went for checkups and got tested for sexually transmitted diseases, and both came out fine.

I rented a cabin in New Hampshire for a week, eager to get away and just savor. Sprax was on a long-planned trip to Alaska, and when he got back, we were supposed to start trying. He had broken up with Lucy, not over our baby-making plans, he said, though they surely had a certain catalyzing effect. Sitting on the cabin balcony, overlooking green September woods and blue-gray distant mountains, I contemplated what lay ahead. It would be funny and wonderful to sleep with Sprax again, I thought. Friends kept asking me if we were getting back together, and I would say "no," and they would say "oh." What could I say? I liked things the way they were, and if Sprax hadn't fallen in love with me before, I certainly didn't expect it to happen now.

In the cabin's musty bedroom, I would put Liliana down for her nap, and after a minute, she would pop up and say "Good morning!" She could say "grasshopper," and of her mosquito bites, "itchy!" She asked for "the Nutcracker book," and knew almost all her colors. I was teaching her "high five," and she burst into laughter every time we clapped. This, I thought, is the definition of "blessing."

Liliana and I drove down from New Hampshire through pouring rain to pick up Sprax at the airport. He was focused on her for the first few minutes, then met my eyes with a beam of quiet happiness. I was the one who initiated the hug. We drove to my dad's apartment and dropped Liliana off for a while so that we could have the time alone we needed to start trying.

As we left my dad's, Sprax said, "This is a very funny situation. I feel like a teenager who's just made conversation with a girl's father before taking her out on a date."

Date, indeed. The fertility monitor said I had entered my most fertile period the day before. There was no time to lose.

I found myself shrugging and unable to look at him. It felt fantastically awkward, and like nothing I had ever read about: this person is guaranteed to sleep with you, but does he even want you? Well, maybe it was like a lot of teenage situations.

We got back to my town house and stopped at the kitchen table for a beer.

"It's not too late to back out," I told him.

"No, I've been looking forward to this," he said.

"Could you please tell me that it's not a chore for you to sleep with me?"

He grinned, suddenly half-shy. "I feel lust for you," he said quaintly. "The only problem there ever was between us was that you were too good for me."

That was the most blatant historical revisionism, and somehow not very comforting. We chatted for a while about Alaska, and that helped. Then we went upstairs, and found ourselves hugging in the hallway.

"You feel so good," he said.

"You do, too," I said.

Later, looking into my eyes, his own liquid and dreamy, Sprax said, "I love you, Carey."

"I love you, too," I said.

The Climb

Carey: "When you climb, your equipment is supposed to hold."

Beth: "Most of the time it does."

Pam: "What do you do if it doesn't?"

Beth: "Fall."

Beth

I WAS ENJOYING MY OWN COMPANY, and I'd mastered a few useful skills in the previous two years: I'd learned how to ride a bike with cleats, I'd muddled my way through buying a house, I'd navigated my divorce and my haywire finances. Now I wanted to climb.

I signed up alone for a multiweek rock-climbing course when none of my friends wanted to join me. Three cold New England spring weekends I showed up with my new harness and purple gummy-soled climbing shoes at chilly rock faces around Boston.

My classmates were friendly, but I spent the most time with an instructor named Chris. He taught me how to tie knots, set anchors, belay, and rappel. He was a lanky, quiet man. Nearing fifty, wiry and fit, he was a distance runner as well as an accomplished climber. He was like a cat, quiet and agile, and so thin I was surprised by his strength. I'd ask lots of questions. He'd smile, nod, answer me, smile again, and then we'd climb.

The final weekend was in New York State at the Gunks—in the Shawangunk Range—an East Coast mecca for climbers, mere miles from where I'd spent my honeymoon with Russell. I joined the group at a muddy campground, and Chris quickly found me at my tent. He surprised me, approaching quietly and from behind.

"All the new climbers are being set up with leaders," he said. It had rained the night before, and he gestured to the damp climbers emerging from their tents. "Maybe you'd like to climb with me?"

I said yes.

The climbs were challenging, gratifying, and a huge achievement. That night, there was a dinner and raffle, and of the eighty people participating, and a dozen prizes, somehow Chris and I had five of the winning tickets. He was embarrassed to pick up all the prizes; we ended up giving two away.

Typically, new climbers find different leaders on the second day of the trip. Chris asked if I'd join him again. I did.

Climbing is an intimate sport; it doesn't matter whether you're the leader or the "second." Your safety and your life depend on your partner. At the same time, you're completely self-reliant. Once you've made the first move off the ground, nobody's going to pull you up the cliff.

My life had been moving so fast for the past couple of years that the incremental movement of climbing was an ideal counterpoint. One foot here. One hand there. Another step. Another pull. On and on for hours. I was pushing my limits physically, and I had to focus so hard that everything, other than the cliff in front of me, the gear, and my partner, was gone.

After the course was over, Chris and I continued to climb together.

Initially, he wasn't a big talker. We'd sit quietly on rocky precipices eating granola bars and cheese sticks. Watch hawks. Enjoy the views from New Hampshire's Cathedral Ledge down to Echo Lake and across to the hills. But I didn't need to talk either. Our shared experience was the climbing. The journey, not the destination. And that was how we learned about each other, by keeping each other safe at the ends of ropes.

One sunny summer afternoon, we took a break just below the six-hundred-foot top of Cathedral Ledge. We tied off and sat down, our legs dangling into clear air and open space. "I love this," I told him, unclipping a water bottle from my harness and offering it to him. "Just look..." I gestured across a vista that was vast, green, high, and cloudless. Panoramic. "I feel like a big bird." He opened a granola bar and passed it to me. I gave him one of mine. "Days like this can change you."

"On days like today, when everything works, it's the best," he said. "Amazing."

I shifted slightly, tightening a knot before turning to him. "And thanks for getting me here."

He nodded and leaned back against the rock. "You did it yourself."

Climbing was so rewarding that I let go of the urgency for a baby. I figured I had a year before I turned forty, and I've always been a skilled procrastinator. But I also thought it made sense to start talking, to prepare everyone in my life for a somewhat less than optimal birth plan.

My parents were supportive but disappointed.

"I'm glad you want to have a baby," my mother said, "but this isn't what I'd choose for you."

I arranged for the seven vials to be driven down the road from Arlington to Boston IVF, a renowned fertility clinic. I wanted a professional seal of approval on my postponement, to be certain that my physiology would wait, too.

Blood was taken, and my FSH level (which identifies egg quality) tested well. In early October I had a hysterosalpingogram to assess whether my fallopian tubes were clear. I drove home, a thirty-nine-year-old single woman in a car, uncomfortable in my belly, stuck in traffic, trying not to cry.

The doctor identified several polyps in my fallopian tubes, and he recommended a hysteroscopy to remove them and increase the chances for insemination. I scheduled the outpatient surgery, which required anesthesia, for the beginning of February.

I didn't see any reason to tell Chris. Our mutual friend and climbing partner Jackie rolled her eyes a dozen times when I denied that Chris hoped for a relationship with me that didn't require a harness.

"No way," I argued. "We're buddies. He knows that."

"He knows that's what you want." She rolled her eyes again.

Why didn't I try to recruit my best buddy as a sperm donor, a man I knew to be kind and honorable, funny and smart, who was tall (but not six feet five) with dark hair and blue eyes?

Because if he did want me, I didn't want to know about it.

Still, it was tempting. As a candidate, he was ideal. Almost. As hard as I tried, and I tried really hard—I could have climbed with him every day—I felt no physical attraction. No spark. It was one of my life's crueler ironies. I was afraid that if I decided to have his baby, he'd want to have me, too.

Then, on a beautiful fall weekend, Jackie, Chris, another climber named Paul, and I went to the Gunks. I planned to share one of the two rooms with Jackie. Chris had planned to share one with me.

"What would Jackie's husband think if she stayed with Paul?" I asked him.

Jackie rolled her eyes some more.

I did my toughest climbing that weekend. When I was struggling to pull myself over a ledge just below a challenging summit, Chris leaned over the rock. "Come on!" he yelled. "You're here! You're done! Just pull yourself over the top."

It took several attempts. I was exhausted. I whined. And then I topped out.

"That was really, really great," he told me, and gave me a loud high five. He might have hugged me, but I was too close to the edge. "You should be proud."

I was.

Rock is steady, and solid, and relatively permanent, all the things my life hadn't been for the past couple of years. So once I was comfortable on rock, I was ready to embrace a little unpredictability. A little foul weather. I started climbing ice.

Chris took me into the woods with my new crampons and mountaineering boots, and put challenges and risks in front of me. Then he encouraged me to meet them. With ice axes in my hands, and spikes on my feet, I spidered up frozen waterfalls. Late at night, after I'd dropped Chris off, I'd park my car and walk home along Charles Street. Down the brick sidewalk, under the gas lamps, past the antiques shops and preppy clothing stores and charming cafés. With my ice tools strapped to my backpack, I felt like a superhero.

One day in mid-December, we left the cliffs as we always did. We organized gear, coiled rope, and hiked out in the dark wearing snowshoes and headlamps. We stuck to our usual plan of dinner, coffee, stay awake for the drive back to Boston. That night, we headed for a Mexican restaurant where there were few other diners.

Before the enchiladas arrived, we were talking about my two nieces. He'd met them a few weeks earlier when we'd stopped for dinner at my brother's house on our way home from the Gunks.

Chris wasn't a big eater, so when he picked up a tortilla chip, examined it, and put it back down, I didn't think much of it. But when he did that twice, I asked if there was something wrong.

"I was just wondering." He held the chip in his fingers and broke off an edge. "You really love your nieces. And I was just wondering, but you don't have to answer if it's uncomfortable. I was wondering if you want to have kids."

Chris had never been married.

"The short answer is yes," I told him.

"And the longer answer?"

"To be honest, I've started looking into being a single mother, and you're up at the top of my list of potential donors."

"Donors."

"Sperm donors."

"Right. Okay." He put his fork down. "I don't know what to say. This isn't what I expected to hear." He raised his eyebrows and shook his head. He looked at the table, then around the room. "But don't get me wrong, Beth. I'm honored. It's just that it's something I never considered. I'd have to think about it."

Two days later, I received this e-mail:

I make this offer with all the sincerity you know I am capable of. This is your journey. That I may be your traveling companion for a time is a treasure for a lifetime. What may be in it for you? Here are some of my thoughts:

Absolute certainty of heritage. I will provide any and all information you need. You can accept or reject this offer based on criteria only you need know. No questions asked.

In turn, I may receive a lifetime of pleasant thoughts. Thoughts that I may have helped another experience life fully. Especially if that other person is you.

I should've kept my mouth shut. Chris had made it clear on more than one occasion—through a combination of kind actions, gestures, notes, and occasionally spoken words—that his deep feelings for me continued to grow, and he held out hope for a romantic relationship. I was certain that if we did have a child together, turkey baster or not, his wish would only increase. If we agreed to be parents, we'd be locked together forever. No more buddies.

The following week, Chris took me to dinner, a real dinner. A date. Afterward he walked me home and gave me a gift. A wooden mountaineering axe with the pattern of my tattoo—"abhaya," the Sanskrit word for fearlessness—carved into it.

"I love you," he told me, as I unwrapped the axe.

"This is incredibly thoughtful. I'm just—" He put up his hand, didn't let me finish. "I know you told me not to say it. But I've already tried being the quiet buddy."

"I'm not sure what to tell you." I held the axe, turned it over in my hands.

He took a breath and stepped back, leaning against the kitchen counter. "Then don't." He shook his head. "Maybe you can think about it."

I called him at work the next day.

"I'm fine, Beth," was his answer when I asked how he was.

A useless question. A way to fill the space. "I'm fine. Hurt, but I'll be fine."

We went climbing later that week, and on the drive home he put his hand on my thigh. "I'm still willing to help you," he told me.

I took his hand—gently, I thought—and moved it.

We climbed together a few more times at the gym, but then he was suddenly busy whenever I called. Nearly a month passed and then I heard from Jackie that he'd accepted a job offer and was moving to England.

"What did you expect?" she asked me. "That he'd say no to having a baby with you? That he'd take it well if you declined?"

I was sorry he was going. I missed him, and I missed climbing with him. But even at the low points, when I missed him most and wished I had fallen in love with him, I knew I hadn't made a mistake. I also knew that 8282 was still there.

Before Chris left, I'd signed up for an ice-climbing class. I arrived early for the first weekend, pulling into Harvard Cabin, a communal bunkhouse set back from windy Route 16 in Jackson, New Hampshire, on a cold afternoon. The place was empty except for two guys.

"Here," said the one with the rakish black wool cap and goatee, patting the bench beside him, "you can sit here."

I did. He raised his fork toward my mouth so I could share his dessert. It was a forward gesture, but I opened my mouth like an oversized baby bird.

And there it was: Meeting Phil was a piece of cake. Chocolate cake.

The rest of my climbing class arrived, knocking snow off boots, peeling off layers, sitting at the long tables. I talked to Phil the goatee guy about his lousy day climbing in one of the gullies with frozen ropes, about how excited I was for the workshop, about the importance of embracing winter if you live in the Northeast. How his truck was a truck, and he wasn't one of those guys who referred to his SUV as a truck. For a while it was so noisy with voices and people banging on the gas stove to keep it burning, that we just sat next to each other in our Gore-Tex. He had dark hair and blue eyes. He was around six feet tall, broad, with big hands that were red from pulling frozen ropes all day. Rugged. Even not talking, he gave off energy.

Eventually, our group started gathering for an orientation, and Phil excused himself and went upstairs to his sleeping bag.

In the morning, he was gone.

By the end of the weekend I knew two things: I wanted to keep climbing ice, and I wanted to find the guy who fed me cake. I had no contact information, so I sent an e-mail to the leader of the ice program, who knew Phil's partner, and the e-mail was ferried along to Phil.

When I got Phil's e-mail address, I wrote something about waterproof ropes, or ice screws, and then asked if he'd want to go out sometime.

"How about Saturday night?" he wrote back.

Carpe diem.

For our first date, he arrived in a black pickup.

"See." He gestured to the flatbed. "A truck. By definition."

I smiled. Hmmm, I thought.

We went to a low-key pub in Somerville, listened to an Irish band with a great fiddle player, drank pints of beer, and ate hearty fare. I've never been one to pretend I eat only rice crackers and fruit. I still liked him, and from what I could tell, it was mutual. He drove me home, miraculously found a parking space, and walked me to my door. "Do you want to come in?" I asked him. He shook his head.

"No. Thanks. Not tonight, but I'd like to another time."

What a waste of a parking spot, I thought.

We started spending a lot of our free time together, going out to dinner, hanging out and watching TV or going to movies during the week. He'd kiss me, but he wouldn't sleep with me. For years I'd thought that sex was the best way to get things going, to jump-start a relationship. It wasn't what you waited for. It was what you did, then you figured out the rest afterward, if you bothered to.

Raised in a big Catholic family, with parents who were more of the 1950s than any other era, Phil was being gentlemanly. I was a little bewildered by his behavior; we'd roll around on the couch, and before anything happened, he'd take a deep breath, kiss me, and leave. It was enticing. Waiting for something worthwhile is a great stimulant.

But the courtliness didn't last. We were going on a weekend ice-climbing trip with his friends Guy and Clare in early February, where we'd be staying in a small cabin, sharing a bed, and the room next door would be occupied. I suggested we might want to start any intimate relationship in relative privacy. He agreed.

Guy and Clare were great. They were welcoming, and good climbers. You can meet people at a party and like them, but meeting people in the snow, and trusting them with your life, and knowing they trust you with theirs, is an intense way to start a friendship. Phil barely knew me, and he invited me so easily, saying something like, "My friends have this ice fest every year where we get together and climb. Do you want to come?" As if he were inviting me to a movie.

We were together every weekend from the beginning, and back and forth to see each other during the week. A forensic auditor at a large financial services company, he had the consummate bachelor pad: a ground-floor garden apartment halfway between the city and his job. Regulation large-screen television. Beige couch that seems to come standard with being an unmarried male over the age of thirty-five. One pot and a George Foreman grill with bun warmer. Some beer, pastrami, and unidentifiable items in the refrigerator.

Pam and I had planned a cross-country ski trip to Vermont's Northeast Kingdom for the end of February, but she had a deadline that prevented her from going.

"I'm thinking I might invite Phil," I told her.

"That's an excellent idea," she said. "But be aware that it's a looooong drive. Either lots of time to talk or lots of time to figure out there's nothing to talk about. But," she added, ever the optimist, "he seems to be worth the effort."

It was indeed a long, dark drive, and Phil and I made many wrong turns. We laughed a lot—about his high school job as a cheese stirrer, another job as a singing waiter, his old beater motorcycle. His family. Mine. I also learned that he hadn't had a relationship lasting more than four months in a decade, but lots that were abbreviated.

"Why not?" I asked him. "What was wrong with them?" An easier question than: "Do you have a commitment problem?"

"I guess it was different each time. Some moved away. Sometimes it just didn't work out. Sometimes it wasn't where I wanted to spend my energy."

I tried not to analyze. Maybe he'd just had bad luck. But a

handsome, smart, funny, employed, athletic thirty-seven-year-old male who's largely been single leaves a couple of questions.

I was able to push those thoughts aside temporarily. It was a beautiful weekend. Plenty of snow and blue skies, temperatures warm enough to lean our skis against a maple tree and have a picnic of apples and peanut butter sandwiches under the branches. We were outside all day. I'm a lousy skier, but he didn't care.

Our room was cold, and sparsely decorated, so when we were in it, we spent a lot of time in bed. It was great. I thought so, and he told me so, which was amazing. I wasn't used to that. Russell was so self-absorbed that he'd say stuff like, "Thanks, babe. That was good. Can you hand me my book?" And all the others were just that: the others. Anchored to a place and time that was desperate and needy. A part of my history I didn't want to forget but surely didn't want to repeat. Phil seemed different. Kind and sarcastic. Self-assured and considerate. Physical and gentle. Funny and sensitive. But he wasn't perfect; he was a registered Republican. Aside from that, only the remark about where he didn't want to spend his time and energy remained worrisome.

Girlfriends who knew my single-mother agenda asked if Phil wanted to have children. "I barely know him," I'd reply. "I'm not really sure. I haven't asked him."

Pam knew how much time I was spending with Phil, and she also knew that 8282, or some other means to the same end, was high on my priority list.

"Don't you think you should find out?" she asked me.

"No, I'm not ready to find out if he's not."

I saw no reason to put the hard questions out there yet. And I'd given myself a year to delay. If Phil fizzled, 8282 was still my guy.

I enjoyed Phil's friends Guy and Clare so much that when they invited us on a climbing trip to West Virginia's Seneca Rocks in early April, and Phil couldn't go, I decided to join them anyway.

But six hours before I was to meet Guy and Clare at the airport, I decided something wasn't quite right. I walked to the pharmacy and bought two pregnancy tests.

I took my time on the way home. I bought a Frappuccino. I stopped at a gift shop and browsed. I bought something for my nieces. I waited for the light to change before I crossed the street. I looked at the view of the river down Pinckney Street. And then I went in the front door, up the stairs, and into the bathroom.

Both tests were positive. I spent one of the remaining five hours sitting on the tiled floor in my bathroom, staring at the wall. I'm sure my blood pressure spiked. I looked down at my belly. Telling Phil made me anxious. Being pregnant made me anxious. Deciding what to do about being pregnant, that didn't make me anxious at all. Knowing I'd already decided, that made me anxious, too.

For the record: this truly was a case of contraceptive failure. Use contraceptives as instructed, and reapply, reinsert, refill, as indicated. Yes, I wanted a baby. But, no, I did not do it on purpose.

I didn't call Phil before I left. I didn't call anyone.

We flew to DC, with plans to drive to West Virginia the following day. We arrived early, so I called my friend Madeleine, whom I'd known since we were fourteen. She picked me up for dinner. We went to a brightly lit place in Adams Morgan that had an extensive beer menu and all-day breakfast. I looked at the beer menu. Then I ordered an iced tea. And there it was, a life decision in a beverage choice. No alcohol. New lifestyle.

I looked at Madeleine across the table and started crying. I hadn't seen her in two years, but at that moment it didn't matter. I opened my mouth. I shook my head. The waitress came smiling our way, and Madeleine asked her to give us a minute.

"What . . . ," she asked me quietly. "What, what is it?"

"I'm pregnant," I told her. "And you're the only person who knows."

She nodded her head and reached over a bottle of ketchup to touch my shoulder. "Ah, Bethy, Bethy," she said softly. "Is this a good thing?"

"I don't know. I guess it's not a terrible thing."

"But I'm the only one who knows?"

"Yes."

"Then it's not an ideal thing."

"No, not ideal."

Those five chilly days in West Virginia we climbed from sunrise until dusk on the soaring, narrow sandstone fins that make up Seneca Rocks. In the quiet moments—in the shower, or when my roommate Bill had fallen asleep, or between bites of breakfast—I was hit by the magnitude of what was happening. I cried a little in the shower, listened for hours to Bill breathing on the other side of the room, and decided that the best way to tell Phil was just to tell him. After I got home.

I didn't take it easier with the climbing. If anything, I pushed myself harder, trying during the daylight hours to concentrate on the routes, and not on the rest of my life.

We flew home at night, so I had the following day to pace and try to come up with the right thing to say: "Hi, come on in, I'm pregnant." Or "Hi, do you want a drink? Have a seat. I'm pregnant." I was one woman in a continuum as long as humanity, preparing to drop a bomb on an unsuspecting male.

Phil was coming over after work. I sat myself on the staircase inside the front door, and waited. I noticed paint cracks I'd never seen before. I listened to voices filtering in from the street. I focused on my breathing. I couldn't stop jiggling my leg up and down.

When the bell rang, I felt it more than heard it, like an electric shock.

"Hey!" Phil was smiling. "Was it great?" He leaned over and kissed me.

"It was great. It really was great. Guy and Clare and Bill are great. The climbing was great. The weather wasn't so great. The place is great. It was all great. Really. It was great."

He stepped inside. "Well, sounds like it was great. Really, really great. And that"—he kissed me again—"is great. I'm only sorry I missed it."

Then, because I'm not a patient person, I shoved us into the next phase of our lives. "I have to tell you something, and I don't know how you're going to take it." I stepped away from him.

He must have thought I was going to end our relationship, even though it had barely begun. "I'm pregnant," I announced, my voice louder than I'd meant it to be. I didn't want to end anything. I didn't know where we were going to go, but I didn't want it all to end.

He looked almost relieved. For three seconds.

"You're pregnant?"

"Please don't ask me if I'm sure."

"I wasn't going to."

"Okay." I really didn't know how to proceed.

"Right. Okay. This isn't the welcome I expected." He took a deep breath and rubbed his face.

"Sorry. I figured if I didn't say anything until later it would be a mistake. Then you'd wonder why I hadn't told you right away."

He nodded. "Yeah. You're probably right. No good time, I guess."

"None that I could think of."

Then Phil stood in front of me and, sooner than I expected, he asked, "Do you know what you want to do?"

This was Phil, who'd been an escort at Planned Parenthood until he took a swing at a fanatic with a poster board. But he was also the son of devout Catholic parents. Religion probably wouldn't factor into his decision, but his single-guy, fried-pastrami-three-nights-a-week lifestyle might.

"Keep it," I said.

"Really?"

"Yes."

"You've thought about this?"

"Yes. What do you think?" I asked.

"I think you've already decided. But you need to give me a little longer to think, to really wrap my head around this." He paused. "You had a few days with this, right?"

I nodded.

He nodded. "You knew before you left." He took another deep breath.

"If you don't want to do this, I'll totally understand." I considered touching his arm but didn't; I had no idea what he was feeling.

He shook his head. "We'll figure this out. You just have to give me a little time."

No shouting. No blame. No "How could you let this happen?" One way to get to know someone is to get pregnant accidentally and then try to stick it out.

I went to the ob-gyn two days later. The pregnancy was

confirmed. What I found most surprising was that after years of foolishness and intermittent unsafe sex, I'd never gotten knocked up. I almost assumed I was infertile. The added irony was the surgery I'd scheduled to remove polyps and unblock my fallopian tubes to increase the chances of getting pregnant. I'd developed the flu the week surgery was scheduled, so I'd never had it. What did occur to me, while I was in a polka-dotted johnny, waiting for the doctor, was that now Phil and I would be forever connected. If I had this baby, Phil would be in my life. Forever.

If things fell apart, we'd never be rid of each other. Clearly, that was not the thought process of a woman entirely comfortable with romantic fantasies. Instead, I wondered if we'd end up in court fighting over custody.

"Okay," he said one afternoon. "Let's do this together. I have to grow up at some point."

I started to look at him as a potential father, and he looked good.

Then Phil took me to meet his parents.

Beverly and Ron were traditional, conservative, churchgoing, gin-and-tonic-drinking, American-car-driving, still-have-the-45-rpm-turntable-in-the-living-room parents. Lovely, but far different from my parents. They welcomed me. But they didn't know I was pregnant.

Phil and his father hung bird feeders and cleaned the grill, and his mother brought me upstairs. She'd had her hair done before we arrived, and it swept in a crisp, sprayed gray wave up and across her forehead. She took a box out of her closet and, after showing me baby photos of Phil, she held out pictures of another boy, a beautiful, blond, smiling boy.

"This is Phil's older brother, Durl," Beverly said. "He died of Reye's syndrome when he was six."

Phil had mentioned his older brother early on, when I'd asked how many siblings he had. His response had been: "It depends on who you ask. There were six. Now there are five."

I sat there on Beverly's king-sized bed, photos spread across the comforter, watching her face. She smiled at the photos as she looked at them and as she put them away. It seemed she'd just brought me through a family rite of passage. She started crying, and I touched her arm. She put her hand on mine. After we went back downstairs and she'd gone into the kitchen, Phil intercepted me in the hall and asked, "Was she showing you the pictures of Durl?"

I nodded, and he shook his head, looked around the corner of the dining room at his mother's back, and said, "I'm sorry." Durl wasn't mentioned again on that visit, but it became clear immediately that he was the missing piece of that family.

My parents were the first to hear about the pregnancy. The beginning of the phone conversation was standard. Here's what's new, things are fine, work's good, the weather's been rainy, I really like Phil.

"That's great," my mother said, "I'm glad. Seems you're doing a lot together."

"Yup."

"Any more trips planned?"

"We thought we might come out to see you and Dad."

My parents lived in Manhattan, with a second home north of the city.

"Really, when? That'd be great."

"Next week?"

"That sounds good."

And then a pause. A legitimately pregnant pause.

"There's something you should know before we come." A quick beat. "I'm pregnant."

"Really?"

"Truly. Even the doctor said so."

"Oh my."

My mother's not an "oh my" kind of woman. It sounded very midcentury, very June Cleaver.

"Can't wait to meet Phil...," she said. Not surprisingly, I detected some sarcasm. Over the years I'd brought home a long line of boyfriends. Some serious, others whose names I barely recall. From high school onward they'd come to Thanksgiving, summer weekends at the lake, Passover, and birthdays. This one, he got me pregnant, and they'd never even laid eyes on him.

Phil, the son of a naval officer, was convinced that my father would chase him out of the house with an axe. He was visibly tense as we drove across the Massachusetts Turnpike to their country place, his chin twitching under his goatee.

Instead of wielding a weapon, when we arrived my father opened a bottle of champagne. It was warm for early spring, and we sat outside. "Here's to health," he toasted. We stayed on the patio until long after dark.

Phil's parents were next. His mother was weepy when he told her over the phone. "Happy weepy?" I wanted to know. "Or distraught, shocked, a baby-out-of-wedlock weepy?"

"Probably a little of both."

We felt like high schoolers, telling them we'd made a mistake, but we were going to buck up and see it through.

We decided during the summer that Phil would move in with me in October; the baby was due around Christmas.

At the next doctor's appointment, I sat in my johnny for ninety minutes, waiting. Phil had taken time from work to meet me, and he was waiting too, in the reception area, wondering if something was wrong. What was wrong was that my doctor, a Best of Boston winner, had forgotten about me.

When he finally showed, he apologized, gave a quick excuse, and we listened to the Doppler sounding of the baby's heartbeat, that gallop of life racing through the electrostatic meter. It was astonishing, like finding a new planet. This was life imposing itself on the world, through me and Phil.

When we hit the three-month mark, I told people. One by one, I made it real. It's different when you're nearly forty. Friends with older kids were amused.

My friend Nancy, whose kids were in high school: "I'm really happy for you, but I'd put a bullet in my head before I'd live with another infant." And Maggie: "Hahahahahahaha! Call me in ten years!" Fiona found it entertaining to inform me that "not too long ago if you got knocked up over age thirty-five they called it a 'geriatric pregnancy.' "

Friends who were nearing or past forty and wanted but didn't have kids were simultaneously happy and sad. "Can you sell me some of that mojo?" my colleague Jane asked.

My amnio was scheduled at Massachusetts General Hospital, but first we had to meet with a genetic counselor.

The counselor we spoke with was sweet to a degree that was off-putting. We had a few issues to be concerned about—hereditary markers that might put a fetus at risk—but nothing major, other than my age. She showed us charts, discussed options, but we'd already determined to have the amnio, and if it showed significant abnormality, we'd terminate the pregnancy. We knew the odds, even at my age, were on our side.

There are many women over thirty-five who don't have amniocentesis or CVS (chorionic villus sampling), opting for less invasive testing or none at all. Although the risk factors increase with age (1 in 1,250 chance of a Down's pregnancy at age twenty, 1 in 400 at age thirty-five, 1 in 100 at age forty, 1 in 30 at age forty-five), some women wait so long, or try so hard to get pregnant, that the risk of a miscarriage from amnio, however slight, is unacceptable. I wasn't one of them.

Then the waiting. There are numerous academic studies assessing the level of anxiety in women awaiting amnio results, and, no surprise, there's hard-core anxiety for the two weeks before the cultures are complete and the results are in. So we waited. It was mid-June; on the late side for an amnio. I'd willed myself out of anxiety and into my fortieth birthday.

We spent my birthday at Crane Beach, a sweeping expanse of protected shoreline north of Boston. It was windy, but warm, and I lay on a blanket, resting my head on Phil, and thinking that our days of reading on the beach were about to conclude. Soon, instead of carrying novels and magazines, we'd be carting pails and diapers.

When the call came, I was in the bedroom, reading an article for work. "Hello, Beth? This is Jenny, the genetic counselor," she said. "I have your amnio results. Are you somewhere private? Where we can talk?"

"Yes?"

"Beth, I'm sorry . . ."

That's all I needed to hear.

I've never had such a strong "shoot the messenger" response to anyone. She went on to tell me that the results showed trisomy 21: Down syndrome. End of story. And for us, end of pregnancy.

It's estimated that up to 90 percent of women who receive a Down's diagnosis for their fetus opt to terminate the pregnancy. We'd made our choice prior to the diagnosis. There are many loving accounts of raising a Down syndrome child, but we didn't feel equipped to take on the challenge. I knew that I would not outlive my child, and I didn't want to live my life fearing my own death and for my child's basic survival.

Jenny asked if I wanted to come in to talk to her. If there was anyone she could contact for me. If I had someone to call. I hung up.

Phil picked up on the first ring. He always did. I could barely speak, could only shout, "The baby has Down's!" and then I lost it.

Soon I heard Phil racing up the stairs.

We lay on the bed for a while, and I asked what if they'd made a mistake? If they'd confused the records? And all the questions I'm sure everyone in our position asked.

I told my parents. My father cried. I took a shower, and examined my stomach as if I might receive a message. Then I went to the kitchen. Phil was sitting at the table, his head bowed, and I thought he was reading. He was crying. I leaned over and touched his arm. He shook his head.

I realized at that moment we were in it together; he hadn't agreed to have the baby just because I'd made a choice. He'd made a decision, too. Then he shook his head again and said, "Please. What I'd like is to be alone." It was at *that* moment I realized we still barely knew each other.

Prior to the diagnosis, I'd changed ob-gyns. So the first time I met my new doctor, the kind, young, bespectacled Dr. Reed, was to schedule an abortion. It was a Thursday, and the procedure was scheduled for the following Wednesday. The waiting room was (to me) a horror show: full to brimming with hugely pregnant women, young children, and parenting magazines. He was apologetic but also businesslike, recognizing that in order for us to get through the information, it was easiest to be gentle yet efficient. I kept my eyes on the floor on the way out of the office, preferring to bump into furniture than to see all the bulging bellies.

The weekend before the termination, I went on assignment for the *Globe* to cover hiking on Mount Washington.

Phil and I smoked on the way up to North Conway, New Hampshire. We drank beer when we got there. We paid a fortune for a modest room with a view of the mountains in a resort hotel. I plowed through a massive breakfast buffet. And the hike. I was four months pregnant, out of shape, heartbroken, and grateful to be climbing—as slow as a mule—the highest mountain in New England. That was the first day of summer; I have a photo somewhere of me standing in a large patch of snow near the top of Mount Washington, throwing a snowball at Phil.

I'd like to believe I closed the *Globe* piece with an anthem to the future, glimpsed from atop the Mount Washington Observatory: "And everything, everything, for hundreds of square miles, was down there, below us. At that moment, as far as the Northeast goes, we were standing on top of the world."

At home, Pam brought food, stayed for about five minutes, realized that we just wanted to stare at the walls, and left.

"I have no idea how you're feeling," she said, handing me a

tray of Chicken Marbella that could have fed twenty people. "I feel totally useless. That's why I made enough food to feed your neighborhood. I didn't know what else to do."

"I don't know what to do," I told her. "Except maybe eat all the chicken and not invite the neighbors."

"Mangia," she said. "Do whatever you need to get through today. And tonight. And tomorrow, start over again."

She kissed me and left.

On Monday a medical resident inserted sticks of dried kelp into my cervix. It sounds, and is, bizarre. Oddly like having brittle sushi shoved into your body. The intensely uncomfortable twigs are called laminaria. They're strongly "hygroscopic," drawing water from their surroundings and slowly expanding. A less aggressive technique for expanding the cervix than metal dilators—so long as the resident inserting them is experienced and skilled. But my resident was neither. It hurt like hell. They sent me home, telling me to prepare for cramps.

Laminaria take time. I was to wait twelve hours before having them checked for sufficient dilation. I sat on a chaise on the deck, reading tabloid magazines, watching the sun move, feeling sad, fat, and uncomfortable.

Twelve hours later, the laminaria hadn't worked. More were inserted. I went home and sat for twelve more hours. That night, before we went to bed to read and not sleep, Phil turned to me and said, "Hey, even though we're not going through with this, I still want to move in."

"Thanks," I said. "I'm glad." And I went to sleep.

The procedure took a very long time. My first ob-gyn had advised against CVS, which would've given us early results and likely allowed the termination to be a simple extraction. Instead, I was forced to deliver a fetus that would die on its way out of me, crushed into oblivion, after twenty hours of labor, after pitocin, after an epidural, with my feet in stirrups—in a heinous imitation of actual birth. When it was finally over, when I heard the awful sounds of the fetus sloshing out of me, I was heaving, and all I could ask was, "Is it over?"

I'd asked Phil to leave the room. And it was only later that I realized how terrible it was for him to sit alone in the corridor, while crying, breathing babies were delivered in rooms all around him. I'd also forgotten that it was his birthday.

Dr. Reed wiped his glasses and looked up at me over the stirrups. "Some people want to see the fetus," he told me. "But this time, I don't think it's a very good idea." I agreed.

Eventually, I fell asleep in the hospital room, and Phil did too, on a recliner next to me, in front of windows that overlooked Beacon Hill.

Shrieking woke me up. Followed by predawn screams from the next room of "Push! Push! Come on, baby, you can do it! Come on, baby, you can do this!"

If I could make one recommendation to hospital maternity wards, it would be to provide, at the end of the hall, and equipped with soundproofing, a room where women terminating their pregnancies can stay far away from the blessed agonizing cries of women in labor. I couldn't believe what I was hearing. I threw the blanket off my legs and jumped out of the bed. "Phil," I yelled, "I want to go home, I'm going home." But I fell, and collapsed on the floor. The epidural hadn't worn off. I couldn't feel my legs. I couldn't stand up. I couldn't leave, couldn't do anything but sit on the floor crying, listening to the woman in the next room giving birth.

Phil helped me get back into bed and we stared at each other.

That summer, I wanted to push pregnant women down stairs.

I felt fat, and for no good reason anymore. There was also my body still thinking it was pregnant. And there were the various leakings, the cramps, the belly, the hormones. But then, eventually, things eased. I got my body back. Perhaps most amazing, Phil and I were still together. Or maybe it wasn't amazing. Maybe we'd circumvented the trivial and superfluous aspects of early relationships, and by steering straight to the core, to the first big crisis, we'd navigated through.

One day I said to him, "I'd still like to have a baby."

And he said, "Yes. I know."

"Are you okay with that?"

"I think so," he told me. "I just need to get over this one."

I'd basically used a megaphone to announce that I was pregnant, and when I wasn't I had to let people know. I didn't want them asking me about my progress. I was intensely jealous of anyone pregnant. "I want to knock that woman down," I muttered to Pam as we passed a woman with a carriage.

"Best not to," she warned. "And besides, that might just be the nanny."

Piece by piece, we started moving Phil's things into my house in September. We moved slowly that summer, no more rush to get to know each other. Our pace was slurred.

The last week in September, Phil had a yard sale and sold his remaining furniture, pots and pans, the bachelor couch and particleboard media center. He locked the door to his apartment and walked away, toward Beacon Hill.

"You're doing the right thing," Pam assured me over coffee in Harvard Square.

"I'm trying to remain optimistic."

"Eventually you won't have to try."

"I'll try to remain optimistic about that, too."

That fall, Phil and I went mountain biking at Mount Snow in Vermont. I wrote about our trip in a travel story for the *Globe,* and, rereading it, I sound happy: "I know that Phil, my partner in all things outdoors and insane, and I have had a successful day when we high-five at the end and congratulate ourselves on simply remaining intact." The summer was over. We were having fun. We were moving fast again, very fast.

Several weeks later, Phil and I were reading in bed. The windows were open, there was noise from Charles Street, and the air was getting cooler. I put my book down.

"Hey." I touched his arm.

He turned to me, didn't put his book down.

"I was thinking."

"Should I be afraid?" he asked.

"Maybe."

"Thinking about what?"

"Thinking about thinking about having a baby."

"Oh, really . . ."

"Yes. Really."

His eyebrows went up. His book was put down. "Can we talk about this tomorrow?"

We did talk about it tomorrow. And we talked about it the next day. And the next. Somewhere in there, Phil told me he'd changed his mind, he didn't want to have a baby. He didn't want to have a baby at all.

"How about that," I said. "We've got a problem."

"I guess. But I'm here because I want to be with you, not because I want to have a baby."

"But I want to have a baby. Remember? We talked about this." My tone was shifting, not in a nice way. "And a baby ideally with you."

He shook his head. "I'm sorry. I don't have an explanation. I didn't plan to change my mind."

"This is a big change."

"I just don't want to do it," he repeated. "The last time I didn't have much choice."

"If I do this alone, I can't imagine you'd want to be here, and where are you going to go? You sold everything you owned for six hundred dollars."

Clearly he hadn't thought this part through. "This isn't quitting," he informed me. "So please don't imply that. You don't get the luxury of quitting if you never got the luxury of choosing."

Later that night I went downstairs. Phil was sitting at the kitchen table. The only light was coming through the frosted window. "This is going to be awful," I said. "Really, really awful."

"I know." He didn't look at me.

"This is going to be worse than what we just went through."

He turned to me. His face was shadowy in the dark and he shook his head. He looked down. He shook his head again. "No." He was emphatic. "It doesn't get worse than that."

The Second Transfer

Pam: "These were no ordinary vials I was getting. They were lucky."

Carey: "Passing along the sperm was becoming a tradition."

Beth: "The ultimate regifting."

Pam

BOYCE RENSBERGER, THE JOURNALISM FELLOWSHIP DIRECTOR at the Massachusetts Institute of Technology, looked around the conference table at us with a mischievous smile.

"Welcome to MIT. Nice to meet all of you. Do you know you have something in common?" he asked. Blank stares. A nervous giggle or two.

As the newest crop of fellows, we were introducing ourselves for the first time over coffee and cookies: Hujun from China, Debbie from Costa Rica, Rehana from South Africa, Kevin from Washington, Steve from New York, and the rest. We couldn't have been more different from one another, apart from being journalists.

"Crisis. You're all in crisis," he said. "That's why you're here, even if it takes you a while to figure it out."

We looked at one another, but no one said a word. Paid to be students for a year, who were we to complain? About *anything?*

"I ain't in crisis," Steve, the senior science writer of the bunch, joked later. He spoke with a Bronx accent and the sonorous tones of a radio announcer. "And if you say I'm in crisis again, I'm gonna start to cry!"

At one low point during a biology seminar, I elbowed Steve. I knew very little about science, unlike most of the other fellows, who had impressive biology and chemistry backgrounds. He looked over as I flipped to the back of my notebook and pointed to a blank page.

"Hey, could you please diagram a cell for me?" I whispered. How embarrassing.

Steve, who knew pretty much anything related to science or Mel Brooks, graciously drew circles and arrows linking atom to molecule and gene to chromosome.

He also scribbled, "You smell good."

There I was: perfumed, single, jobless, financially insecure, and planning on motherhood. That was my crisis. But I had precious months ahead of me with no serious responsibilities, and I decided the fellowship year's mantra would be: "Receive, receive, receive." Let the universe come to me. And do what I wanted to do, not what I felt I should do. Zero gravity, baby.

Samuel Palmer, a knowledgeable and enthusiastic astronomy professor, promised to teach us the laws of the universe beneath a copper-sheathed rooftop dome that housed what was once the largest telescope in the country.

That night, his opening lesson on luminosity—the quality of emitting or reflecting light—had a decidedly human element. Sitting in front of me was a handsome man with a long, straight nose and blue or maybe green eyes. Dark brown bangs swept over his forehead, and a black leather jacket draped over the back of his chair grazed my knees. With a calm and patient expression, he was listening to the ramblings of a wild-eyed student to his left.

I pictured sitting on a bench next to him when we were much older, with him listening to me with that same compassionate gaze. As we moved from the classroom up to the Harvard College Observatory, I found myself thinking, I'd like a man like that. I followed him onto the rooftop, with the glinting Boston skyline spread out before us and the stars above like a canopy of fireflies.

"Beautiful night, isn't it?" I said.

He smiled. "Yes, it is."

I detected a slight accent. I also detected another woman, petite, with an asymmetrical haircut and red lipstick.

"The professor seems very engaging," she said.

"Yes, he does," the man replied.

"And a great explainer," I chipped in. "Which is good, because I get a stomachache just thinking about doing math." The woman nodded empathetically.

"When he showed one star pulling matter out of another," the man said, "I thought that was really fantastic."

The other woman and I enthusiastically agreed, saying, "Oh, yes!" in unison, as if this good-looking fellow himself could pull matter out of stars.

"I'm Pam," I said.

"I'm Mark."

I don't remember what her name was. Honest.

"What brings you here?" I asked him.

"I've just been interested in astronomy for a long time, and

I've enjoyed taking classes at Harvard for many years now," he said. It was some kind of British accent. "It's such a wonderful opportunity to learn and meet interesting people. And you?"

"I'm on a fellowship at MIT," I said, "which basically means for a year I can learn and meet interesting people, too."

I moved closer to Mark, and the other woman drifted away. We moved into the dome, where it was dark and I could barely see the outline of his face.

"What do you do when you're not taking classes?" I asked quietly. He worked in information technology.

"I always thought journalism was a wonderful profession, and you must be so talented to do it," he said.

I blushed. "You'd be surprised at just how unglamorous it is."

I sensed Mark's eyes on me as I stepped forward and peered into the telescope at the bright planets above. I waited for him to take his turn, and we asked our lecturer some questions. Only a handful of people lingered. As the observatory viewing came to an end, I slipped down the stairs and followed Mark out to the sidewalk. Our conversation was instantly personal. He was Welsh, from a place I could not pronounce, and he had just discovered a half sister in Australia.

"My mother and father divorced when I was two, and I've rarely seen him," he explained. It came as a complete shock to his mother, Ruth, when she went to the supermarket and an acquaintance casually asked her about Mark and Mark's father's other child. "*What* other child?" Ruth asked. Some sleuthing uncovered a daughter whose mother had a failed relationship with Mark's father and moved to Australia with the girl.

"It's remarkable that I have an immediate affinity by virtue of blood with someone who is no more than a complete stranger," he said in his Welsh lilt, as we walked down the hill from the observatory. The streets were empty and quiet.

"Have you spoken to her?"

"Yes, many, many times over the phone. I regarded myself as an only child for so long, for four decades, and now I know it's not the case," he said. (Okay, so he's at least forty, I thought to myself. Good. And no wedding ring.) "I do have someone who is out there. That's truly new for me."

We approached the street where Mark had parked his car.

"Would you like a lift home?" he asked.

Tempting, I thought. Dangerous, too. It was almost eleven p.m., and I didn't know him, though everything in my being felt that he was safe. Better than safe.

"No, that's okay," I said. "Thank you anyway."

He grinned. "Nice to have met you. Good night, Pam."

"Good night."

I smiled all the way to the subway. All the way home. All the way into bed. I hadn't felt butterflies like these in years. The kind that are whirring around so fast that your hands feel jittery and your legs twitch, as if you've had too much caffeine.

The next morning, sitting next to Debbie in biology class, trying hard to concentrate on a genetics lecture, I wrote in my notebook, "I met a cute Welshman last night." She gave me a big smile and an elbow nudge, pressing for details.

I showed up early for astronomy class the next week. Mark came in late and sat near the door. Our eyes met, and we mouthed "hellos." I picked up my handbag and notebook during the break and moved next to him. After class, he slid his notebook into a backpack and turned to me. This time, I could tell his eyes were blue.

"Do you know Caffé Paradiso?" he asked. "Would you like to go for coffee there?"

Hell, yeah. "Sure," I replied. "That would be nice."

We made our way to the café, ordered drinks, and settled into a table by the window. A few other people read books or chatted quietly.

We connected the dots of our lives: This is where I grew up, went to school, traveled. Mark lived in a modest suburb north of Boston. He had been a U.S. citizen for nearly twenty years and traveled a great deal, including many times to India. He had a busy social life seeing films with friends and taking classes, and he was interested in foreign affairs. He had a background in mechanical engineering and toyed with the idea of getting a graduate degree or doing something creative like photography and filmmaking.

Mark spoke softly and listened with that kind expression I had first seen a week ago. He also seemed sadder than I remembered. He poured some cream into his coffee and began stirring.

"So, are you involved with anyone at the moment?" he asked.

"No, I'm not," I said, taken aback. He was certainly direct. "Are you?"

"Yes, Pam, I've been married for a number of years," he said. His spoon slipped out of his fingers and dropped to the floor. As he bent to pick it up, his head ducking under the table, I inadvertently swore under my breath. Damn. Damn, damn, damn. How could this be? Had I misread the signals? Why did I have such bad luck?

"It could be said that I have a complicated relationship, and series of relationships," he said wearily, and it sounded as though he had explained this before. I wondered how many other women he met in classes and invited for coffee. He said he and his wife led independent lives.

"What does that mean, if you don't mind my asking?"

"Our other relationships are a way of achieving something we can't get at home," he said. "Companionship that doesn't exist."

He seemed so genuinely pained by his situation that it was hard to think of him as a cad. But still, I was taking his word for it. The "unhappy marriage" line was the oldest one in the book.

That said, Mark seemed intelligent and interesting, and I decided that if I could just tread carefully enough, he could be a friend and nothing more. He dropped me off that night on a street corner near my condo, and I e-mailed him the next day.

"Thank you for the car ride, cappuccino, and conversation last night," I typed, self-consciously spell-checking "cappuccino."

He replied that evening. "My pleasure. Did you say you're going away this weekend? If not, would you like to get together sometime and have a drink? Perhaps a walk around the Charles or something?"

In class the next morning, Jackie and Debbie asked about the Welshman. I shook my head and told them he was married. Jackie, who was engaged, groaned and patted my hand. We sat in an enormous auditorium-style classroom at MIT filled with young men and women who took assiduous notes and paid rapt attention to the lectures. Harvard undergraduates typically scanned Facebook.

"Oh, Pam! That's too bad," said Debbie. "Don't worry. You'll find someone. We'll both find someone."

"I'm not going to worry about it," I lied.

As attracted as I was to Mark—and that was very—I had to let him know that under no circumstances would I get romantically involved. Period. I accepted his offer of a stroll that Sunday and practiced what I would say to him over and over again.

It was a crisp fall day, and the neighborhood buzzed with students and shoppers, joggers and dog walkers. We decided to walk along Massachusetts Avenue to Harvard and down to the river, stopping along the way at an outdoor bistro. I waited for the right time to deliver my statement. There wasn't one. I just had to do it.

"So, I was thinking about something, and maybe it's totally off base and it never occurred to you, and I don't want to presume anything, and maybe I'm wrong here, but I feel like I need to be understood, at least for me, maybe not for you," I stumbled. This was not going to be the articulate and succinct speech I had rehearsed. "I feel like there is attraction between us, and I know other women haven't cared about your situation, and you were entirely open with me, but I need to tell you, for the record, I will never get involved with you."

There. I held my breath.

"For the record?" Mark said. He laughed.

"Yes," I said, blushing. "For the record. I'm a journalist, you know."

"And a very sweet one," he said.

Didn't he just hear what I said? I thought. He can't say things like that!

"I completely understand. It's a good choice," he said. "But we can still be friends?"

"Yes, of course."

"Good."

I excused myself to go to the bathroom. I had hoped to feel some emotional relief. It wasn't that simple. There was regret, too.

"Am I unusual in feeling the way I do about not getting involved with you?" I asked him when I got back to the table. Even though most of the students passing along the sidewalk in front of us wore earphones, listening to music, I lowered my voice.

Mark said that friendships with women sometimes blurred into more, and he had had dozens of lovers in his lifetime: affairs with adult women when he was a schoolboy, airplane encounters, multiple Frenchwomen in multiples. It sounded exotic and wild to my relatively innocent ears. He was raised by women, he loved them, and they loved him. That much was obvious.

The next time we went out after class, we sat outside on a brick patio in Harvard Square where a guitarist strummed Beatles tunes. Mark had quit his job and taken a consulting position at a nearby company involved in aerospace engines. The schedule would be lighter, the commute a breeze. But his shoulders slumped, and his face seemed cast in shadow as he discussed his marriage and how friends had urged him to get out of it time and time again.

"They think it's awful," he said.

He went on to tell me that his wife had manic-depressive illness, full blown and barely controlled. A year ago, she was admitted to McLean Hospital for several weeks after a difficult period marked by violence and anger.

"The person I once loved and tried so long to fix is gone," he said.

"Have you ever considered leaving?" I said. I was curious, and I wouldn't be honest if I didn't admit that a tiny piece of me thrilled to the idea that he might one day be a single man.

"Yes, I have left her, but not for very long. I felt responsible, and it was always a tentative sort of departure," he said. "There can be periods of calm, but you always know there is going to be a relapse."

I had dated someone with manic depression and knew others with the disease. What Mark said was convincing, not a ploy of sympathy and seduction. It was a matter-of-fact accounting of despair.

That fall in anatomy class, I held a human heart for the first time in my life. The size of at least two of my fists with delicate valves and vessels for blood to flow through the tiniest spaces, it seemed a hopeful organ, with a lot of possibilities for any one person to carry around.

"Really," remarked Donna, my best friend, "you just can't wash your hands too much after holding a human heart."

I was reluctant to tell her I also had held a human brain and, more than any subject, neuroscience had me in its thrall. The field, long dormant in some ways, had come alive with advances in genetics and imaging. For the first time, psychologists were talking to chemists, and molecular biologists to geneticists, trying to link behavior to biology. And I was beginning, only just beginning, to understand them.

Mom, who became a psychotherapist in midlife, began to swap articles and discuss mental health with me at length. I grew excited at the thought that having a child would be a personal joy and a fascinating experiment in watching a developing mind learn and grow. To have everything I studied come to life.

"Things happen faster than you can ever imagine," Mom told me. "I learned more from watching you than you ever learned from me."

From time to time, she would ask if I had met anyone *interesting*. She understood that I wasn't giving up on love just because the prospect of motherhood on my own, never far from my mind, was becoming more real.

In mid-September, Beth and I had gone to Walden Pond.

We swam there as often as possible on warm summer days, but it had gotten too chilly for bathing suits so we walked along the perimeter path. The sun was out, and a pair of red-tailed hawks circled above the trees, which were starting to turn.

Beth was feeling better, annoyed by some extra weight from her ended pregnancy, but over the worst. I was feeling better, too, about being single.

"Your fellowship sounds great, really interesting," she said.

"Not a perfect trade-off for love and family, but still a wonderful thing."

"Yeah, I understand," she said, glancing at me as we stepped through the first fallen leaves. "So, is it a good time to ask if you want the sperm I got from Carey?"

I laughed. "Nice segue!" I threw a stick into the water. "I know, I spent too much time on men with no prospects, so maybe it's time to consider other options."

Beth was the kind of woman who would never tell me outright to ditch a boyfriend, especially if she knew I wasn't ready to hear it. She would just let me read between the lines by saying things like "I hope it works out for you the way you want," then waiting for me to come to my senses.

"Look, Carey met me the same day she gave me 8282, and she probably had no idea of the magnitude of her gift," Beth said. "You're one of my best friends, and while I can't give you a new boyfriend, I *can* give you this."

"From Carey to you to me."

"Precisely, because you know you can have it." She snapped her fingers. "Just like that. Voilà. Seven vials of sperm are yours."

"You're sure you're ready to let it go?" I knew that her offer was a tacit acknowledgment of two things: that she believed Phil was the right one for her, and that she thought I was prepared to become a mother, even if I had to go it alone.

"He's a good guy," I said of Phil.

I meant it. Beth and Phil had a quick banter that might surprise someone who didn't know their sweeter sides, but I understood how deeply they cared about each other.

She nodded.

"Okay," I said, holding out my hand to shake hers. "I accept."

"Maybe you'll never have to use it."

"Maybe."

She sensed my wistfulness. "If you do, that's fine. If you don't, that's even better." She patted my back as we rounded a bend in the path. A striped towel hung from a tree branch at the water's edge, and I could see a flash of moving arms and legs in the distance. Someone hearty enough to brave the chilly waters.

"I hope I meet someone, but it's nice to know the sperm's there," I said.

I didn't know much about 8282's credentials. All I knew was that he was a very tall scientist, and he had been good enough for Beth and Carey, two of the brightest women I knew.

Soon after that talk, Beth and Phil's relationship ran into trouble. I hoped they worked things out because I wanted them to be happy together. I didn't tell her this, but I also selfishly feared that if Beth was on her own again, I would have to return the vials and find a new donor. Not impossible, but a daunting process, Carey and I agreed over lunch one day. For now, though, she said she was thrilled I had the sperm.

Okay, it wasn't really lunch. It was a midday sugarfest of carrot cake with rich cream cheese frosting, banana bread, and hot tea at a local coffeehouse. Carey and I grabbed the last available seats as high school students rushed the front counter, and baristas barked orders. As we dug in, we talked a little about 8282 and the perils I might face as a single mother on the dating scene.

"I enjoyed Neil's company, but then he told me he didn't love Liliana. That he thought he would one day, just not then," Carey recalled. "Loving her filled me up so completely that maybe he sensed that and it put him off. And I had to ask myself, could I be with someone who didn't love my child?"

She pointed to a spot on her lip where I had some frosting on mine.

I wiped it away and asked, "I understand how you felt, but do you think it was realistic? For him to really love your child as much as you do?"

"Yes, yes, yes. I see step-parents fall in love with their spouses' children all the time." She mentioned a mutual friend of ours who was engaged to a man with two teenaged sons as proof. "Look at my own dad! And Liliana is, well, so lovable, isn't she?"

We split the last piece of banana bread. Then Carey said something that surprised me.

"Sometimes," she said, "I wondered whether I might love Liliana too much to possibly love anyone else, to make room in my heart for another person. I didn't even know if I wanted to."

As Carey's friend, I had seen her pine for companionship and work hard to find and hold onto it. I couldn't believe she would ever have considered giving that up. I had loved in many ways, as a daughter, sister, girlfriend, friend. Pet owner. Never as a mother. Love for a child might just be enough for a lifetime, she was suggesting, making me even more curious about how that kind of love might feel. Now, with Donor 8282, I had the means to find out.

★ ★ ★

I thought Mark would appreciate seeing Russia's Kirov Ballet troupe perform at a concert hall in Boston's tiny Theater District.

"Would you like to have lunch and head to the performance?" I asked him. He responded, "With pleasure, and perhaps a tipple of champagne afterward?"

Too much like a date. My close friend Ellen had given me a detailed playbook based on her own affair with a "permanently separated" man, an affair that went on long after she swore it would end.

"Tell me and your other friends what you are doing with him, when you are doing it, and draw strict parameters," she said. "Secrecy breeds temptation. I should know."

I called Mark back.

"I'm so sorry, but I have a morning appointment that might run late, so I'll have to skip lunch," I fibbed. "Why don't we just meet at the theater before the performance for coffee or tea in the main hall?"

If he guessed what I was up to, he didn't let on. "Of course, Pam, whatever works for you," he said. "I'm looking forward to it."

When the day came, I wore casual trousers and a long-sleeved black turtleneck. Not an ounce of exposed flesh to send the wrong signal. Mark, on the other hand, entered the ornate French Renaissance grand lobby in a dashing overcoat and dark suit, looking very James Bond. It was all I could do not to clasp his hand once we were seated and the lights went down.

I made excuses to skip the champagne afterward—"I have a long day tomorrow, early seminar, late classes"—and he drove me home. We sat in his warm car outside my building, the sparks between us almost tangible.

"I wish I could have held your hand tonight," he said, reading my mind.

I nodded.

"I want you to find someone to make you happy, although it makes me sad to think of us not being together. I think I could fall in love with you," he said, turning to me. A momentary pause. "In fact, I already have."

I melted, but opened the passenger door. Cold air rushed in. "I just can't."

"As she flees from the car," he said, with a gentle smile.

I was out, running up the front stoop. And he was driving home to his wife.

There's a reason why they call it heartache. Your heart really does ache.

"Mark told me he loved me tonight," I wrote in my diary. That's all I wrote. It was all I could bear.

He called the next evening and left a message: "Thank you for a wonderful afternoon, and thanks for being so candid about your feelings," he said. There was a pause. "I only wish, as you know, that circumstances could be different. Being your friend can be hard sometimes, but I would never change it."

I tossed and turned in bed that night, finally dragging myself over to the computer sometime before sunrise. My cat jumped into my lap and circled once to settle herself as I sat immobile before the flickering screen. A distant siren blared, garbage trucks rumbled down the alley.

"I need to accept and respect that your circumstances do reflect your desires, on some level, while I am seeking to be chosen by a heart that chooses to belong to no other," I typed in the semidarkness. "What you told me was not entirely unexpected. It made me feel happy and sad. Being your friend can be hard sometimes, but I would never change it."

I shut the lid on the laptop, gently lifted the cat off my lap, and went back to bed.

Mark told me he understood, even though we both recognized how much we could feel for each other given the chance. "I hope you'll find a wonderful mate to share your life. Seeing you happy will make me happy, too."

His message was well intentioned and loving, and it flattened me. I realized that I already could not imagine life without him, and part of me was not prepared to rule out the possibility of a future relationship. By now, I trusted him. I had met his friends, some of whom were friends with his wife, too, and all of whom confirmed the status of their marriage. There were no inconsistencies, as far as I could tell, and the one or two friends of mine who met Mark liked him and felt he was honest.

I wanted to protect myself from getting hurt. I also had to consider if I was prepared to abandon the moral high ground after so many years of trying to stake it out. The full story of Mark's marriage resided not just with him, but also with his wife. If I honestly believed marriage was sacred, whatever the circumstances, and if I wanted to be a sister to every woman, not just to my friends, the right thing to do was to end the relationship with him then and there.

I had been betrayed after college by a boyfriend who fell in love with one of my closest friends. I never forgave them. I had comforted wives and girlfriends whose partners had affairs. Beth suffered terribly when her husband left her for another woman, and now I could be the one to cause pain.

Still, I could not let him go.

"Mark, your message reminds me, too, of how much I already feel, for we have obviously known each other much longer than this year."

He responded within the hour. We didn't speak. We just wrote.

"Pam, I feel the same way. You are very special to me. I've only experienced this sense of affinity with two others in my life, and it was the same—an immediate attraction and an almost definitive sense that the person is right. A soul mate."

It was a turning point. And then, nothing. We traded superficial and chatty e-mails for a few days. My heart felt leaden. I repeated the message that was beginning to feel so worn and dishonest, the one that ruled out a relationship even as it opened the door to one.

"I guess you know I would want to be with you if you were free. Maybe I just needed to say that once out loud."

We arranged to see each other the next day, without discussing why. Mark came over with a bottle of the new season's Beaujolais nouveau, and we sat on my deck high amid the changing autumn leaves. It was my favorite time of year, and the annual wine release one of his favorite rituals. He held his glass in both hands, sitting forward, elbows on his knees.

"When I met you, my heart began to breathe again, Pam." He looked into my eyes. "I want to be with you. Tell me what you need me to do."

"I need you to not be married. And I need you to get therapy." (I was my mother's daughter, after all.)

"Okay."

We put down our glasses, and I took his hands in mine. We didn't kiss, and we didn't have sex, even though my bedroom was mere steps away. We just sat together up in the trees.

I told Donna. With brown ringlets and blue eyes, she was a beauty from Boca Raton who dated several men at the same time, on top of her board memberships and a full-time journalism job that required trips everywhere from Iowa to Dubai. At work, when necessary, she wore a helmet and a flak jacket. At home, she sorted matching bra-and-panty sets into dresser drawer organizers and threw bridal showers and cocktail parties with an attention to detail that rivaled Martha Stewart's.

"Hey. I have a couple of questions," she said. One reporter to another. "Like, what are the financial implications for him if he leaves his wife? Is she funding his education? Is she American or British? What's he studying anyway? How old is he?"

"He's forty-three," I replied. "He knows that I want to get married one day so we would move in together with the understanding that this is a commitment. And he knows that it's still hands off each other while he does his work to straighten his life out. Any more questions?"

"Yes, of course I have more questions," she said, with pretend indignation. "So you would live together, and it would be hands off? Hands off what? Your good china? Because I've been to your apartment, and there's only one place to sleep."

We hadn't even kissed. Sex was off the table until he told his wife, I explained.

"What's his immigration status? What's her nationality? In which country were they married, because an Irish divorce requires a four-year separation before filing, I believe. I hope to holy heck they got married in England. Do they own any property jointly?"

His wife was American. They owned a house.

Donna went on, "I'm worried about health insurance. I wanted you to marry a man with health insurance provided by a company before you decided to get pregnant. Breeding is an expensive proposition."

* * *

Not long after my conversation with Mark, I took a brief trip to Chicago.

Robert, a lanky, handsome friend from high school, joined me to see a play downtown, and we went for cocktails afterward. We reminisced about our formative years as geeks hanging around our school's hundred-watt radio station when eight-track tapes were still in. He told me about his prestigious new executive position and how he had broken up with a longtime girlfriend. I told him about the fellowship and a little about Mark. Robert looked worried and expressed some concern about how that would pan out.

I told him how, in any case, I wanted to get pregnant sometime within the next two years, perhaps with the donor sperm that had passed from Carey to Beth to me. Talking about this with Robert was relatively easy; his mother taught sex education at our high school, and he had half a dozen siblings.

"I know Mark wants children, but it's way too early to know if he'll be ready when I am," I said.

Robert sat up and pretended he was on a date: "So, what kind of work do you do? What are your hobbies? And, by the way, how about a boy and a girl?"

I laughed.

We sat by a window nursing strong wintry cocktails and watching bundled-up pedestrians tromping home through the snow. I told him how I planned to get my finances in order and undergo fertility testing before trying to get pregnant. He nodded understandingly.

I looked at him, at this face I had known since I was thirteen, and asked, laughing, "Wanna be a dad?"

Without hesitation, he said, "Absolutely."

I was floored.

He told me that he trusted me, and he knew we would always be in each other's lives. "We'll be talking to each other forever," he said.

He had reached the same point I had in terms of being tired of waiting to find the right person to start a family. I asked him if his offer would change if he met someone, and he said no. I couldn't say the same for myself, especially with Mark in the picture, and he understood. We didn't discuss specifics. I thought we'd likely go the turkey baster route rather than have sex with each other; he was like my brother.

"If we end up doing this, do you mind if I stay in Boston while you're in Chicago?"

He said not to worry. "We'll work it out."

I burst into tears, happy and overwhelmed. When I woke up the next morning, I wondered if I imagined the whole thing. I called Robert.

"No, it's true," he said. I pictured his wide, toothy grin. "It'll be fun. Keep me posted." Very casual, very Robert, just like always.

Still, I could barely believe it. I could have a child with any of three men: an anonymous stranger, a possible soul mate, or a lifelong friend. As soon as I had accepted Donor 8282's sperm and let go of my frantic search for a husband who would make a family with me, I suddenly found love and potential fathers beyond my wildest dreams.

Mom flew in before Christmas to meet the married man with whom her daughter was falling in love. I needn't have worried. The minute he showed up at the door, with roses for me and carnations for her, her face lit up.

"Look, see what he does?" I said, accepting my bouquet and kissing him hello.

All smiles, Mom pecked him on both cheeks. "It's so wonderful to meet you," she said. We stood there beaming for a minute.

"You, too, Joan," he said, taking her hand. "I'm sorry that your daughter is wrapped up with someone in such a complicated situation."

"Life is complicated," my mom said. "And it ultimately led you to her. And her to you."

We drove to a restaurant that was dark enough to be intimate but not fancy enough to be intimidating. Over dinner we discussed school, work, Wales, and I squeezed Mark's hand to let him know he was doing fine even though he didn't seem particularly nervous.

At one point, I stepped away, and when I returned, Mark and my mom were huddled together, desserts untouched, and Mom was wiping away tears. Mark had apologized to her again for any difficulty he had caused me and, as I hoped, she trusted me and had seen through the man on paper—the one in an open marriage—to the man in real life who had stood by his wife in tough times and now wanted monogamy and love.

"He is exactly the kind and smart man I always imagined for you," she said.

"I'm really happy you feel that way," Mark replied, his own eyes welling up. "Because I love Pammy very much." Mom cried some more.

For Mark, too, meeting a member of my family and discovering she was sane and loving was a relief.

"My heart knows that you are the one," he told me afterward.

He wanted me to commit to him before he ended his

marriage; I needed him to end his marriage before I could. It didn't take long for us to realize that, to all intents and purposes, we already were committed, and that was the least of our concerns.

He tried to be gentle with his wife, first telling her that he was going to see a therapist, a few weeks later that he was moving out to his own apartment, and finally that the marriage was over. She knew I existed and had once given me a message from him when I called their home instead of his cell phone by mistake.

"Mark wanted you to know he's running a little late," she said, betraying no emotion.

What an odd relationship, I thought. Still, hearing her voice, I felt instant and deep remorse. When she later found a love note from me among his things, I felt even worse. She must have realized that, unlike his other relationships, this one might be for keeps. Some days, Mark told me that she agreed they should split up; other days, she furiously rejected the idea. Sometimes she wouldn't talk to him. Part of it was her changing medications, but surely we caused her pain.

Even though Mark did what he said he would do, I had insecurities carried over from my past relationships. I also had heard perhaps more than I should have about Mark's sexual past when we were just friends swapping stories, and that made me wonder if I—or any one woman—could satisfy him for the rest of his life. He had swum in the ocean, and now I was the only fish in the fishbowl. On top of that, I wondered if his most recent companions understood that our relationship was different, that it did not have fuzzy boundaries to be trespassed from time to time. He insisted they did.

"I'm confident my friends will support us and wish us well," he said.

That didn't always turn out to be the case. One woman continued to test the waters even as she congratulated him on his newfound love. Another ignored me to flirt with him at a dinner party where we sat across from each other. But I found, even if it took Mark a while to see what was happening, he put a stop to it even at the cost of their friendships entirely.

Apart from Mark for our first Valentine's Day, I traveled with my fellowship group to Mexico, touring pyramids and hiking to Sierra Chincua, a monarch butterfly sanctuary high in the mountains. Mark and I exchanged gifts, to be opened on February 14, before I left. I gave him a book of love poems; he gave me a soft brown leather diary wrapped with a red bow. A card depicted two furry creatures hugging and facing a heart rising like a sun over a mountain. I opened it, and a handful of tiny gold hearts and metallic pink stars fell onto my hotel room floor.

"Be my Valentine, and Thank You for Sharing My Life," the card read. Below that, Mark had written, "And that is what I want. To share my life with you."

By spring, we were in the full throes of a passionate love affair. Even Donna, my most skeptical and protective friend, approved.

"I'm so happy for you," she shouted, grabbing my hands and whirling me in circles in my living room after she met Mark for the first time. She nearly spun me into the kitchen counter. "Fiiiiiiinally! He's wonderful! And he's hot, too."

Mark liked Donna. He also liked Beth and Phil and, like me, was rooting for their relationship to work out. Beth liked Mark, too, though she couldn't help mocking me about all of his love notes.

"You never write *me* love notes," she once told Phil, laughing. "But what would you write, if you did?"

Phil was the kind of guy who'd show up with flowers for no reason, or new climbing gear if he knew she needed it, but love notes weren't part of his repertoire.

He thought a minute, then, smiling, said dryly, "You don't suck."

I was sticking to my two-year plan, and I had to let Robert know Mark and I had gotten serious.

"We're planning a future together, and I didn't know how to tell you because I didn't want to hurt you or let you down," I told him the next time I was in Chicago.

"Pam, I'll always be happy for you if you're happy," Robert replied and smiled. "We agreed: life can happen. And it did. You can always tell me anything."

"I know, I know. So you don't mind being the backup plan if everything somehow disastrously falls apart?" I asked. Backup plan—it sounded so awful. And so unfair.

"Nope." What a guy, I thought.

"I know you'll be a dad one day, with or without me. And a great one."

"I will." He seemed sure, and he seemed okay, which was a relief.

Of course, more than anything, I hoped Mark would wind up being my mate and also the father of my child. But I couldn't count on his time line coinciding with mine.

Mark and his wife had tried to reach a mediated settlement, yet as the months wore on, her mental health wavered and her family stepped in to protect her assets. He also was taking classes to finish the remaining three credits he needed for an American college degree in case he decided to go on to graduate school. Juggling a divorce, new girlfriend, job, and homework, he was exhausted, but he did it, and I admired him.

Just days after my fellowship concluded, and Mark received his degree, Dad called.

"Poppop's very ill," he said, using the nickname my brother and I had for his father. "It's hard to say how much time is left, but I think you should come into town."

Poppop had Brezhnev-style eyebrows and, like the former Soviet dictator, was used to running the show. He was not the type, especially after my grandmother died, to suddenly start counting blessings in his last days after a lifetime of measuring others' shortcomings. After several weeks at his bedside, I missed Mark terribly.

Flying out to Chicago for a weekend, Mark met my last grandparent, Dad, Ben, and my stepfather, Patrick. He did this, in the worst possible circumstances, when other boyfriends did not make a single trip to my hometown in the best of times. And he did it with tremendous grace.

I had been nervous about telling Dad I had fallen in love with a married man, as any daughter would be, and he was concerned. Still, I could tell he instantly liked Mark by the warmth of his greeting and how Dad opened up to him, crying when the two were alone in the waiting room. Even my grandfather approved.

"Have him sit down, close to me. I want to watch him," Poppop said, pushing a button to raise the head of his bed when Mark entered the hospice room. Mark, trying to be respectful, didn't say much. The room, with a low sofa and long window on one side, smelled of antiseptic and apple juice.

"He seems like an okay guy for my granddaughter," Poppop told us, with a fake grimace. "And he's good-looking, too." My grandfather died two weeks later.

It wasn't as if I needed any more confirmation that Mark was the man for me. We were more in love than ever, and he happily teased me about my less-than-subtle desires to be with him, live together, and have a family.

"I see it all before me now: the kids, the dog, the house," he said, feigning horror.

"Don't forget the separate bathrooms!" I replied with a kiss.

He called it the "Divine Plan." But we were only human.

The Cake

Beth: "You got your cake."

Carey: "And I couldn't believe it."

Pam: "Which is funny, because the vast majority of women do have families. It's not exactly front-page news."

Carey

In the New Hampshire cabin, I felt an amazingly blissful change, as if a circuit had been closed between Sprax and me, so that now the current could run round and round through all three of us. It gave me a glimpse of what a wonderful feeling family could be when the family was yours. The people who have anything like this, I thought, are by far the richest people in the world: You see your partner in your child and see your child in your partner, and love each of them all the more for it. You're cuddling in bed, and you feel the flesh of an arm against the flesh of your arm, and you don't need to know whose it is, because whoever it is, you love them and are happy to be touching them.

We did plenty of trying, and otherwise largely mooned around in a lovestruck daze. In pictures from the cabin, I see the glowing haze of a halo around Liliana, her Cupid's work at long last complete.

So did she teach us how to love? Most couples make the transition from mate hunting to acceptance with a wedding. Turns out we were helped across the divide by our child. I think she also helped us by making us even more unique to each other in a world of a million possible partners. We could date forever, but among all the multitudes, our beloved child had only one other parent. And, certainly, she brought us together a thousand times. But no, I don't give her the credit—except that she helped us each grow up a little.

We took Liliana to see the Disney film *Brother Bear,* and it had quite a few phantasmagorical, psychedelic scenes of the northern lights. The lights even lift up the central character and transform him into a bear. Afterward, I asked Sprax whether the lights had produced any magical effects on him. He had finally seen them for the first time on his Alaska trip, out on a remote glacier.

"The lights gave me an intense feeling of luck and prosperity," he said. "It was like: there were these things that I wanted, but I already had them, if I could just see it."

"Like what things?"

"Like family . . ."

Liliana entered the toddler language explosion. Not yet two, she started throwing together sentences like "Do you wanna read book?" and "I don't want it!"

"It's so striking," Sprax said. "It's been almost two years now, and it's new all the time."

I hoped we kept feeling that way about each other, too. Sometimes I felt overflowing, and sometimes I felt edgy. It was often a challenge, next to Sprax, to feel all right about myself physically. There he was with his still fat-free superathleticism;

there I was with the extra ten pregnancy pounds that refused to come off no matter how I tried, the bags under my eyes, and the white strands in my hair.

"It does make you understand better the need for a formal commitment," I told Liz. "Being stamped with that all-powerful 'yes' must neutralize some of these nasty self-esteem challenges."

I turned forty-three years old. There were bad things afoot—my aunt was dying of pancreatic cancer; my sister, Morgan, had troubles—and I was not pregnant. But I still felt beyond blessed.

We went to a town near Albany for the wedding of Sprax's climbing friend, Paul. It was near twenty below at night, the coldest I ever remembered, including in Moscow. It was the trying time of the month, but it was hard to imagine any cells deciding to multiply in a world so cold. Then, in the middle of the ceremony, a migraine walloped me between the eyes. I brought Liliana back to the hotel room, driving carefully in the icy cold, and collapsed into bed. Sprax returned later, and it was only our own supreme devotion to duty (and the plentiful room in the king-sized bed that let us do our trying without waking Liliana as she slept next to us) that convinced us to give it one last attempt for the month.

I like to think that's the one that did it. I was just in the midst of making an appointment with a fertility doctor, and getting a printout of my ovulation patterns for the last four unsuccessful months from the accommodating Clearblue folks, when my pregnancy test came up positive.

I didn't dare get too happy. If I'd been old with Liliana, now I was positively ancient. The chances of a miscarriage at my age were up near 40 or 50 percent. When I sent Liz an e-mail the next morning telling her the news, the subject line was, "We know how little this means, but . . ." I sent Bob, our obstetrician, a message as well, asking if he'd have me as a patient again if I got that far, and he phoned two minutes later, to congratulate me and schedule me for a seven-week ultrasound.

For the first weeks, I had no symptoms at all, except fatigue a bit beyond the usual. I felt myself up incessantly, twiddling at my nipples for the reassuring bit of soreness that was the only telltale sign. When Sprax and I went in for the ultrasound, my heart was leaden. Somehow, the good ultrasound during my pregnancy with Liliana couldn't erase the trauma of the ultrasound that had clinched my miscarriage.

The cheery ultrasound technician asked, "Do you have any children?"

"Yes," I managed, as she slid the wand around in my nether regions. "One."

"Well, you're going to have another!" she said, and pointed out the beautifully beating heart on the screen.

I burst into tears, and only then realized how heavily the dread had been pressing on me. When we were left alone, Sprax and I kissed, hard.

It all felt like such a fully shared experience—so different from the last time.

The time went slowly, though, so slowly. I wanted a chorionic villus sampling so I would know if the chromosomes were all right by my twelfth week. The procedure carried about a one percent chance of miscarriage, possibly a bit higher than amniocentesis, but I had seen what Beth and others had gone through with late terminations; I wanted to know as early as possible, and I wanted to know for sure. Only then would I begin believing in this pregnancy.

A few days later, somehow sooner than I expected, the genetic counselor called. I didn't even have a chance to freeze in terror. She said the chromosomes all looked great, and that we were having a boy. "A boy!" I repeated. Sprax was sitting in bed next to me, watching as I burbled gratitude to the counselor, and we stared at each other, unbelieving. It was bingo, a jackpot, a girl and a boy.

"There is so much to look forward to," he said.

I thought: Sounds like fatal last words.

It was so much luck, I could barely absorb it. It was off the charts.

It boggled my mind that soon we would be indistinguishable from any white-picket-fence family with their 2.2 children. We, who for so long seemed un-mate-able, unsolvable. I felt my love for Sprax deepening and, simultaneously, found it hard to believe that we really got to be this happy and harmonious.

Liliana kept amazing me, picking up phrases like "Maybe so, but I'm not afraid of you!" She also got a bit more two-ish: occasionally, when thwarted, she would emit inhuman screams, and somewhere along the way she picked up the idea that a bleated "Maa!" meant no.

She could recite "Humpty Dumpty" and sing the alphabet. She got wildly excited at little things: "An ant! An ant!" And she loved to turn on the demo song of her little electronic piano and shout, "Dance with me!"

She went to art class with me and music class with my dad and gym class with Sprax. We were applying to preschools for her, and the delightful little school right on our block turned out to be the "Harvard of preschools," only it was a little harder to get into than Harvard. I got my first taste of trying to pull strings for my child's sake. The school was into Cambridge-style diversity, so I emphasized my single-mother status, even though it was true only on paper these days. Then I poured every drop of skill I'd ever developed into writing a persuasive essay about how I wanted my child's first real experience of the big world out there to be in the kind of environment the school provided.

Sprax got a new job, at an optics company in Cambridge, and put his condo on the market. He moved in officially, filling the basement from floor to ceiling with boxes and outdoor gear.

My belly grew. I was dressing one day when Liliana wandered into my room.

"My tummy is getting big!" I said. "That's because your little brother is inside."

Her eyes widened. "You mean you ate him?"

Beth and I went for a hike one humid day near Hammond Pond, a serene spot in the shadow of a huge shopping mall. With maternal concern, we talked about Pam.

"So what do you think of Mark?" I asked her.

"Kind of hard to tell—I haven't spent much time with them—but she seems happy so far."

"They somehow look right together," I said. "I wonder if she'll still end up needing the sperm."

"I hope not."

"What I worry about is that she's so thin that she may not have enough body fat to get pregnant easily."

I wished for Pam to get pregnant in a flash. To confess, I also found a bit of comfort in the idea that, in one thing at least, it was an advantage not to be a sylph.

When I was about thirty weeks along—forty is full-term—I had a bit of spotting. It was the barest bit of pink on toilet paper, but it terrified me. The triage nurse at Bob's office said it was likely just my cervix softening a bit, but that I could come in for a checkup if I wanted. Usually, this is nothing, Bob said. I didn't go in, but I stopped everything: exercising, heavy housework, picking up Liliana, all of it. I spotted no more, but Leeza said she thought I was suddenly carrying lower.

At just over thirty-one weeks, I went to get the scraggles cut off the bottom of my hair. The hair salon was a sitcom joint, all the stylists ribbing the owner for arguing that a small cut on his scissors-finger meant he could not work.

When my trim was done and I stood up, I felt fluid flow into my underpants.

What went through my mind was: huh?

I paid, and as I walked out the door, I could feel droplets course down my legs. Hell. My shorts were quickly soaked. I got into the car and called Bob's office, telling them I was having a major fluid leak, and called Sprax to tell him the same, and headed straight for the hospital, barely able to concentrate on the route. Something was wrong, something was really wrong, this was clearly an amniotic fluid leak, and that should not be happening.

It brought back some deep childhood sense of shame, to walk into the main entrance of Massachusetts General Hospital wearing soaked shorts. I had to stop now and then to rub my legs together to wipe away the tickling droplets. The elevator took forever. At the obstetrics office, I went up to the receptionist and said, "I have an emergency. I have a fluid leak." In an exam room, a nurse used a paper strip to take a sample of the fluid soaking my underwear. She left the room to get it analyzed, then came back and said, "We're sending you right upstairs. You should plan on staying here."

I called Sprax and told him, trying not to cry and failing.

In the triage room upstairs, a kind nurse told me that I was far enough along that the outlook was very good.

"Very good" did not sound very good. She attached a fetal and uterine monitor to my belly and started IV fluids.

Bob arrived a few minutes later, and gave me a big and much-needed hug. "You said, 'Usually it's nothing,' but sometimes it's something," I said, rubbing it in.

"This is going to be very disruptive to your life," he said, "but the chances are fifty-fifty that you will still be pregnant in a week. The big balancing act now is trying to keep the baby inside for as long as possible versus the risk of infection."

If we got to thirty-four weeks, he said, his method was to test the baby's lungs for maturity, and base the delivery decision on that.

Sprax arrived in the middle of Bob's talk, dripping with sweat from the bike ride through the heat. He looked grim, but steeled. He stayed by my side, and as time passed and my contractions abated, we both dozed.

A Newborn Intensive Care Unit nurse came to speak with us. She said the baby's outlook was very good, but that there might be some rough sailing and setbacks along the way.

If I did deliver now, she said, his lungs would probably be so immature that he would need to go on a ventilator for a few days, but he was far enough along that it would be highly unlikely that he would have the kind of brain bleed that could cause later neurological problems.

The main thing I heard was "brain bleed."

The baby would probably need a feeding tube that would go down through his nose, because babies couldn't tend to work out the suck-swallow-breathe sequence until they were thirty-five weeks or so. He would be in a nifty new warmer called a Giraffe that let nurses do procedures without moving the babies. Premature boys did tend to do a little worse than girls, she said, but we could expect to be able to take him home by his due date if not before.

It was so hard to accept that things would not be perfect, hard for some spoiled child in me to assimilate the fact that this pregnancy was going badly awry, despite all my previous forebodings. It was even harder to stomach the idea that we would have one of those poor little NICU babies, all wired up in tubes and monitors, unable to be held most of the time. And for all the stories about how preemie babies do great these days, I seemed to have heard as many stories about how preemies—at least the really early ones—ended up with lifelong problems that made their survival not quite such a miracle.

By evening, I was moved to a regular prebirth obstetrical ward, and Sprax brought Liliana in for a quiet visit. She didn't want to leave, and Sprax told me later that she said "Mommy" about two hundred times in the car.

It was a hard night. I was teary and in turmoil, with a bad case of adrenaline-laced terror, and it was impossible to fall asleep with all the IVs and blood-pressure checks and endless trips to the bathroom to purge the masses of fluid they were pumping into me. Then, as I lay in the dark, I made the giant mistake of thinking of my mother and wishing she were there, and the tears flowed in earnest. My roommate heard my snuffling, and she kindly talked me through it. She had cried her first night, too, she said.

It was just such a strange place to find myself in, and such a shocking turn of events, somehow, and the maternal fear for the baby mixed with helplessness and with concern about Liliana and the surreal feeling of being in the hospital in an ugly mash. I felt, too, a profound lack of spiritual places to turn. Praying to God, "Please let this baby be okay," helped only a little. I tried to meditate on my breath. I tried to imagine myself soaring above a park. I thought of my love for Sprax and Liliana, trying to think of it as a refuge or source of succor. I thought of friends and family, of the outpouring of kindness from work colleagues. None of it seemed to help much.

I worked on what Beth called "cognitive reframing." I told myself that modern medicine would handle whatever happened; I was in the best place possible for all of this; bed rest could be glorious, a wonderful time to catch up on sleep and reading and thinking and writing and learning. All true, but no help. I tried to quash that spoiled child, replace it with an adult who rolls with the punches and takes each thing as it comes, never expecting storybook perfection. Right.

In the end, I concluded, it takes a day to absorb such a blow. At least. Sprax said that at the end of that first day, he just couldn't believe that it had all taken place in just one day. By the next morning, I was eons better, and allowing myself the temerity to imagine keeping the baby in beyond thirty-four weeks.

The days blurred together. I passed the thirty-two-week mark. I read endless Internet accounts of PROM, premature rupture of membranes. Almost all were encouraging in terms of outcome, and all were permeated with bafflement, stories of women sitting quietly watching TV and suddenly feeling a pop and gush of fluid. Why in the world? No one knew.

One night, at about two a.m., my roommate, Sharon, woke up with cramps and found that she was bleeding. She was having contractions every six minutes or so. The nurses brought in the night doctor, who decided that she should be moved back upstairs to the labor and delivery ward. You could hear the panic and fear in her little voice. I tried to encourage her, but she said, "I don't think I'm going to make it"—not "make it" in terms of survival, but in terms of keeping the pregnancy any longer. Even though her odds were great that her baby would be fine, I felt overwhelming pain for her. It took a long time to get back to sleep in the empty room. This is getting to be kind of a battlefield experience, I told Sprax the next day. You bond with your comrades, and then some of them get taken out.

When a whole week had passed, the attending doctor said I now had a better than fifty-fifty chance of making it to thirty-four weeks. Bob stopped in and said he was so pleased I was doing so well. I was adjusting. The only hard part remained the rise and fall of fear as various strange feelings rose and fell in my innards and various strange colors and chunks appeared on my sanitary pads. Every time I went to the toilet, I thought, You cannot live your life in fear.

I told Sprax one night: "This was unlucky, but everything else has been so very, very lucky."

We had plenty of time to think about names, and Sprax—it was his turn to choose—had all but settled on Tulliver, a creative mix of some of his favorite consonants. I was a little unsure about a name quite that unusual, but had a thumping vision of a boisterous crowd at a basketball game chanting, "Tul-li-ver! Tul-li-ver!" I agreed to it, tentatively.

The next morning, I suddenly felt especially strange—a flash of double-vision weirdness, only a moment, but a definite signal. Within minutes, I was spiking a fever, and contractions had begun again. That meant infection. It was time.

I chattered through the C-section, an old hand at the operation now, happy that at least the end was in sight. Sprax was quieter, but held my hand firmly.

Tully pulled a fast one on the resident who delivered him. A week earlier, an ultrasound exam had shown him to be head down; but during the emergency C-section, the obstetricians were shocked to find he had somehow turned breech. The first part of him to emerge was a big purple left foot.

He also got a bit stuck, and ended up coming out with prize-fighter bruises. But to my unspeakable relief, he was generally in wonderful shape for a premature baby: He weighed nearly four and a half pounds, a good pound bigger than expected; he was eighteen inches long, a reasonable length even for a full-term baby; and he could breathe room air right from the get-go. He squalled appropriately, turned a lovely pink, and showed no sign that the infection that triggered his delivery had affected him. I had been steeled for all kinds of awful possibilities, and most fell away so quickly I could barely wrap my mind around them. This wasn't a simple, joyous birth, but I began to dare to hope that perhaps it would not be a tragic one, either. In the hours to come, Tully digested well, too, and I began pumping colostrum and milk for his tube feedings right away.

He was in the Newborn Intensive Care Unit for only a couple of days, then moved down to a pleasant lower-level nursery, where he would mainly just be fed and monitored. At twelve days, he hatched out of his incubator to an open crib, and a head ultrasound showed that his brain was normal. Still, I was slow to bond, concerned that something would happen while he was in the hospital—some evil hospital infection, some human error, some fluke—and he'd be hurt or even die.

He was a beautiful baby, though, at least to me, the visible sutures of his skull plates making his head look something like a big walnut, his features regular and already identifiably male. He had brief periods when he opened his eyes and gazed up with that foggy newborn look. Really, I kept reminding myself, he was, by rights, still only a fetus. He had a triangle of blond fuzz coming down his forehead, just as his sister did in her infancy, and his legs looked like hers, too—long from the knee to foot—but his feet looked enormous.

Liliana would lie down on the couch and say, in a baby voice, "I'm Tully," and pretend she was too little to do anything. Tully spent a month in the hospital, and weighed only about five pounds when he came home. But then he began to pack on the pounds, and grow as if intent on not just matching but surpassing his peers. Leeza was once again a heroic feeder, unfazed by his tiny size and determined to catch him up. We rented a scale that could detect a change of even a tenth of an ounce, and reassured ourselves once a day or so that he was still growing. On the back of his head, one side had flattened out, a common phenomenon now that babies are all laid on their back for sleeping to avoid SIDS. We brought him to a specialist who recommended a custom-made orthotic pillow that Tully loudly refused to sleep on. We kept him rolled a bit on one side with body pillows, and decided that if he kept the flat spot, he could just avoid shaving his head when he grew up.

Counting his hospital time, the exhausting newborn period lasted two or three months longer than usual, and the fatigue hit an unheard-of intensity. Sprax did the late-night feedings, and found himself compulsively ripping hundreds of CDs and ordering more to create a massive personal collection on hard drives.

Sometimes I suspected I was depressed, and then reflected that it was exhaustion—which didn't mean it wasn't depression, too. When I saw mothers of small children now, my first emotional reaction was sympathy as I thought of their fatigue, even more than I thought of the joy they were surely experiencing as well. I tried not to wish that this phase would pass quickly, but I couldn't help it. I just wanted a time when I would be able to sleeeeeeep.

At a party for Liliana's preschool class, a father who was a brilliant literary critic told me he had been blindsided, simply blindsided, by the enormity of the difference between one child and two. Hear, hear. I told him that being the single mother of one had been far easier than being the partnered mother of two.

I got an IUD. When a woman has had one premature baby, her chances of having another are multiplied something like sevenfold. I told people, "It's amazing how quickly you go from wanting a baby more than anything in the world, to not wanting another baby more than anything in the world."

There were jewel-like moments as well: Tully's smile, Liliana's I-love-you, a few stolen moments in bed with Sprax. An acquaintance asked Sprax how the married-with-children lifestyle was, and Sprax said he couldn't believe it was real sometimes. He wasn't saying it like he had won the lottery, though he wasn't saying it negatively either—he was just disbelieving: "Can life really change *this* much?"

The dregs of the winter hit. Tully got hopelessly constipated, and only Leeza's old Russian trick of slipping a sliver of soap up his butt finally got him to go. He started on solid foods a bit early, technically, though we were never quite sure whether to consider his age dating from his due date or his actual birth date. I found myself writing a letter to Marty Baron telling him how enormously I was looking forward to going back to work; I said my respect for stay-at-home moms had grown exponentially, as had my certainty that I didn't want to be one of 'em.

Liliana was thriving at school, and constantly proclaiming "I'm a hippo!" or "I'm a dinosaur!" Sprax and I went to a "next schools" meeting, and faced the daunting news that Cambridge-area private schools were nearly impossible to get into, and we could not even be guaranteed that Liliana would get into a public school close to our house.

So we pooled our resources and bought another house, an old Victorian we couldn't really afford, in an urban suburb with excellent schools that is a bit like Boston's equivalent of the Upper West Side or Brooklyn Heights. It needed a lot of rehab, and my dad helped with it enormously. The move was excruciating. I got so stressed that one day, having just unloaded the rear of my station wagon, I closed the car's hatchback onto my face; I was just too distracted to move out of the way.

We had now completed what Sprax had once called perhaps the most significantly committing move a couple can make—buying a house together—but it seemed a simple matter of course. Taking on a mortgage together was nothing compared to taking on a toddler and a preemie.

When Tully was about six months old, we brought him out west to see Sprax's ninety-two-year-old grandparents in Arizona, and his parents drove down from Utah as well.

I was a little hurt that neither of his parents said they were happy that Sprax and I had worked things out. His mother, Emeline, said she remembered me telling her when we visited with Liliana that he and I just weren't right for each other.

"Yes," I protested, "but that was because of his behavior at the time."

She still looked dubious.

I went back to work and felt like groveling at Marty's feet in gratitude. But my weekdays off were nice, too: walking Liliana home from preschool and playing a shadow-chasing game that got her laughing uncontrollably; Tully's blue eyes above a smiling mouth smeared orange with apricots. When I was dating online, I'd written in my ad that I wanted a man with "a thick streak of sweetness." Sprax had that, and Tully had inherited it in spades; even the nurses in the hospital had commented that he was quite the sweet baby—though I had assumed they said that to everyone, because how could they possibly tell?

Sprax and I had "date night" once a week. On one, we were sitting across from each other at a noisy restaurant, and he said, "It's so great to go out and eat good food with someone you love instead of making conversation at a party."

By summer, we were all settled in; Liliana, now three and a half, started at her new preschool, and instantly joined a proto-clique with two other little girls, Madison and Gabrielle. The playdates began. Tully had four teeth and had started cruising around the furniture, but cast away our hands when we tried to help him walk. Liliana was a deeply kind older sister, protective and already trying to teach him the ways of the world.

It may seem a small thing, but one day I told Sprax my actual weight: that it had been stuck at 180 (on my five nine frame) since Tully's birth. It was a confession I could never have made during most of my life.

I wondered how much of this new self-acceptance was simply age and how much was motherhood. We learn from loving our children that none of them is perfect, but that they are the wellsprings of the deepest, truest love—and it is such a short jump to the fact that we all are children, and all worthy of love even in the depths of our imperfection. If that is what "motherly" means, it is a good thing, I thought.

One summer night, Sprax and I went out for a spin in a used double kayak we had just bought. The boat was a flat, heavy tub, a sharp contrast to the sleek fiberglass Selkie of my youth.

The double kayak seemed like a potent metaphor: My wonderful old Selkie was so much swifter and more maneuverable, and paddling in it seemed like so much more of an adventure. On the other hand, at times I could just sit back and relax in the double while Sprax paddled, and we could really talk to each other; and if we were going to take the kids out, I wouldn't want boats that could get separated. So, yes, we were weighed down now, and couldn't help but have some nostalgia for the wild old days—but it was better this way. And this period was finite, too: our children would grow, and we would be freer again.

It started with Sprax saying things like "We should get married," and me saying, "Uh-huh."

Then it progressed to a moment when he really did get down on one knee by the kitchen table and ask, "Will you marry me?"

And I laughed and said, "Yes, I suppose I will."

There was one little rub. We had to get married by the end of the year if we wanted to save many thousands of dollars in taxes on the sale of my Cambridge town house. That determined the timing. I don't know when we would have gotten married otherwise. Certainly not in a year that also included raising a premature baby, selling one house, and rehabbing another. But we would have, eventually.

We started warning people that we were going to do a teeny-tiny town hall wedding, and then have a celebration at some later point when I could stomach handling some logistics. Don't be offended, we said, we're not inviting anybody but the kids.

First we brought the children to town hall to fill out the paperwork; I misunderstood the clerk's instructions, and we ended up having to do it a couple of times before we got it right, but we did, eventually—a nice metaphor for our relationship, of course.

As we were walking to the car that day, Sprax said, "You should congratulate me. I'm marrying the most wonderful woman in the world."

I said something similarly fatuous back. We were strangely happy. I'd thought, after all we'd been through, that marriage would feel like a mere formality. It didn't.

Liliana had a small concern: "When Mommy and Daddy are married," she asked my dad, "will they still be my parents?"

He reassured her.

I was too busy with the house and children and work to even focus on a wedding date, but suddenly we had settled on one a week away, and it was all becoming real. My colleagues at work got me a cake, and I blushed and teared up as they presented it, feeling somehow like an imposter.

The town clerk was not available on our designated day, so we decided to have a justice of the peace in a nearby park. Recommended by the town clerk, he was a soft-spoken former pilot with a gray ponytail and southwestern bolo tie. He offered to recite a special Apache blessing at the ceremony, and we happily agreed.

On impulse, I took the week off from work and got a facial and a haircut and bought a thrift-store dress in maroon velour. I felt no desire to wear white; some of that pivotal sloughing of romantic ideals remained in force. On the morning of the day, Sprax played a long, hard session of pickup basketball, then shaved carefully and put on a gray suit he'd had since his twenties. I put on more makeup than I'd worn since before Liliana's birth nearly four years earlier, and I pinned up my hair in a "careless" do that got ever more chaotic as the day progressed.

It was the perfect New England autumn day, crisp and coppery. The October sun slanted shafts of late light into the open-air rotunda next to the pond at Larz Anderson Park, a huge, hilly oasis in South Brookline. The rotunda had caught my eye on a visit to the park's playground one day. Only after the ceremony did we find out that it was called the "Temple of Love."

I'd always known that I'd invite my dad, but at the last minute I also asked my sister, Morgan, and Liz, who flew in from DC. Sprax's best man was his dear friend Tim, a bighearted inventor so footloose that when he turned up you never knew whether he had just been carving canoes in Africa or sailing a small craft to Cuba. Leeza and her family came, incurring a $300 traffic ticket in their rush to be on time. And the children were there, Liliana as flower girl and one-year-old Tully as stroller-bound witness, resplendent in a blue sailor suit.

In a frilly purple dress, her gilt hair lit from behind by the low sun, Liliana did her job all too well, carefully scattering her orange petals all around the rotunda, around and around. When we finally cued her to stop, she asked, "Can I be a flower girl again soon?"

Len, the justice of the peace, read the Apache blessing in a voice so faint we had to strain to hear.

"Now you will feel no rain, for each of you is shelter for the other. Now you will feel no cold, for each of you will be warmth to each other. Now there'll be no more loneliness, for each of you will be companion to the other. Now you're two persons, but there is but one life before you. Go now into your dwelling to enter into the days of your lives together. And may your days be good and long in number."

Sprax and I stood together before him. Our eyes locked, for longer than they ever had before, and I swear I felt some science-fiction energy phenomenon, some shazzam!, coursing between us. I had suspected that getting married would make us even happier. But I'd had no clue that the ceremony itself would hold such power. Yet there we were, doing something like a Vulcan mind-meld. As if the molten wedding-energy was purifying us of all our myriad doubts and insecurities, our past sins and slights.

I do not really believe in wedding vows. That is, I believe that no matter what people say at their weddings, they will ultimately do what makes the most sense given the state of their relationship five, ten, fifteen years later. But I meant my vows, and Sprax spoke his words with quiet conviction.

"With this ring I thee wed, and pledge to you my faithful love for now and for all that will come..."

For all the ceremony's power, it also felt uncomfortable. It is surreal, to obey the regimented rules of a rite that your culture imbues with cosmic importance. It felt obedient in a not entirely pleasant way. In general, I would rather play the anthropologist than the native. So for all the good juju, I was a little glad when it was done. We all signed the license.

Tully said, "Ahhh—yah!"

Liliana said, "Mom, let's go to the playground! Playground time! Everybody follow us!"

We crunched through the fallen leaves to a picnic table near the park's playground. We poured champagne and cut a flowery cake.

My dad raised his glass. "Carey. Sprax. You didn't come into this marriage in the conventional way, but I guess neither of you are conventional types. The main thing is that it feels like there's a lot of love going on between you, and that trumps everything else. So a happy, long, wonderful life with these two wonderful kids. *Mazel tov!*" We sipped.

"Can we go back to the playground?" Liliana asked. Denied, she occupied herself by snitching fingerfuls of frosting.

Liz raised her glass. "Liliana and Tully, I'm going to tell you a little story. Your mommy and your daddy are both very courageous people. Your mom took off to Russia when it was still behind the iron curtain, and your dad climbs up ice walls and sheer cliffs. And, Carey and Sprax, that courage is going to serve you both very well as you launch yourselves into this journey of marriage. It's just one more adventure, and I wish you great joy and urge you to dive into it together, and trust your love, believe in each other, and hold on tight."

"Eeeeee!" said Tully.

Tim asked Liliana, "Do you want to say anything?"

"I love my mommy!" she announced.

"What about me?" Sprax asked.

"I love my daddy!"

Tim's toast: "I'm always giving people advice based on your lives," he said. "Because you're my example of smart people who have found a way to be happy anyway.

"So," he concluded, "don't screw up."

Liliana had begun systematically taste-testing all the different colors of frosting on the cake. Always a picky eater, she was high on sugar and her own newly adventurous palate.

"Mom, Dad, can you believe I'm eating cake?!? I used to not like cake! I tried the orange and I tried the yellow and I tried the purple! Could I try the green, please? Can I have some green? Can I have some green?"

Leeza, elegant in a black leather suit, chatted with Liz in Russian.

"I keep thinking," she said, "what's better, to do it at twenty or forty?" Back in Ukraine, Leeza had borne her daughter, Dasha, at age nineteen, and her son, Kostya, just a couple of years later. She had earned her degree in aeronautical engineering in the midst of new mothering.

"It's hard when you're forty," Liz said.

"It's hard when you're twenty, too," Leeza said.

Liliana was distracted by the small bride-and-groom statue on the cake, and proclaimed it the "marrying trophy."

"Whoever gets married, wins! Mommy, you win the trophy!"

"Thank you, sweetheart."

"Now let's go celebrate!" Liliana declared. "To the playground!"

The Adjustment

Pam: "Can you keep your identity when your whole life changes?"

Beth: "The appropriate answer is, 'Everything improves.' The honest answer is a little more complicated."

Carey: "Who has time to think about it?"

Beth

PHIL DIDN'T LEAVE. But if I could box up the four days we barely spoke, and set the box sailing, I'd do it.

He stayed late at work those four nights, then went out, somewhere. I was with friends, or asleep, or pretending to be asleep, when he got home and pulled a pillow over his head on the couch. I arranged work that required early morning departures.

Then, on the fifth night, he came home from work, and said, "I want to stay here. Not on the couch." He paused, sighed, and added, "I'd like to bring my pillow back upstairs. And figure out how to do this thing where we try to have a future and a kid."

I took a bottle of wine out of the refrigerator, and we went up to the deck. He grabbed a bottle of Scotch as he passed the liquor cabinet. "I need something stronger," he told me.

It was one of the last warm days of Indian summer.

"I'm sorry," I said, once we sat down. He opened both bottles. "I get selfish sometimes. I owe you a big mea culpa. I didn't give you a chance to make a decision."

"No," he replied. "You didn't."

He'd lived alone for a long time, until I engineered this reverse domesticity: (1) get pregnant, (2) move in together, (3) break up, (4) get to know each other, (5) try to get pregnant again.

He poured himself a drink. "I'll probably never see the Himalayas, but, hey, neither will you. The idea of giving up the rest of my life just isn't as scary the second time around. Live and learn."

"Don't write off Kathmandu. I'm talking about a baby, not a jail term."

He sipped the drink. "Right, that's what I said."

I listened to Carey and bought a Clearblue Easy. Turned out my cycle was around thirty-one days, which shifted the small window of ovulation from what I'd predicted, the standard twenty-eight. With the monitor, I didn't have to guess. And then, voilà. The week between Christmas and New Year's, I was pregnant. Synchronically, coincidentally, oddly, it was the week the first pregnancy would have come to term. And I was petrified.

If there'd been some sort of machine I could've strapped on to tell me that everything was okay, every minute, I'd have had it on in a flash. I don't think any first-time pregnant woman over thirty-five considers pregnancy as a breezy dream, but if you've had a twenty-four-hour termination of a chromosomally imperfect fetus, all bets are off. I scheduled a CVS.

* * *

In late February, Phil and I joined my family in Mexico, at a villa north of Puerto Vallarta. Things were better. They were, in fact, good. We were comfortable together, and it felt easy. We swam, bodysurfed, watched the sun set over Banderas Bay with my parents and my brothers and their families, sat in the sun, played with my nieces and nephew, ate tortillas, and waited. The CVS was scheduled for two days after we got home. But when we arrived at the airport, our flight had taken off four hours earlier. We had no explanation, just that we both had the wrong time in our heads.

It was school vacation week. There were no seats available for three days. We drove back up to the house, and I got on the phone to Brigham and Women's Hospital, one of only two hospitals in Boston where CVS are performed. The secretary was terse. No waiting list for cancellations.

I immediately called Beth Israel hospital, the only other option. The receptionist calmed me down. No, the fetus's chromosomes wouldn't shift because I'd missed the flight. No, I wasn't a bad mother. She scheduled me for a CVS the week after we got home. Protocol required that we see Beth Israel's genetic counselor. I made it clear that I didn't want any preamble when she called with results. I knew the stats. I knew I was a year older.

I went to the CVS alone, as if the procedure was just another thing I did and not critical enough for Phil to take time from work. We didn't want to know the gender, same as with the first pregnancy, because to us, gender was identity, and that was too scary. The CVS was uncomfortable, but my years of creative visualization and breath-focused relaxation calmed me, even with a long plastic tube winding its way through my cervix and into the delicate placenta.

And then the call.

"It's Lisa," she said. "The genetic counselor. The test is fine. It all looks good."

"It looks good," I repeated.

"It does. Everything looks good."

"Thank you," I said, and I wasn't sure what else to say. I paused on my end of the phone. I opened and closed my mouth.

"It's okay," she said. "I know it must be an enormous relief. I'm glad I was the one who got to tell you." She waited for me to agree, but I didn't say anything. After a moment she added, "This is the beginning of the good part."

I might be stoic when it comes to soldiering through the big stuff, but I cry at almost anything: TV commercials, animal shows, heartbreak, joy. After I hung up I cried. I called Phil, then drove to his office. He left early that day and we went out for Chinese food.

"Hello," I said, as the sizzling platters arrived. "I'm Beth. It appears that I'm going to have your baby."

"Pleased to meet you." Phil reached his hand across the table, and we shook. "I'm glad to hear that." He smiled in a way I hadn't seen in a while.

Boston offers myriad options for birth: hospitals, birth centers, doulas, nurse-practitioners, home birth attendants. But what I wanted was four blocks from our house: a premier hospital with a large maternity ward, and Dr. Reed. I didn't want to investigate Lamaze, the Bradley birth method, water birth, herbal salves versus pharmaceuticals. I didn't care about the Scientologists' "Silent Birth" practices. I wanted as much Western medicine as I could get, as many potential safety hatches as existed. Many people would argue that a hospital isn't where the best care resides, but I didn't buy that argument. If I had to have a C-section, so be it. I just wanted a healthy baby. My friend Katie was due with her second baby at the same time as me. She showed me pictures of the Cambridge Birth Center; it looked like a bed-and-breakfast with flowered curtains, vases of daffodils, cushioned glider chairs. I nodded and knew I'd never give up the scuffed linoleum, antiseptic, and uniforms.

In March, I went hiking in the Utah desert with my friend Anne. I recognized that I was slowing down when I couldn't keep up with the fastest group of hikers, and I didn't even try. One afternoon, I drove alone into the desert, in and out of Mormon communities full of young families. I saw women fifteen years younger than I was with five children.

I worked hard that day, slipping in and out of envy, and anxiety, and finally heard myself say, and repeat: "I am going to be a mother," which was amazing, and true.

I ordered a home Doppler. When my anxiety rose, I lay down on my bed, applied some goopy ultrasound gel to my stomach, put on the headphones, and listened to the quick, astonishing heartbeat. I'd close my eyes and relax.

In August, Carey went into labor, and Tully was born early. The timing was off, the events out of sync. We expected my baby first. Both of us had worked hard to get to the Massachusetts General maternity ward; and this wasn't a race worth winning. We simply wanted the norm.

Tully was a skinny little guy. I visited him in the hospital more than once, where Carey sat in a rocker holding him for hours at a time.

I sat next to her, and we looked down at Tully, curled on her lap, not with pure unbridled joy for his entry into the world, but with tension and a feeling that it might not be safe to love him too much just yet.

"Don't get your hair cut," she warned me. "I'm sure that's what did it. I went and got my hair cut and I went into labor."

Of course she was joking, but any mother frightened for her newborn would want an explanation, no matter how far-fetched, as to why her baby was in neonatal intensive care and not at home. There was always something to be scared of, and this proved it. Things can happen. There's a Yiddish term, *kineahora*, which means that you shouldn't ever feel too secure because if you get too secure you might get arrogant, and that's when you get slammed. So, in some part of me, I held my breath to the end.

The due date was September 21. The equinox came and went. On September 22, I went into labor. I was in the den, on the daybed, and as the hours passed, the sharp, gripping pains left me breathless.

At three a.m., Phil drove me to the hospital. When the doctor checked me, she said I was only three centimeters dilated. "I know it hurts," she said, with a degree of sympathy I couldn't detect, "but since you live nearby, you might want to go home and wait there until you're further along."

I wanted to stay, but Phil helped me drag myself, like an old woman, back downstairs, into the car, and back to the house. I stayed home for twelve hours, and at some point, when Phil and I weren't timing contractions or staring at each other in shock, I called Carey. "This really, really hurts!" I told her.

She laughed, in a sweet, knowing, kindly mocking way. "I know," she told me. "But it's so, so worth it."

At three p.m. I fell into the ward and was essentially loaded onto a bed. "You're eight centimeters," the resident said. "Why didn't you come in earlier?"

There I was, back at MGH's maternity ward. Next door to the room where I'd been a year earlier. The first nurse I had was a proponent of natural birth, so she found me an exercise ball and I sat on it, bouncing in the shower for three hours. Then I paced. The Red Sox game came on and Phil alternately helped me count breaths while he looked over his shoulder at the game. Six hours had passed. Another nurse arrived and asked if I wanted an epidural. "Can I?" I'd moved back into the shower. "I can get one now?"

"You could have had one hours ago," she told me. I realized that, eager to please, I'd hoped to meet the earlier nurse's expectations and see through the natural birth. This nurse didn't care, and suddenly neither did I. "Yes," I told her. "I really want an epidural. I'd really like an epidural now." Then another contraction. "Right now!" I grimaced and curled up, as much as a pregnant woman carrying forty extra pounds can curl up. I dragged myself out of the shower and, dripping wet, crawled onto the bed. When the nurse left the room to call the anesthesiologist, I recognized her as one of the women who'd been on shift the night I terminated the pregnancy. She didn't remember me. But even through my haze, I recalled her tenderness, and her face, immediately.

I got the epidural, and that changed everything. The doctor on the floor that night was seven months pregnant, and she'd stop by, see how I was doing, and waddle down the hall. The Red Sox game went on for twelve innings, so once I was pain-free, it was a great distraction.

Six long hours later, the doctor said it was time to push. I pushed. Nothing happened but pain. It was time to change the balance of the world as one more soul entered, but still nothing happened. The resident used a giant purple suction cup and lacerated the baby's scalp. No budging. When we both started to show signs of a fever, the doctor said it was time to change tactics. In seconds, I was rolled out of the room, Phil was taken to get scrubs, the doctor was gone, and I was in the OR. The doctor, who was short, stood on a footstool. My arms were taped down. Anesthesia was administered, and I felt loopy. Phil was up there somewhere, occasionally talking to me. A sheet was draped over my belly, but I could see Phil's face staring down at my guts. Then he looked up, panicked, and there was a lot of scurrying, doors opening and closing, a sense of unanticipated chaos. I lay there, no idea what was going on. A nurse leaned down to my face, and it was another woman who'd been there the night I terminated the pregnancy. I tried to explain and thank her, and she smiled.

Then the baby cried. I'd done it. We'd done it.

Somebody appeared from around the curtain carrying my boy. My tiny, wrinkly, pink, ten-toed, ten-fingered boy. I had to wait to hold him, but there he was. The three of us were all there in that room. Lots of other people were there too, but it didn't matter. My family was in that room. "That's him!" I said, crying, as Phil came around the curtain. "He's here!"

"He is. That's him," Phil said. "You did it. He's here."

"He's really here."

Then a smiling Asian man in scrubs appeared. "Congratulations," he said. "He's a very beautiful baby."

I had no idea who the man was. I looked at Phil. "Who's that?" I whispered.

The surgery had been more complicated than anticipated because of a large fibroid. The pregnant ob-gyn had already delivered two sets of twins and another baby by C-section before they rolled me into the OR. She started on me, realized it wasn't going to be simple, and midway through the operation, with my innards lying outside my body, my son on a heating table across the room, she'd opted out, and a second surgeon was called in to put me back together.

I never knew his name (hers was on the birth certificate). He was kind of like Zorro arriving in a surgical mask.

We had a baby. A boy baby. Baby Boy Jones had a scrape on his head, and he was intubated, but he was indeed perfect. We had a list of names, boys' and girls', and the final inclusion, scrawled by Phil the day before, was the winner. Baby Gareth. Baby Gareth Daniel, his middle name selected by my mother after my grandmother Dorothy and Phil's brother Durl. We had three quiet days in the hospital. Then we were shoved from the nest.

Gareth was a gorgeous, easy baby. Phil had a few weeks off, and we walked around the neighborhood in the flush of new parenthood, convinced ours was the most miraculous of all children.

Gareth and I took a baby-mommy class, and I realized that I wasn't the only mommy who knew nothing about my crying, wheezing, coughing, charming, glorious bundle of joy. Things moved into a rhythm, and although we continued to gaze at Gareth with head-shaking, stunned astonishment, life became "normal."

The one thing that didn't feel entirely normal was my age. As I pushed my first baby carriage at age forty-one, other Beacon Hill mothers appeared uniformly young, pert, beribboned, rich, and Waspy. I felt incredibly old (and fat, and disheveled, and Jewish).

Then I met women I'd never known were there, the nearly-or-already-over-forty crowd with babies, who lived within shouting distance. One took early retirement from an airline after twenty years of service. Another was a real estate agent who lived with her boyfriend and whose daughter became Gareth's best friend. And, of course, there was Carey.

"I feel old," Carey muttered over a cup of coffee when we met one morning at the *Globe*'s offices.

"We *are* old," was my standard reply.

"Experienced, we're experienced." She looked half-asleep.

"That doesn't necessarily make us wiser."

"Ahhh, but we're more patient." She wagged her finger at me.

"Because we move more slowly and we're always tired."

We'd lived full lives, waited, and worked hard to have kids. Many of us dated into middle age, several needed fertility drugs. Denise, the real estate agent, and I had unplanned pregnancies. London's *Guardian* newspaper published an article titled "Our Strange Fear of Older Mothers."

I don't think we're that scary. But we're out there. The number of over-forty pregnancies doubled between 1991 and 2006. And it keeps increasing. We are legion.

I have friends who took other routes to create families. In her midforties, a friend and her partner spent a month in Kazakhstan before taking home their son. Another couple traveled to Ethiopia for their daughter. One girlfriend went to Colorado and came home the single mom of a two-week-old daughter. Another is single and seven months pregnant with donor sperm. My cousin Laurie and her wife have three kids, all full biological siblings, conceived with donor sperm.

Other friends, some single, a few in relationships, carefully considered the option of having children, and opted out. "It's just not for me," one told me. "I know that much about myself."

Phil hadn't wanted kids. But he loved Gareth unconditionally. For a man who never planned to be a father, he didn't look back. In bed, they shared a pillow.

* * *

There are babies who log more miles than Gareth, but he did plenty. From the very beginning, we have pictures of him on Caribbean beaches, crossing ice fields on Phil's back through the Rockies, bundled up in lavender fields in Provence, in front of the Eiffel Tower, playing in tide pools in Hawaii and along the Cape Cod seashore. I'm grateful he might have those fuzzy memories, because I have them, too.

I kept writing for the *Globe,* as a nanny who was Mary Poppins with an Irish accent helped with Gareth. Phil and I tried to go out every other Friday night. I read books that weren't only about child development.

I pressed a single, childless friend for a character assessment.

"Have I changed?" I asked. "I really want to know. Not just, Do I look more tired, but am I still me?"

"I'll be honest," she said. The pause that followed didn't bode well. "You haven't been absorbed by your child," she told me. "You might have less time, but I don't think you've changed."

But I had a hard time keeping up with my work, and my editor scolded me for making mistakes.

And I had changed. On a cold January day, near a pizzeria on Charles Street, a man stepped in front of me. I looked up. It was Russell.

"Hey," he said.

"Hi." I wouldn't have noticed him if he hadn't blocked my path.

He pointed to my chest, where Gareth was slung in a carrier. "Is that yours?"

"He's mine," I told him. "I'm not the nanny."

"Wow." He shook his head. "How about that."

I nodded my head. "Amazing but true."

There was nothing else to say. Or nothing else I would bother to say. The pain was old, and far brighter things had replaced it. And what did it matter? I had my scrumptious boy.

We celebrated Gareth's second birthday at a pub on Cambridge Street in Boston with my parents, my friends Marie and Jake, chicken fingers, and chocolate cake. Never one to sit still, Gareth kept sliding out of the booth and running behind the bar. We wondered how much of his high energy was innate, and how much came from his parents, who loved to roam.

On an unseasonably warm October night, Phil and I went to dinner in Boston's North End. Our reservation was at a romantic restaurant on Hanover Street, at a table overlooking the busy sidewalk. It was the middle of the week, but the restaurant was buzzing.

"I'm really happy with our life," Phil said. "I'm really happy with you; I'm really happy with our boy; I'm really happy with all of it."

"I am, too," I told him. "I'm happy with all of it." I was looking at a good man across the table.

He nodded, and paused, and held onto my hands, turning them over, looking down at them, then up again. "Then, will you marry me?"

I had absolutely not anticipated that question. This was not something I had actively hoped for, or even had time to wonder about.

"Yes," I said. And I meant it. He gave me a sapphire ring.

I waited months to research wedding venues. "You realize," said Marie, verbally slapping me around, "that postponing the venue search is tantamount to neglecting Phil's proposal." Pam offered to help me look. Eventually, I shook myself from my nuptial paralysis. It was true, if I was going to marry Phil, I had to take some responsibility for making it happen. And I had to admit that yes, I could still retain my identity, even if I was married.

Many people say a first marriage is training for the second. Russell was a good instructor. He taught me that it's important to marry someone who actually wants to spend time with you, who shares your interests and your pleasures. Not just your religion or your address. Someone who makes you a better person, and who you wouldn't threaten with a carrot peeler.

Phil was not Russell.

Ultimately, I had to admit that marriage isn't a life sentence, at least not in the way it's usually defined. Marrying Phil wasn't a step toward incarceration. It was love. So I took a breath, and stopped fearing what I might lose if I got married, and thought instead about what I was gaining.

The Grand Isle Lake House was a mansard-roofed turn-of-the-century hotel on a wide lawn at the edge of Lake Champlain. It was beautiful, even on the frigid, rainy winter day when we first saw it. It was the only venue we visited. We set the wedding for a Saturday afternoon in early July.

The skies opened half an hour before the ceremony, drenching all the fresh lavender strewn across the lawn, the white chairs, the potted ferns that were meant to frame us in front of the deep blue lake. Instead, we were married on the side porch, with plastic awnings lowered against the downpour. With 150 guests squashed on that narrow whitewashed porch, we were surrounded by people we loved.

I started crying as soon as I stepped out the door. We had rings from a small Boston jewelry maker, and she'd made a silver bracelet decorated with stars for Gareth. We kept the ceremony brief and brought our own vows.

"It was very cold the night I met you," I said to Phil.

As I think back to that January night, that cold, our ice axes leaning against a wall at Harvard Cabin, your rakish hat, your nips of Scotch, the crumbled chocolate cake, it's not difficult to see how we arrived here, at this warm July afternoon. I set out to find you as soon as I left the mountains. Evidently, you were looking, too.

I don't know that I believe in fate, but I believe that sometimes we actually find what we want, as well as what we need. You, and Gareth, are more than I hoped for, and you are surely what I need. We are very, very fortunate, and have been blessed, I think, by something larger than ourselves.

As my wise grandmother said: we all wish for a lifetime of happiness, but it's up to us to make it happen. We have become each other's responsibility. Our actions, our words, our candor and honesty, matter. Everything is not hinged to hope.

Today I let go of my trepidation, and my past poor experiences of love.

I anticipate the rest of my life with you and with our very beloved son, in this world of wonder that surrounds us, and with the people who love us. I will do my best to keep us safe, and when confronted with adversity I will uplift our strong little family.

Please be with me forever.

Phil had driven off earlier in the day, alone, to think about his vows. His were extemporaneous. He held my hands while he spoke, and kept his eyes on mine. "I was looking for you, too," he said. "I didn't remember your last name, but I knew I'd find you. . . . I loved who we were before Gareth, and who we are now with him. I love watching him grow, and I love watching with you. . . . You inspire me." The rain had stopped. The sun came out.

After the ceremony, we walked off by ourselves for a little while. We sat in two white folding chairs and didn't talk much. We drank wine. Phil took my hand and held it on his knee.

"This is perfect," he said. "A little wet, but perfect."

Gareth was dancing with his cousins on the porch, chewing on his new bracelet. The grass smelled of crushed lavender. Everyone stayed late, dancing on the lawn, playing bocce as the late sun set over the lake.

"Hey," Carey said as I approached the table where she and Pam were sitting. "Have a seat." I did.

"Great party." Pam raised her glass. Everyone else at the table was off dancing or running after fireflies with the kids.

"Can't say I ever expected it," I told them.

"Maybe you didn't expect enough," said Carey.

"Hear, hear," added Pam.

"Now we just need for Pam to catch up," Carey said, lifting her glass.

Mark was kicking a soccer ball on the lawn, and we all looked over at him, then back at one another. "I'll drink to that." I smiled, and we clinked our glasses.

Gareth's sitter told us that after she'd taken him upstairs to bed, he stood for hours in his porta-crib, dancing and singing.

Late that night Phil and I sat on the porch steps. The bottom of my dress was muddy, and his pants had lost their crease. "This feels like frosting," I told him. "Like we already got everything. We have the family, we've lived lives we're happy with. This feels like an amazing extra life I hadn't known would happen."

He kissed me. Then he played poker until three in the morning with his siblings, and I fell asleep.

My friend Jode had traveled from Colorado for the wedding, and she asked if we wanted to go to Montreal with her after the Lake House. After an initial knee-jerk "no, we have to go home," we realized we didn't. Phil had quit his job, planning on a six-month hiatus when we'd travel and spend time together. So we drove up to Montreal for the jazz festival and spent three days dancing to free music all over the city, walking up Mont-Royal, eating *moules frites* and croissants. This was our perfect honeymoon: sunny days in Montreal accompanied by our son and a great friend.

Back home in Boston, a real estate agent called. The house was in a leafy suburb still close to the city, and not far from where Carey and Sprax had moved. We were looking casually. "I think you should see this place," the agent said. "But there's already an offer on it." Our initial plan had been to pack up and go live in New Zealand for a few months. Instead we moved a few miles away.

When I became a parent, time took on a parallel course: there was regular time, the time of clocks and days and work and the far past and getting everything done, and then there was the time of Gareth. The distance between his birthdays, his evolving milestones, his new school, his extraordinary advances and bumpy passages. The hours of watching *Curious George* when I was too tired to suggest the library, a walk, a book, a museum, or a puzzle. His kicking and screaming tantrums. His life as inseparable from, yet entirely independent of, ours.

I don't know many men who are fathers who would have so easily said yes to their child's mother traipsing off on safari in Africa. But it was Phil who encouraged and convinced me to accept my friend Claudia's invitation to a twenty-day adventure when I was reluctant, my ancient fear of disaster alive and blazing.

The trip went fast, very fast. And then, after a thirty-eight-hour, four-leg return flight, I was home.

I cried when Gareth opened the front door. The babysitter handed him flowers to give me. I knelt on the splintery porch and held him, saying over and over, "I missed you so much. So much." He hugged me and kissed me a hundred times. But that night, he had a screaming tantrum, and I yelled at him. I felt guilty for days; he was probably just confused about my coming and going. And I was tired and disappointed that we didn't achieve a perfect evening. But that, too, is life. Perfection is when Phil and I can shrug and admit that everything isn't within our control, not each other and perhaps most of all our child. So on we go. A little blithely, a little blindly, and, when necessary, with some caution.

Going away, and returning home, made me realize, again, just what I have. I have a partner, in all senses of the word. And nobody else will ever, ever be Gareth's mother. I find a great deal of comfort in knowing that there is someone in this world to whom I am completely irreplaceable. Eventually, he'll find lovers, partners, hopefully someone he loves forever. But even then, I will remain his mother. To him, I am indelible.

The Friendship

Pam: "We shared an experience, just not the one we expected."

Carey: "It helps to have friends who've been there."

Pam: "I was so glad to have you. And you."

Beth: "Friends who can point the way forward."

Pam

IT WAS A CLOUDLESS SUMMER DAY. Beth was eight months pregnant, and I envied her belly as she lumbered across the warm sand and into the ocean, Phil keeping a watchful eye on her. Mark ran past them, diving in, jumping up and giving his head a good shake like a dog. Dark hair whipped around his face, and his pale, lean chest shone against the blue water.

To me, Mark was an unusual man: He built a computer from scratch and shot fine art photographs. He read history books about colonial India and loved lowbrow British comedies. He did martial arts and prepared homemade sorbet. He listened well, and he never made me feel stupid or clumsy even when I did stupid or clumsy things, like locking my keys in the car or burning dinner.

Mark shaded his face with one hand and waved to me

where I sat on the shore. I waved back, and he dove in again. A burst of white surf. We had all gathered for a wedding in Rhode Island, and this was the first time he had spent a whole weekend with my friends. Even though we were doing well, and all signs pointed to future happiness, Beth sensed that the recent spate of marriages and baby showers might not be easy for me. She knew as well as I did that it's one thing to be headed for marriage and motherhood. It's quite another to get there.

"I hope you'll have what you want," she said that day, settling onto the beach blanket and reaching over the hump of her growing belly to brush sand off her legs. "I feel certain you will." She gave my arm a gentle squeeze.

A wedding was not in the works for Mark and me any time soon. He needed a break from marriage, and I understood. I told him a ring at some point would make me happy as a tangible symbol of our commitment and, one day, a small ceremony before family and friends. No rush.

A baby was another matter. A year had passed since the fellowship began and I had vowed to be a mom. I didn't want to put off talking to Mark about having a child—with him or not. I couldn't.

In recent days, I had noticed that my breasts felt sore, and my period was late. I was shocked, happy, and scared about what might be in store for my body, my relationship, and my life. Mark was reading in the living room, engrossed in a book about India.

"I think I might be pregnant."

"Really?" he asked. Eyes wide. Closing the book.

"I'm not sure, but I seem to be having some symptoms."

"What sort?"

"Well, for starters, I haven't gotten my period yet."

"You should probably take a test." Pragmatic. Not the reaction I had hoped for.

An accidental pregnancy had never occurred to me, as stupid as that sounds. We always used protection. ("A diaphragm?" my mom said later, shaking her head.) I was a planner. I had expected to plan the timing of a baby. I hoped to have a better home and a bigger paycheck, though my prospects had improved. I was managing to eke out magazine articles and work as a freelance radio producer, and my grandfather left me a generous inheritance. Enough to give me the flexibility of working part-time while raising a child, and that was a huge gift.

I was lucky in so many ways. I knew that. Still, that wasn't enough because I desperately wanted to be a mother. So for all the bad timing, the tension with Mark, the unknowns, I wished the pregnancy to be true.

"Stop worrying about it," Donna said. "If it happens, no matter when it happens, it'll be a blessing. No one is ever ready for it."

As it turned out, we didn't have to wonder for long.

Before a test could show I was pregnant, I began bleeding at home, much more heavily than with a normal period. I went through pad after pad, and finally stood in the shower to let it wash away. I called Mark, and he came right over. Even if we could never confirm a miscarriage, the cramps were more painful than usual with dark red, clotlike pieces of blood and tissue that made me wince with disgust and sorrow. It felt strange to grieve something that may or may not have been.

Mark did his best to comfort me. But I knew my sadness, unlike his, was not tinged with relief.

The bleeding and cramps lasted for several days, and I went to get a checkup to make sure everything was okay. It was. But as long as Mark and I continued to have sex, I could get pregnant again, and I didn't want it to play out the same way. We needed to talk about where we stood and whether I should consider other options.

This was not a conversation that my mother could have had, or her mother before her. This was a twenty-first century discussion, even if it was still about one of the oldest issues in the world: love, commitment, children, timing. How to be a family.

I told Mark more about Donor 8282's frozen vials and about Robert, reassuring him (whether he needed reassurance or not) that Robert had no romantic attachment to me and wanted only to be a father. We sat on dusty plastic chairs on the tilted, second-floor porch of Mark's rental apartment overlooking a small yard. A child's voice could be heard from the unit below.

Mark said he didn't think he'd be ready to have a baby for another year or two. For him, it was too much, too soon. He told me he had just finished taking care of one person, his wife, and said he needed a break before taking care of another person, a child. Things between us had moved fast.

At this rate, his divorce proceedings would coincide with childbirth classes.

"It would be good to have our relationship founded just on us," he said. "To get naturally to the point where we have children. Not force everything through at the beginning."

Not now, he was saying. Did he really mean not for a long time? Or not ever? I faced the painful and paradoxical dilemma of having found my soul mate only to possibly lose him because he wasn't ready to be a father.

He felt rushed. I felt slowed down. I wanted to relieve the pressure on both of us, so I presented him with some alternative scenarios that seemed crazy to me even as I said them out loud.

"What if I went ahead and got pregnant with the donor sperm? Or with Robert? Could you and I still be together?"

He looked at me in bewilderment. Like, Are you *nuts?*

"How, exactly, would that work?"

"I don't know." I hadn't thought it out.

Mark looked frustrated. He began kicking at chipped paint on the floor slats until a splintered triangle of bare wood emerged.

"I don't really want to go down that road. I want to have a normal relationship," he said.

I agreed it would be awkward, to say the least, and I didn't think even I could handle it. As if sensing my impatience, the child downstairs began to cry. I couldn't keep it together much longer.

"Do you want to have a baby?" I said. "I love you. I don't want to lose you. But I want to be a mother, my time is running out, and I really need to know."

Yes, yes, he said. "I want to have a future together, and that includes children."

"When?" We sat without talking for several minutes.

"Let's say, within a year." It felt like we had stepped back from the edge of a precipice, and we settled into our relationship with a renewed sense of commitment.

In November, on my thirty-ninth birthday, I woke up in Mark's bedroom. A sliver of sunshine shone between the closed curtains, rippling in a bright line across the floor and over the duvet. Already awake, he reached under his pillow and handed me a square, tiny blue box tied with a white bow.

"Happy birthday, my love," he said.

Inside lay a simple yet elegant white gold band. The pull tab from a soda can would have done fine.

"A year ago, when you were in Chicago, my heart ached for

you! Now it is a year later and all that you are is more important to me than life itself," he wrote in the birthday card. "I love you."

That winter, Mark and I hunkered down and counted our blessings. We watched Laurel and Hardy films from an inflatable mattress in his living room and walked in the cold around Walden Pond, its surface feathered with ice crystals. We read books in front of the fire, made love, and ate chocolate and drank champagne in bed. We listened to folk music and told stories by candlelight when snowstorms knocked out the electricity.

The baby question lay dormant, and I didn't mind. I was enjoying this period of peace after all the drama of recent months.

Post-fellowship, I was trying to establish myself as a freelance science writer. I produced radio programs and wrote features for online sites, newspapers, and magazines, making for a semblance of routine. Life outside a nonstop daily newsroom, as Beth and Carey knew, could be pretty sweet.

As spring peeked around the corner, Mark seemed to emerge into a fresh state of being, too. He seemed almost jaunty in his "bachelor" apartment, everything arranged to his liking, the new bath towels hung just so, the kitchen plates and mugs fresh and white. It made me laugh. It also pleased me seeing him in his own space, and he made me feel better by saying it wouldn't be for much longer and suggesting that we break our hibernation with a holiday.

"It would be nice for our world to consist of just a room, a beach, and a couple of restaurants for a few days," he said. "No distractions. No complications. Just us." Us. I wondered if he knew how much his saying that word meant.

A colleague recommended Harbour Island in the Bahamas,

and it was paradise: endless beach, warmth, and light. We went scuba diving and snorkeling, bicycling and swimming, and we spotted the supermodel Elle Macpherson wheeling around town in her convertible. In a red-striped cabana on the beach, Mark turned to me.

"My life, with you, has taken a turn for the better," he said. I know mine had. Videos from that time, shot by Mark with an outstretched arm, show us kissing and laughing, the pink sand shifting in translucent turquoise waters around our bare feet. Everything easy and happy.

Back in Boston, the significance of a new season, with its intimations of rebirth, was not lost on me. It had been more than seven months since our last baby conversation, and I was eager to get things going. As a step toward that, I brought up the subject of moving in with each other, and Mark agreed to the fall as reasonable. I figured we would try to get pregnant soon after that, exactly in line with my two-year plan. When June rolled around, I began casually reviewing rental apartment listings in Cambridge, where we both felt at home.

As luck would have it, our MIT friend Jackie and her husband were moving out of their place near Harvard Square. It was a big one-bedroom with a spacious layout, three fireplaces, a private yard, and reasonable rent. Mark, who came along to see it, didn't expect to be checking out apartments so soon, but we agreed it could work and stopped at a grocery store on the way back to his place.

Somewhere between the bread aisle and the dairy case, Mark clutched a box of rice to his chest and said he had to tell me something. He looked panicked.

"I need a bit more time alone before we move in together," he said. "I thought I'd have until the end of my lease. That was the original plan." His lease expired in November.

When we first met, Mark did everything he said he was going to do: he left his marriage, he started therapy. Out on his own, however, he was balking at moving forward, and I wondered if a bite of freedom had given him a taste for more.

I abandoned our grocery cart in the aisle and walked out to the car, where I burst into tears. Not my proudest moment, having always encouraged him to share his feelings with me, but true. Back at his apartment, he told me that he wasn't having doubts about our relationship. It was just the same old story: too fast for him, too slow for me.

"I just needed to tell you so that you would appreciate my need to have space," he said.

"And what do you expect me to do with that information?" I was still visibly shaken and sat on the edge of his couch, ready to bolt at the first sign of rejection.

"Understand it."

"What does that mean?"

It meant that much as he would have liked two more months in his own apartment, he was willing to break the lease as long as I accepted that he would need a lot of time to himself in our shared home.

"Okay. I understand now," I said, though it crossed my mind that he might just be going along with things to make me feel better.

We signed a September 1 lease the next day.

Perhaps it was the jolt of Mark's telling me he felt rushed, even if he would go on to reassure me that everything was okay. Perhaps it was the change, good, but change nonetheless. I had never lived with a man before and hadn't moved in eight years.

Maybe it was that everything seemed to be working out with us, and, as positive as that was, I found it hard to trust.

Perhaps it was a stretch of family illnesses and deaths that began to wear at me and make me more anxious than I had ever felt before. My grandfather had died, then my aunt. A few months later, my stepfather, Patrick, was diagnosed with late-stage esophageal cancer.

Perhaps my anxiety also was due to the fact that, as a journalist, I wrote mostly about tragedy and disaster. That was news. I witnessed the gory aftermath of car accidents and murders. I met dying children and interviewed grieving relatives. I viewed homes flattened after storms and saw the reassembled fuselage of a plane whose nose had sheared off in midair, leaving doomed passengers to face open sky.

I worried about Mom and about Patrick. I worried about Mark, about Dad, and my brother, Ben. I worried about everything and everyone. I imagined Mark dying in a car crash on the way to work. I imagined burglars breaking into Mom's house or her drowning as she swam in Lake Michigan, Ben getting shot, Dad having a heart attack.

Mom, also an anxious person, who now treated anxious people, called this "awful-izing"—as in, always coming up with the worst-case scenario. Mark had another word for it: "controlling." I asked him to do things that, in my mind, reduced risk. In his mind, I was just telling him what to do.

My pleas went something like this: "Promise me you won't drive through the Big Dig tunnel." He agreed. "Will you please schedule a checkup with your doctor? You haven't had one in two years." He nodded. "We should get those tickets this week before they sell out." He rolled his eyes.

It took him a while to understand that I was trying to

minimize my anxiety by planning around it, which didn't always make it easier to take, though sometimes made it less annoying. This glass-half-empty state of mind, though, was getting uncomfortable even for me to live with. I feared I would be a neurotic and overprotective mother, and I could understand how it might grate on Mark in years to come. I wanted to get over myself, so I went back to therapy.

"Maybe you can start believing that there are other endings," said my therapist, Alice. She was willowy and elegant, with reddish hair and pale skin, and she spoke with gentle authority. "Good ones. Happy ones."

I recited mantras in my head: *Mark can go to work and come home to me safely. Mark can go to work and come home safely. Mark can go to work and come home safely.* I thought Alice was good, smart, and focused, and I knew she would help me make some sense of the past few years and move forward with less anxiety and fear of loss. I wanted to embrace joy and love fully and not expect it to disappear.

I turned forty.

My brother, Ben, newly married to Dena, called to wish me happy birthday.

"Can you believe how old I am? Insane."

"I know! That means I'm old, too."

"How are you guys doing?" I asked.

"Great, but work is busy," he said. "How's the new place working out?"

I looked around at the paintings and photographs we had started to hang, the new pot rack over the stove. The pile of collapsed cardboard boxes in a corner.

"Good. We're *nearly* all unpacked, settling in. How's Dena?"

"Great."

We raced through the updates: Mark, how Mom was working too much, how Dad was exercising too little.

"Anything happening on the baby front?" I blurted. Boy, I thought, talk about an annoying sister. I knew they wanted to start a family, but it was really none of my business.

"We've been trying for a few months. Nothing yet, but I'll let you know when there's news to tell!"

As soon as I put the phone down, I realized that I didn't want to wait anymore either, and I was afraid that even now I had waited too long. What if I couldn't get pregnant? What would I do? At the same time, I realized I had been nervous about broaching the subject with Mark. It would be much harder, if not impossible, to consider other options—the donor sperm, Robert—now that we were living together, emotionally committed. But it was time.

My fears were groundless. It turned out that in recent months while I was waiting for him to bring up baby, he was waiting for me. Mark was a man of his word. He had not forgotten the time line we had compromised on. If I hadn't mentioned getting pregnant to him soon, he told me he would have said something in a matter of days.

"I just didn't know if you were ready," he said.

"I'm ready."

We got started that night.

My gynecologist measured my hormone levels. They weren't great, as in "you can take all the time you want to try to have a child," but they were good enough.

"Try on your own for three months, and we'll take it from there," she said.

For his photography class, Mark documented everything, from me taking my basal temperature in the morning to the paraphernalia of pregnancy attempts: prenatal vitamins, ovulation charts, the Clearblue Easy Fertility Monitor urged on me by Beth and Carey. While some people might think it odd, I found the photographs beautiful and loved seeing Mark's pleasure in creating a permanent memory of this time. I also was happy to see him tapping new energies and pursuing a creative path he had long desired.

On Valentine's Day, we traded cards, candies, sex toys, and scented potions. We lingered in bed. Five days later, I took a pregnancy test even though I didn't expect to be pregnant. I had convinced myself that it would take a while, maybe even a year, to conceive. It was more curiosity than anything else.

So this is how it works, I discovered: unwrapping the plastic, uncapping the stick, peeing on it, finding it impossible not to get pee on my fingers, making sure the stick remained level, waiting three minutes, wondering if I would be able to distinguish one faint line from two.

But this dress rehearsal turned out to be the real thing: Positive. Undeniably positive. Solid pink. Pregnant. I took another test: same thing. We'd been trying for less than two months.

I crawled back into bed with Mark, tapped him on the shoulder. His brown hair was tousled, and one eye half opened with a smile. I loved that in the morning. He nodded in silent greeting, and I told him the news.

"Congratulations, honey. That's wonderful," he said, turning onto his back so I could nestle my head in the nook between his shoulder and neck. His body always radiated warmth. "Did you just find out?"

"Yes, can you believe it? It's exciting."

"Of course I can believe it. I always knew we could." He kissed the top of my head.

We lay there and savored the moment. For a second, I felt wistful and regretted that we had not had more time alone together. I had waited so long to find him, and we had barely begun to explore the world as a twosome. Given how much I wanted a baby, it was a surprising emotion.

Mark and I got dressed and walked to the pharmacy to buy more pregnancy kits, just to be sure. As a woman pushing a stroller passed us, I felt as if I was hovering between worlds—the world of people with children, of *strolling,* and those without. Not better or worse. Just very, very different. Four more tests confirmed the earlier news. I was, as the Welsh say, "up the spout."

Photos from later that morning show me standing by the kitchen counter with a vase of red roses, right next to a plastic cup of urine. There's a close-up of my face looking serious, dipping a stick. There's another photo showing a slice of my face against a bright blue sky, and you can tell I'm smiling from the crease lines in the corner of my eyes. You can see me calling my family, holding my hand to my face, smiling at Mark. The expression is one of happiness and disbelief.

"Put the phone against your belly so I can talk to it!" Mom said. Dad cried.

"Mark looks absolutely delighted, but also as if he can't quite believe the evidence of his own eyes," his mother, Ruth, wrote in an e-mail to us from Wales. "I know that it is said that pregnant women have a distinctive 'glow' about them, but you, even at this very early stage, are positively radiant!"

What a day, I thought to myself. Hope it stays true.

It had been a heck of a week. Mark's divorce had become final four days earlier. He sought a fair division of assets, which were ample, but wound up walking away from the house and joint bank accounts with little more than his nine-year-old Taurus and a modest retirement fund. Dad was diagnosed with colon cancer the same day and would go on to have surgery.

Around the same time, a stranger turned to me in the subway and gave me one of the most memorable compliments of my life. He must have thought I could use it. "You look like someone," he said. "You look like a good memory."

It was strange to get such good news and bad news all at the same time. I tried to keep it in perspective. Mark and I made our first prenatal appointment and got our due date, which seemed propitious: November 1, his mother's birthday.

The first day of spring arrived, and with it, the first sight of our ever so little one. Looking part alien, part tadpole, the embryo was developing nicely, and I cried out of relief at the sight of the heartbeat, a dot thumping like crazy on the screen in front of us. We gasped at the fuzzy outlines of the placenta and the yolk sac, and we both felt we could have watched the images for hours, even days. Mark showed my ob-gyn the printout, one of thousands she must have seen. The only one of ours.

This, I thought, is a child of love.

We scanned and e-mailed our family the ultrasound images. Because of the embryo's size, Poppyseed became its nickname, and we not so secretly hoped it was a girl. My mom sent me a morning-sickness music CD and a chocolate care package addressed to "Mama and Papa." Dad sent a check with "baby food" written in the memo section and stamped with little yellow ducks.

As the weeks passed, I became bloated, moody, and tired. I had stopped drinking coffee, which didn't help, and had

Olympic-class hormone swings. I gave up pottery because of the metals in glazes and declined work due to nausea that made it impossible to sit for long at the computer. Our sex life had come to a screeching halt because Mark sensed my discomfort.

Nearly two months into the pregnancy, I noticed some spots of blood on my underwear. I feared the beginning of a miscarriage, so I called Mark and my doctor. We went in for an ultrasound. Everything was fine. The fetus was nearly two inches long; the heart pumped at 163 beats a minute. We could see two brain hemispheres, the umbilical cord, arms, legs, and even fingers. Relieved, I realized that, whatever I felt on bad days—foolish, foolish me—I did want this baby.

Carey, because of her own miscarriage, knew how scary spotting could be. I decided to take it easy and try not to do so much gardening and lifting, which seemed to make me bleed. Carey usually told me when she thought I was overreacting. She didn't this time.

"Thank goodness for the ultrasound!" she said, checking in with a call on her way home from work one day. "It's so hard not to exert yourself, but in the unlikely event something does go wrong, you're going to need to know one hundred percent that it was nothing you did. So whatever level of rest you need, take it."

I knew how deeply she analyzed everything, so I suspected she must have had to work through guilt over her own failed pregnancy. It didn't matter that miscarriage was one of the most natural occurrences in the world. It was a terrible loss that could stir all kinds of emotions, and I felt grateful that she was trying to spare me any possible future remorse.

"You're right," I agreed. "I would need to feel that I had done everything I could."

"Still, it's ridiculous," she said. "How many women are pregnant with one kid and have to carry two others, and still do fine?"

Mark and I went to the hospital several days later for the mandatory genetic counseling that preceded a CVS. Genetic defects, we learned from the counselor, could be caused by errors in one or more genes passed on or inherited by the parents, by a missing, damaged, or extra chromosome, or by a mixture of genetic and environmental factors. Risks increased with maternal age, and chromosomal disorders were most often the result of an error that occurred when the egg and sperm joined. Most such defects resulted in miscarriage. Some did not.

We already had received good results from an ultrasound test called nuchal translucency, which correlated an estimate of the thickness of the embryo's neck with the risk of Down syndrome. For this test, though, the doctor would insert a long needle into my cervix (just how long I wouldn't know because I didn't look) and draw cells directly from the placenta. The cells would be cultured, and we would get results within two weeks.

I had tested negative for cystic fibrosis and Tay-Sachs disease, among other hereditary illnesses, and the genetic counselor told us I had a second-trimester chance, based on my age, of 1 in 70 for Down syndrome and 1 in 40 for chromosomal abnormality. That was equivalent to about 2.5 percent.

"Pretty good odds, all things considered," Mark said.

We walked to another part of the hospital for the test. I lay on my back, one crinkly paper gown covering me below the waist, another hiked up over my chest above my belly. Mark stood by my side and held my hand. I had to turn my neck to see the ultrasound, and we watched as the doctor moved the probe across fuzzy images on the monitor before saying he had to postpone the test for a week. Previous measurements put the embryo at about eleven weeks. It looked like that was an overestimate. Still, everything seemed all right.

When we returned a week later, the doctor began the procedure by saying, "This could be risky," because part of my bowel was in the way. He moved the needle up and down as Mark watched, and I closed my eyes and winced in discomfort. It felt like someone was pinching me from the inside out, but it went fine, and we just had to wait. We sent out more images of Poppyseed with a happy note. We saw hands developing, even bones that appeared bright white on the screen.

"Amazing to see tiny fingers and long legs (must be your genes at work)," we wrote our parents. "According to the doctor, Poppyseed is developing to plan and everything (that can be seen) is where it should be. Stay tuned."

Mom could barely contain her excitement at the prospect of becoming a grandmother and on a visit to Boston, eyeing the too tight waistband of my jeans, insisted it was time for a maternity wardrobe.

"How about this? Or this?" She ran around the store like a toddler on a sugar high, returning with armloads of clothes and wheeling an extra rack outside the fitting room to hold even more. One minute she was showing me soft elasticized sweatpants; the next she was offering me free juice and granola bars and suggesting a full-length body pillow.

"Are you hungry? Are you thirsty? Isn't this *cute?*" she crowed, thrusting another Empire-waisted blouse in my direction.

Her enthusiasm was contagious, and we walked out of the store hundreds of dollars later with gorgeous flowy skirts and tops, silky nightgowns, and stretchy pants to accommodate me and my growing belly through the summer months. I was officially a pregnant woman.

Days later, Mark and I left for a long weekend on Martha's Vineyard, where we had vacationed the two previous summers. We stayed at a guesthouse in rural West Tisbury run by a doula, a type of pregnancy and labor assistant, and her husband, a onetime fisherman. Lobster traps and seashells decorated the lawn and back porch, and when she learned I was pregnant, she gave us a compilation of soothing music for newborns. I tucked it into a bag for safekeeping.

Mark and I planned to relax and also to collaborate for the first time on a travel story for the *Boston Globe.* I would write the article and he would shoot photos. My nausea had abated, and I was feeling good. I pushed the prenatal test to the back of my mind and concentrated on the work at hand.

Monday morning rolled around, gloomy and overcast, and my cell phone rang. It was Karen, the genetic counselor.

She said, "You've probably been waiting for this call."

"Yes." I signaled to Mark.

"The test was inconclusive," she said.

"What does that mean?" I had expected a one-word answer: "good." Maybe even "bad." Not ambiguity.

"I'm sorry to tell you this, but it showed an extra chromosome in all of the sampled cells. It's called trisomy 22, but it's hard to tell whether it affects the fetus because the cells were only from the placenta," she said. "That's why they say it's inconclusive."

"How do we find out for sure one way or another?" I asked.

"We'll schedule an amniocentesis in another two weeks," she said. She might as well have said two years.

"What does trisomy 22 mean?" Down syndrome was trisomy 21, but 22 was a rare and poorly understood condition, and she had no information.

"Pam, do you want to know the sex?" she asked.

"Yes, please," I said. I wasn't thinking.

As if to break our hearts into a zillion more pieces, it was a girl.

We slunk off the Vineyard a day early. It felt too strange to be there, on an island, cut off from family and friends. The minute we were home, I launched myself onto the computer and manically searched every science and medical site I could find. Mark retreated to his office and tucked himself away. I had learned through therapy not to expect the other shoe to drop. Here it was, dropping, dropping, *dropping*.

"I'm trying to do as much research as I can, but I'm still in shock, and it's hard to digest all the information," I told Betsy, a close friend who sat next to Carey at the *Boston Globe* and was one of the most resourceful people I knew.

"Of course it is. Let me help you find whatever you need," she said. Over the phone, I could hear typing as I gave her the details. "How is Mark doing?"

"He's just terrified of serious birth defects," I said. "If the next tests show the problem is only in the placenta, then okay, we'll go from there. If not, we're going to end it. But I can't even think about that after getting this far. It feels surreal." I started crying.

"Oh, Pammy, I'm so, so sorry," she said. "It's such a horrible thing, not knowing."

I learned that it was extremely unusual that I had not miscarried earlier. Full trisomy 22 was frequently seen in first-trimester miscarriages and second-trimester spontaneous abortions, and the babies that survived beyond that died shortly before or after birth. I wondered if my efforts to prevent the spotting also prevented what would have been a natural process of rejection.

Partial trisomy 22, in which only some cells were affected

by an extra chromosome, didn't seem like a cakewalk, either. The placenta could fail to develop properly, causing complications for the fetus. There could be any number of possible defects, small and large: tiny brain, abnormal ears, webbed neck, cardiac abnormalities, kidney problems, cleft palate, fingerlike thumbs, gastrointestinal malformations, clubbed feet, contracted pelvis, seizures, and on and on.

I read on the Internet about the experiences of parents of newborns with the condition. They wrote of multiple surgeries, slow growth, and developmental disabilities. Stories of hope were few and far between. "I had a boy with trisomy 22," one mother wrote. "He was born in 1993. He died in 1997. If anybody wants information, please send me an e-mail."

Mark and I each saw pictures of trisomic fetuses that made our hair stand on end.

"I can plainly say, I don't want that. I know there are no guarantees, but I want a healthy child," I told him.

Mark woke up one morning and rolled over to face me. His eyes were bleary and swollen from lack of sleep, and I stroked his cheek, creased from the pillow. "No one should have to live through this," he said. "The waiting."

Our family was loving and supportive, but I had a hard time talking to them when they called because it felt as if my body was letting everyone down, and I was ashamed. I had nightmares of jumping over rooftops because someone was chasing me, of failing to memorize twenty pages of script for a school play, of bleeding in a public restroom and trying to hide the stained toilet paper from view.

"We continue to pray and love you beyond words," my mom said.

Beth had some sense of how I was feeling. She understood

that I felt as if I were masquerading as a pregnant woman, looking like one and not wanting to be identified as one because I might not be for much longer. I didn't want to respond to smiles or questions about the due date and gender, and I felt guilty that I had not understood the depth of her own trauma.

We sat on the living room couch, where I had spent a lot of time lately, napping and watching television. I had gotten out of my robe and into some sweatpants and a T-shirt after she called to say she was coming over.

"I can't believe what you went through. I had no idea what getting that news must have felt like until now," I said. "I'm so sorry I wasn't there for you more."

"It's okay. How could you possibly understand? I wish you didn't have to," she said. "Just so you know, though I'd hope you already do, if you want to talk any more about your anxiety, or just sit with someone other than Mark and not talk, just let me know." She was telling me, *I needed that.*

"That might be good. Thank you."

A teenaged neighbor walking a dog passed in front of the apartment, talking on her cell phone. An older couple, looking lost, stopped near the front door to check a street map. If I had had my usual energy, I would have felt inclined to offer assistance. Instead, I looked at Beth, put my feet up on an ottoman, and sighed.

She said, "If you want a drink, I won't tell anyone. I know the waiting is exhausting."

"I just dread having to end it," I said.

"I really hope you don't have to do that because it's awful. It's going to be worse than you expect it to be," Beth said. "But if you do, you have to know that it's the right decision and just go forward with that."

I waited a moment, unsure whether to ask, whether it was fair.

"What would you do?"

Because Beth was my friend and knew what it was like to want answers when there are none, she told me.

"I would agonize, and I would try to get as much information as I could, but I would terminate the pregnancy," she said. "And I did. I made the decision that felt like it was the best one. It was heartbreaking, but I don't have any regrets."

"And you and Phil? How did you manage?" Mark and I had been through stressful times. Nothing like this.

"We're different from you two. Phil and I barely knew each other, and if nothing else, it gave us more time to figure each other out," she said. "It took the summer to recover, and I knew I was doing better when I felt like shoving pregnant women in the side, but not knocking them down completely."

As the days passed, I read news articles and reviewed research papers with titles like "Molecular Mechanism of Rearrangements on Chromosome 22q1." I felt grateful that the fellowship taught me enough to decipher some of the dense technical language ("...the mechanisms of either trisomic zygote rescue and UPD..."), but I barely managed. What did other people do?

I tracked down genetic researchers around the world. No one could give me the odds of having a normal child, and they didn't dare try to advise us what to do, even though I wanted them to. "Trisomy 22 is quite a difficult one to counsel, as there are very few well-studied cases out there," one told me.

Desperate, I tried to locate the one woman who might be able to tell us something. A Canadian scientist had studied this chromosomal disorder more than anyone else. I e-mailed her former colleagues. They had no idea how to reach her.

*   *   *

Mark and I went for an ultrasound before the amniocentesis, and the first technician called in a second technician. Together, they peered at the monitor screen glowing in the dark and pointed to a blinking red dot that marked the heart.

"There could be a problem," the first one said, "but we're not sure."

We would need to wait a week for another ultrasound. They looked worried. Worse, the fetus was small, at least a week behind schedule, and the placenta had not finished merging. We realized it always had been small, causing us to shift due dates at least twice and to postpone the first CVS.

My ob-gyn came in and reviewed the information. I sat up on the table, my bare stomach still sticky from the ultrasound gel.

"What do you think?" My voice trembled. I reached for Mark's hand.

"All indications are that you have an abnormal pregnancy," she said.

"What does that mean?" Mark asked.

"It doesn't look good."

The stress already had taken its toll on us individually and on our relationship. Mark didn't think he could handle several more months of not knowing what was to come. Our baby had the equivalent of a time bomb in her genes. Even I conceded that she faced an enormous uphill struggle before she was born, if she was even born. The physical defects and slow growth compounded with the genetic anomaly forced our hand. We agreed to terminate the pregnancy the next day, and my doctor, without telling us directly what to do, said she might make the same choice.

Mark felt confident of our decision. I didn't, and my insides churned. The previous day, someone had forwarded me the e-mail address of the husband of the scientist in Canada and suggested that I try to reach her that way. With nowhere else to turn, when we got home I gave it one last shot.

"I know there are no absolutes, but your insight as a respected expert would be greatly appreciated at this difficult time," I wrote, detailing the situation.

Later that night, before I went to bed, I checked my in-box. And blinked hard. She had replied, saying she had no idea how hard it was to locate her.

"Fetal trisomy 22 is not compatible with normal development," she wrote. "The fact that your latest ultrasound findings showed delayed fetal growth and potential heart abnormalities suggests to me that most likely the whole conceptus (both placenta and the fetus) could be trisomic for chromosome 22."

She told me I could call her at home with any burning questions, and because the time difference meant I still could catch her at a decent hour, I did. I had less than twelve hours to go before I had to be at the hospital.

Our situation was extremely rare, she said, and in her experience, all signs pointed to a tragedy in the making. More than that, she said we would be sparing the world another child with defects so great it would be a cruelty to do otherwise. She was informative and comforting. By the time I got off the phone with her, I knew we were making the right decision for us, for now.

The next morning, four months from the day we found out I was pregnant, we rose early and boxed up my maternity clothes, baby books, and ultrasound and pregnancy photos, shoving them into the back of a closet.

Mom and Dad insisted on being with us, and I could

appreciate the generosity and slight oddity of it: How many divorced parents would fly into town for their daughter's abortion? They would have been grandparents, and they put their own grief and disappointment aside to come together and take care of us.

I took the suppository that my doctor had prescribed. Naked and alone in my bathroom, I began having cramps and realized, in a moment suffused with horror, that the pregnancy was over. Many of my friends had abortions for one reason or another; no one had warned me about this part. It was not a procedure done under anesthesia in which I would go to sleep pregnant and wake up not. It began with a deliberate action before we even got to the hospital, and my body would still think it was pregnant long after it was not.

As much as Mark and I told ourselves and others that we didn't think of this as a baby, as a real child, I would regret for the rest of my life knowing that it was a girl. I still didn't regret our decision, but I stood in the shower, sobbing, my whole body shaking against the cold tile wall, and telling her I was sorry. I was so very, very sorry.

My parents were sitting in the hospital waiting room when we arrived. A social worker handed out pastel-colored paperbacks with poems and essays about grief by parents mourning their "angels." It left all of us cold.

In the hospital room, my doctor sat down next to me, said very little and held my hand. Mom and Dad told me later that she said we had made absolutely the right decision. The anesthesiologist came in. I slipped into unconsciousness. A few hours later, once I woke up, after Mark and my parents had seen me, I stood for the first time, and blood gushed down my legs and onto the floor. It wouldn't stop. Embarrassed and horrified, I bent over and futilely tried to wipe the puddle away with a tissue before a nurse came in and put me back to bed. I closed my eyes but could not sleep.

For the first day or two, Mark and my parents seemed surprised that I was rather chipper.

"You're doing so well, baby," Mom said.

"You're such a strong woman. I'm so proud of you," said Dad.

The truth is, I was in shock.

Mom and Dad cooked and washed dishes together and helped me plant flowers in the garden. One night, we even clowned for the camera in silly hats and makeup. Friends dropped off meals and cards and took me for walks. My brother came to visit. A friend from high school sent me a sympathy message that he said he rewrote twenty-five times. Another e-mailed one simple line: "I love you."

Mark came to bed with me every night. He had been so strong, but he cried when I had a glass of wine, the first alcohol I'd had in months. Slowly, ever so slowly, I began to fall apart, too.

My brother told me that he and his wife were going to Wisconsin with some friends, and I sobbed after talking to him because I didn't know when I'd feel that light and carefree again. My belly began receding: the abrupt curve from my breasts to stomach disappeared, and only a bulge remained. I felt aching, twisting, pulling, as my body reversed course, and the blood flowed out. It was like moving back in time, the ultimate emotional whiplash.

The hormones were hammering me. I still tested positive for pregnancy weeks after the abortion, and just when I thought it couldn't get any worse, I noticed round wet patches spreading across my T-shirt one afternoon. My breasts had begun leaking milk. I drank coffee every time my mood dipped, which put me on a weird caffeinated plane, neither normal nor depressed. My hairstylist opened her salon early one day so I could color my hair without the caterwauling of other clients and stylists.

I tried not to "get ahead of my headlights," as my stepfather, Patrick, advised, and focused on the smallest of decisions: what to put in my coffee or what shoes to wear. I noticed that as evening came, the sadness caught up with me as if I had left it behind on the road during the day and now we were both pulling into the same motel to spend the night. Looking back, I probably should have taken some kind of antidepressant, despite Mark's misgivings, or forced myself to start working again.

Mark and I saw a counselor to ease the tension that was getting worse between us. My depression triggered painful memories of his ex-wife's mental illness, causing him to withdraw. I knew he wanted me to be better, to be my old self. I couldn't rush it and felt pressured. I wanted him to be with me constantly, but he was grieving, too, and so I spent hours communicating with other women through an anonymous online message board. The weirdest thing of all was that sometimes I thought I was still pregnant. Even though I knew better, I found myself wondering what November would bring.

Mark came home after a night out at a pub with Phil. Their usual conversation was a back-and-forth of jibes and insults, laughter and banter. Mark played up his cool British irony, Phil his gruff sarcasm, even as their genuine affection for each other grew. This time, as private as he was, Mark said he had confided in Phil.

After a few pints of Guinness, talk turned to their dashed

expectations of fatherhood and their shared experiences of loss. Mark said he described to Phil his anguish at the lack of information and statistics, of not knowing what course of action to take.

"Utterly, utterly frustrating," he told Phil. "And just when I had come around to thinking about what it would mean to be a parent. A father."

"I'm really sorry, man," Phil said. "I understand. It's a hard thing to go through." The bar was dark, and Phil had begun to cry, but Mark doubted anyone else noticed the tears.

Mark told me how moved he was by Phil's empathy. "He was virtually holding my hand, and it felt good," he said.

When I finally went for a follow-up appointment with my ob-gyn, she told me the results of the tissue autopsy: the fetus was an entire month behind schedule with severe growth retardation and signs of deformities consistent with full trisomy 22. We probably would not have had a live baby. She also told me my chromosome blood test was normal, and soon we would find out that Mark's was, too, making it likely we could have a healthy pregnancy in the future.

That news helped speed our healing process in the coming months, despite occasional reminders of that horrible time.

One afternoon, Mark and I decided to check out the Museum of Science's exhibit on the human body, a one-of-a-kind plastination project that depicted preserved corpses in various poses and highlighted anatomical specimens. It was accompanied by an IMAX film, and I thought the science would be fascinating.

The film, it turned out, was largely about pregnancy, with the main story line of a woman expecting her first baby. There we were, Mark and I, emerging from our grief, confronted by three-dimensional, apartment building–sized images of a woman having an ultrasound, embryos developing, and a newborn baby being swathed in a blanket. I began simultaneously laughing and crying.

Carey recalled how she had gone to anatomy class during her Knight fellowship when she was six months pregnant, only to find out it was the day that birth defects were being discussed.

"All the babies born without intestines and throats and you name it . . . sheesh!!" she said. "I'm so sorry you guys were hit with that. The only bright side is that maybe it was so in your face that it could act as an exercise in desensitization." Maybe. Maybe not.

To celebrate our third anniversary that September of the day we met, Mark and I brought a bottle of champagne to our astronomy professor, Sam, who happened to be conducting a special lecture in the observatory. Mark gave me a square card printed with black-and-white stars. For all we had endured, we had not lost each other.

"It has been three years since we met that night under the stars. You were a stranger, yet I felt your soul was familiar, attractive, a lost part of my own," he wrote. "And, in the weeks that followed, I knew that I had found my soul mate."

I felt the same way. "Your love gives meaning to my life and warms it with the depth of your compassion, the heat of desire, and the spark of kinship," I wrote him.

I had begun freelancing and taking science classes again, slowly rebuilding my life even as something loomed: the due date. Mark was willing to just ignore it. I couldn't.

"I don't care where we go, but I really don't want to be home that day," I told him.

"I understand. Where would you like to go?"

"A totally different environment. A cabin in the woods. The Ritz-Carlton. The Fairmont?" I didn't want to risk sliding back into grief. Nature or luxury, or both, would be distracting.

When we arrived at the hotel, the receptionist surprised us with an upgrade, courtesy of a friend. To the Presidential Suite. We dined at a long dining room table fit for dignitaries, made love in a four-poster bed surrounded by antiques, luxuriated in a giant bubble bath, and had breakfast in fluffy white robes at a table overlooking Copley Square.

Beth joined me there for coffee after Mark left for work, agape at the sheer size of the suite, and we pretended to be celebrities taking a break between interviews on our publicity tour.

"If I have to answer the same questions about what I'm wearing another hundred times today, I think I'm going to lose my mind," she teased. "And the flashes from the paparazzi cameras are blinding me."

"Oh, me, too. Me, too," I said in a bad British accent as I raised my pinkie to take a sip of coffee.

I nearly forgot that had things been different, I would have been a mother that day.

Several weeks later, Mark and I took his mother, who was visiting from Wales, to spend Thanksgiving with my family. Before joining everyone at my brother's house, we brought Ruth over to Mom's and asked if they'd like to go for a walk with us. No, no, they said, shooing us away. Go ahead.

Mark and I strolled along red cobblestones to the Baha'i temple down the street. It was one of my favorite places in the world, a towering lacy dome overlooking Lake Michigan. We walked up the steps, and Mark drew me to one side.

"Is there a place where we can get a good view?" he asked. Construction scaffolding encircled part of the temple. "Let's stop here a moment. Look at the light. Look at how it arcs across the whiteness."

He tilted his head up to the bright blue sky, and I followed his gaze. We often paused in silent moments like these together. He reached inside his camera bag and, to my utter shock, he pulled out a small blue box.

"Go on, open it," he said, smiling. For the first time, I noticed he was a bit nervous and excited.

I did, and inside was a sparkling diamond ring. There was no mistaking it for anything but an engagement ring, except that we had never done the traditional thing, and I had never expected it. I wore the white-gold band every day and had assumed that would be my only ring for the rest of our lives.

"It represents my love for you," he said, slipping it onto my ring finger. The sparkle of the gem, the happiness in his eyes, the blue of the sky, the white of the dome. The flutter of my heart.

He told me how he had conspired to find out my ring size, hiding a caliper under our bed, and that our mothers were waiting for us to share the news. In fact, I half expected them to come bursting out of the bushes. His card read, "I've been married to you from the moment we met. You are the origin of all that is fine and good in life."

Our life was good. We traveled for a month to New Zealand, a kind of nonmarital honeymoon capped by a week on an idyllic South Pacific island. In that short period of time, I became pregnant but quickly miscarried on the island. Disappointing and sad, yet it felt like a victory because Mark and I came through it with our relationship more intact than ever, handling each other lovingly, and to me that made all the difference.

"Our daughter is coming," he said time and again. And I believed him.

★ ★ ★

Strange, feverish symptoms gripped me days after we returned home from overseas that February. My joints ached and felt brittle, as if they were made of fragile glass. I suffered chills and sweats and diarrhea for days until I suffered dehydration severe enough for Mark to take me to the emergency room. My legs turned beet red, and my platelet count plummeted. The diagnosis: dengue fever.

I stayed in the hospital for one week and came home six pounds lighter with my legs still pinkish, but with the pain in my bones (no wonder they call it "break-bone fever") beginning to fade. A few weeks later, and I was back to my old self. And more, besides.

I was pregnant.

The first ultrasound showed that all was well, as the familiar technician repeatedly reassured us.

"You can ask me over and over again if everything is all right, and my answer will be the same," he said, smiling. "It's normal." Normal. We couldn't say it enough.

The sight of the heartbeat, that pulsing little light, made me gasp with relief and astonishment. This time around, though, we tried to be more detached. I continued to drink my morning coffee and understood that chromosomes were beyond my control, and I could not know for sure what was going on at a level too minute to comprehend. I knew I would be relieved if our other tests came out okay, and the real worries could begin—the routine ones, the ones I thought I could handle.

I went to the maternity store (Destination Maternity—were it so simple). When the cashier asked for my e-mail, I requested to be taken off the mailing list to avoid the deluge of baby supplies newsletters and parenting magazines we had received the previous year.

"We're waiting for our genetic test results," I explained, and she nodded and somberly handed over the bags.

Friends offered cribs and baby clothes so often it would have made any other pregnant woman giddy with anticipation. Mark and I did not hesitate to decline, even if it meant losing the goods no one wanted to store: Thank you for your offer, we replied, but no, we don't want anything until we are much closer to having a child here, in our arms, in our home. We know you'll understand.

We had the CVS and were told the chance for a chromosomal abnormality to happen in a subsequent pregnancy depended upon the type of chromosomal abnormality. In general, it was 1 percent or less. This meant there was a 99 percent chance that it would be fine, although my age increased the odds. Karen, the genetic counselor, told us we could get preliminary test results in two days, but there had been cases where those had been wrong. Normal had turned out to be abnormal; abnormal, normal. No thanks, we said. We want certainty.

A week passed. The wait was grueling. The anxiety I pent up during the day bubbled up in nightmares when I was asleep. I rolled over and put my arms around Mark one night, waking him up.

"You're not worried?" I asked.

"No, I'm not. And I wish you wouldn't worry so much, honey. There's no point," he said, brushing hair off my face and cupping my chin in his hand. "We can't control what's going to happen. We can only hope for the best."

It took me a while to notice that he was spending an inordinate amount of time on his computer, in the dark of his office, headphones on, eyes glued to the screen. He wouldn't admit it, but, yes, he was anxious, too.

We had no idea what the next few months would bring: Would I be having an abortion this month, or preparing to sign up for childbirth classes? Would my parents come in to comfort or celebrate? I didn't map out any scenarios in my head because I knew how easily one could be overturned by another.

I called Karen on a Friday. She said she would call us early Monday morning if she had results or in the afternoon if she had an explanation of why the results were taking so long. Monday came and went. Tuesday morning. It was twelve days after the test—no call. I couldn't sit still any longer and headed out to Target to browse the anonymous, crowded aisles. I was looking for something, only it wasn't on any of those shelves.

Somewhere between the women's underwear section and handbags, my cell phone rang. It was home.

"Karen called. Everything's okay," Mark said, "and it's a girl."

The words streamed out of him, and I could hear his happiness and relief, and his desire to give that to me over the phone. It felt unreal, his disembodied voice, the fluorescent lights, the bright red shopping carts. We were going to have a baby. A girl.

"Really? Are you kidding? Really? Everything's all right?" Tell me again, and again, and again, my voice pleaded.

"Yes, honey, everything is fine. Perfectly normal," he said, laughing.

"What did she say, exactly?" I asked.

"She said, 'This is Karen. Everything is fine. Do you want to know the gender?' And I said, 'Yes!'" Mark told me. "And she said, 'It's a girl.'"

I was speechless. My arms full of paper towel, shaving

cream, and batteries, I was ready to bolt from the store. I couldn't get home fast enough and, when I did, I ran into Mark's arms. He had a broad grin on his face.

"It's everything we want," he said.

Our due date was early November. Mom called and whooped with relief, and Dad laughed. The rest of the family was overjoyed. We called and e-mailed close friends.

"Thank fucking God. That's wonderful news," said Anna, my college friend. "I almost cried when I read your e-mail. And yay, yay, yay, it's a girl!"

As the weeks passed, I had difficulty breathing as the baby grew and pressed my internal organs up into my chest. I was claustrophobic and needed the windows and curtains open at all times. I gained forty-five pounds and got hemorrhoids for the first time in my life. My fingers and ankles swelled. Our bed disappeared under body pillows.

I loved it.

We hired a doula, and I made lists of supplies. We read books to my belly at night—*Mouse Paint* and *Goodnight Moon*—and stacks of parenting books piled up on my nightstand. My friends teased me that, ever the student and journalist, I was studying how to raise a baby. We had a name. And even though we sifted through thousands of choices, it was the same name we always returned to because, as Mark told me so often, this was the girl who would always come.

By late October, the baristas at the corner Starbucks anticipated my order when I waddled up to the counter: "A tall coffee, and a baby, please," I wheezed. Ba-da-bum. It always got a laugh.

I began having contractions weeks before the baby was due, occasionally for hours at a time. Donna came to visit the first weekend in November, and my contractions grew stronger as we worked on a giant and intricate puzzle that showed a map of the world. By the time she left, everything save the endless blue pieces of ocean had been assembled, and still no baby came.

The due date passed, and we decided to be induced two days later to avoid any unnecessary risks by waiting too long. Our entire family flew into town.

"Ready to have a baby, honey?" Mark asked me that morning as we called our doula and headed out the door, the car packed with pillows, a cooler, birth ball, and clothes. It was a brisk and sunny November day, my favorite time of year.

"I am," I said, kissing him and winking at the sky.

I labored for hours, the contractions winding up, then slowing until nearly imperceptible. The doctor stripped my membranes, ratcheted up the pitocin. Labor up, labor down. My cheeks flushed, and Wanda, the doula, massaged my swollen feet. Mark rubbed my legs. Mom held my arm. We decided it was time to break my water, knowing that a C-section could be in the offing if things did not progress.

People told us birth would not be what we expected. They weren't kidding. We intended to go natural, and now I was having just about every intervention you could ask for.

The umbilical fluid rushed out warm and soothing, and suddenly it felt as if a razor was slicing my abdomen into shreds. Not only was the pitocin maxed out, but there was no longer a cushion between my baby and my body. It was her against me, me against her. It hurt more than anything I had ever experienced in my life.

Was I ready to have a baby? Mark had asked. Yes. *Now.*

Wanda told me to relax my shoulders and breathe deeply. Mark had one hand on me, one on the video camera. A minute or two passed between the contractions, and I clenched my jaw. My whole body clenched.

"I can't do it. I need a painkiller," I said until they could tell I really meant it.

The nurse was out the door. Twenty minutes later, the epidural was in, and Wanda told me to rest. I slept for nearly an hour. When I woke, the baby's heartbeat was slowing. I was ten centimeters dilated, and she was there, ready to go. The doctor, not my ob-gyn, but a pleasant enough woman from her practice, rushed in. Mark and Mom each held a leg. White-coated women clustered between them. I pushed.

They told me I was doing great.

"You're almost there," the doctor said.

"Just a little more," said the nurse.

I stopped believing them, and I focused on the sharp ache below that felt like my pelvis was about to crack. I filled my lungs and visualized the baby moving down, down. They held up a mirror so I could peek at the top of her head. It was only an itty-bitty sliver, a glimpse before she retracted back inside of me. All this time, had I been doing *anything?*

"Take the mirror away," I moaned. "Put the video camera down!" I couldn't be distracted.

Two hours passed, a shock of dark hair poked out. And she was here, pink and wailing and kicking. Exquisite.

Dear family and friends: Emma Lulu was born at 9:06 PM last Saturday after a fairly short labor. She's a healthy 7.4 lbs and about 20 inches long. We're overjoyed! She seems to be a very alert and happy baby—and we'd swear she already knows how to smile. She has huge big toes and a killer grip! And after the initial exhaustion, both mother and babe are doing very well.

Epilogue One: Carey

I went to my mother's grave the other day. I almost never go there. For me, she's not there. But Liz was visiting her in-laws in central Massachusetts, and as I drove to their house, I felt a creeping sense of mournful déjà vu. Sure enough, the Jewish cemetery where most of my Worcester relatives are buried was just a two-minute detour away.

The ruts in the dirt road made my car bounce like a boat in choppy water. The lot where I parked was deserted, the trees bare, the winter sky as granite gray as the headstones. I started crying as soon as I headed up the pathway toward my mother's grave. It wasn't just that I missed her. It was that all of us, her family, were so cruelly deprived of her. And even worse, that *she* was missing so much—never to meet her own grandchildren, never to grow old with the loyal man she loved.

I stood before the half-empty stone, one side left blank in anticipation of my dad. In my bones, I could still feel the exact sensation of hugging her, the fragile shoulders and soft, tousled curls. My own shoulders hunched higher, and my hands dug deeper into my coat pockets.

"We're doing really well, Mum," I said softly. "Sprax is an amazing father and husband, and the kids are totally delightful. And of course Dad is the best of all possible grandfathers."

A deep, trembling sigh. "I just wish you were here. You would have loved them so, so much, and you would have been the best grandmother in the world. As you would say, it just really sucks. That's the simple truth."

I swiped at my eyes and nose, blinking hard and looking around at the nearby graves. Many had pebbles on top, to show that visitors had stopped by.

"It's hard for me sometimes, being a mother. I'm not as relaxed about it as you were. I wish I could take it more for granted. I'm afraid, a lot. But any good qualities I have as a mother, I know I got from you. I understand you so much better now, and it comforts me to know that we must have made you as happy as Liliana and Tully make me. I'm so glad we did that."

I thought of my friend, Robin, who had recently died of cancer at fifty-four, leaving eleven-year-old twins. She had met her husband-to-be right after turning forty and giving up on marriage. When she got her diagnosis, she told a friend that she had gotten everything she wanted in her life, and could accept her fate, if not for leaving her children.

I would feel the same way, I thought. I know I would. Like my mother, Robin had been horribly cheated out of decades, but before she was cheated, she had been very blessed, and knew it full well. I had new things to fear, but one thing no longer scared me: that I would miss out on what for me is the center of life.

"I hope I don't die for a long time, Mum," I said. "But even if I die tomorrow, I'll have had everything I could ever ask for."

I thought of myself at thirty-nine. I had desperately wanted a baby. I felt an abstract emptiness in my arms. But I knew so little about what the fulfillment of that wish would mean. I did not know, I could not understand in advance, that my life would fill with richness—and change, and change, and change again, as babies grew into children, as marriage wore off its rough edges, as the years marched forward not for me alone, but for all of us together.

Epilogue Two: Beth

WITH FAIR REGULARITY, I COME SKIPPING HOME like a ten-year-old to inform Phil that I've made a new girlfriend. I might be part cynic and skeptic, but I believe the world is full of people I want to meet.

My girlfriends are scattered across the globe; some I've known for over forty years. But their embrace, which is fundamental to my life, is only a phone call, e-mail, walk around the block, train ride, eight-hour flight, away. Maintaining friendship requires work, but the very best kind. There are so many things we give each other: laughter, companionship, unyielding support, emergency childcare, prescription drugs, advice, our hearts, in ways we never give to men.

Carey, on the day she met me, gave me hope. And Pam gave me Carey. We make a funny little triumvirate. Three women connected first by a stranger's sperm, then by friendship, and ultimately, by a triple love story. Without Carey and Pam, and the shove 8282 gave me, there might be no Gareth.

And at this point, five years into his life, I don't know who I'd be without Gareth. Without every piece of him, down to the birthmark on the bottom of his right foot. He's my child, and I love him without reservation, but if I had the option of changing anything, would I? Maybe. I'd give him a higher frustration threshold, make the world a place that hadn't, at such a young age, turned him into a nail-biter.

As a kid I bit my nails, too. Sometimes I still do. At times, the world is big and scary for all of us, and I know there are times I'd rather batten down the hatches, pull the shades, and turn off for a week. But I no longer have that option. Someone depends upon me. That, too, is scary. There are so many things I could screw up, and I'm convinced at least once a day that I've done something to permanently chip away at Gareth's ego. I hold him too hard when I'm angry, I get in his face and yell, I hear my voice in his when he's frustrated. I fear that I don't appreciate the good moments sufficiently.

But the love. The overwhelming, limitless love I feel for my son. No matter what he does (though I say this prior to his becoming an adolescent), everything falls in line behind the love.

One night, long after I put Gareth to bed, I heard him calling. "Ma-ma... Ma-ma...," in a sweet singsong. When I opened his door, he was lying in his Captain Hook bed, patting the space next to him. "Come be with me," he said.

I lay down next to him, and he put his arm around me. "Please stay," he said. "For a long while."

"Forever," I told him.

Recently, I found a piece of paper. It was the amnio report from my first pregnancy. Stamped on it was "Patient Does Not Want Information on Gender of Fetus." And there it was. Information on the gender of the fetus. It had been a boy. Without warning, six years later, I knew what I'd lost. It's true that some moments simply, and physically, take your breath away.

I immediately called Pam. And began to cry about a decision I didn't regret. She was in Chicago, a thousand miles away, but that didn't matter. She was there, with her own experience, her own Information on Gender of Fetus, and her true, true friendship.

I count myself lucky. Very lucky. Once I gave up chasing the dream, I found it. First in a cryogenic freezer, then in the middle of winter in a lodge with a slice of chocolate cake. Before I met Phil, I hadn't given up hope for a family. I'd actually found it in the form of a stranger's sperm.

Maybe this is a story of luck tripled. Carey took the leap to buy the sperm. Didn't need it. I took the sperm, didn't need it. Repeat with Pam. I'd argue that we would have met our goals for families regardless, but instead of just meeting them, they were exceeded. We got to have not just birth stories but love stories as well.

So I start up a "Book of Beautiful Things." A book that lists three things, every day, that are beautiful in my life. And it's so easy: Gareth in the tub; Phil coming home at the end of the day; apple picking; my mother always calling on the full moon so she can look at it with Gareth; going to dinner with girlfriends; love. And there it is. With no effort, *six* things. Six beautiful things.

Epilogue Three: Pam

Emma is two years old. She's a blue-eyed blonde, tall for her age. She begins every day with a smile, and she quakes with excitement at the sight of a book. Her skin is as soft as a peony petal, and her body smells like biscuits. She is delicious.

We live north of Chicago these days, both Mark and I working from a rented home several blocks from Lake Michigan and mere miles from where I grew up. We came here for many reasons—for the love of extended family, for a change of environment.

I can't help but wonder if Donor 8282 gave Carey the patience for Sprax, and Beth the strength to reclaim her life after a failed marriage and dashed dreams. To me, 8282 gave hope—hope that, despite the bad choices that left me unhappily single at thirty-eight, I could remain true to my romantic ideals.

In accepting donor sperm, I also accepted that I could script my life and not wait for it to happen to me. I could follow an untraditional route and still be happy. I trusted those instincts, and walked straight into a love story.

Motherhood is the best thing I ever did, apart from being with Mark. I have a little person who has his eyes and my laugh—the trademark guffaw that one friend compared to a pig seeking truffles. It is also the hardest thing, as mothers since time immemorial can attest. The relentlessness of the tasks required in tending to a small child is just that: relentless. Diapers, feedings, baths, laundry. Sometimes I can't get enough of taking care of Emma, her happy and good little being; rarely it's too much. This is, after all, what I signed up for.

Carey described how her family is like a closed electrical circuit. I know the feeling. My own power dims when something is wrong with Emma or Mark—a runny nose, a disappointment at work—and shines brighter in their moments of joy—a new word or a beautiful photograph.

I will be lucky to see Emma's children, if she has any, but most likely will not meet my great-grandchildren. Mark, who grew up as an only child, and I go back and forth every day about whether to give her a sibling.

"I guess I'm just an optimist at heart and believe you can bring wonderful people into the world," he told me one night as we sat outside a restaurant, Emma sleeping in her stroller beside us. He shook his head and smiled. "I just can't imagine life without her."

We wonder about our energy and resources. There are no guarantees that our children would be close friends or that a little brother or sister would be healthy (at forty-four, I am terrified of faulty genetics). There is no evidence that having two makes you fear less for one; in fact, the opposite may be true. In any case, I know that Emma will grow up surrounded by loving family and friends.

We never had a baby shower for her. But on the hundredth day after her birth, some of my closest girlfriends threw a party welcoming her to the world—and to our sisterhood. More than a dozen women showed up at Beth's house, including my mother, loading countless dishes, from curried chicken salad to lox and bagels to a strawberry "Happy 100 Days" cheesecake, onto a sprawling table decorated with white-and-pink tulips and yellow rubber ducks.

They each contributed something else: A letter to Emma. With advice and well wishes, all bound in a linen book with her photo on the cover. They wrote about the fragile, upside-down times we live in. About the importance of kindness, learning, and speaking the truth. How Sean Connery is the best James Bond, and, while a lot of things can disappoint, getting a driver's license is not one of them. How no one knows the big answers, and everyone makes mistakes. How they would help protect and love Emma always. How much she was wanted.

"You are blessed with parents who worked so hard to have you, and who loved you years before you ever arrived," Beth wrote.

Later that afternoon, after we had noshed and chatted and drunk and laughed, everyone sat in a circle on the living room carpet. Emma nestled in my lap, warm and content, while two of the women introduced an ancient ritual with symbolic objects to predict her future. If she showed interest in a needle and thread, she would live a long life; if a book, she would become a successful scholar.

Kneeling in front of us, Carey slowly slid a dollar bill before Emma. No response. A spool of black thread, a small bowl of sugar, one of salt, and a worn paperback. Still, nothing.

"How about this, sweetie?" Carey said with each try, nudging the object forward. Emma drooled down the front of her pink flowered dress.

A blank notepad. Carey was determined this time. One push, another. Emma raised her right arm toward it, delighting the writers among us.

Beth gently tied a red thread around Emma's ankle for protection, and we each wished something special for my baby girl, like Sleeping Beauty being blessed by the fairies. These workingwomen—white and black, single and married, childless and mothers—offered from personal experience what they had discovered a girl really needs in this world. ("A different kind of list than my generation," remarked my mother.)

"Humor," Mimi said.

"Inspiration," said Lisa.

"Flat abs and a small ass," said Maria. Resourcefulness. Health. Peace of mind. Wisdom. Passion. Vision. Being able to dance. Hope.

"Love," Beth said.

"Luck," said Carey.

"Friends like these," I said, feeling weepy.

As I stood up to thank them, balancing Emma in my arms, I stepped on a plate of birthday cake, prompting Carey to amend her wish.

"And grace!"

Everyone laughed. I glanced over at Carey and Beth and knew we were probably thinking the same thing: That here we were, mothers, and our longed-for children might one day be reenacting this very scene—all grown up, perhaps with children of their own. A piece of their hearts, exposed, for all the world to see.

Coda: The Sperm

You are wondering, of course, what happened to the sperm.

It did not languish forever in its ice-encrusted vials. It did get used. With all three of us ensconced in loving relationships, Beth heard that Lynn, an old college acquaintance, was seriously thinking about becoming a single mother at forty-two. Beth got in touch with her, and after a few rounds of e-mail, the vials were once again on their frozen way, this time to Manhattan.

But Lynn had some fertility problems. It didn't work.

We followed her progress from afar over e-mail, rooting for her, and when it became clear that 8282 had doubly failed—for Lynn neither became pregnant nor met her true love—we could only feel sad for her. Back to Real Life, with all its usual disappointments.

A few months later, we stumbled across the Donor Sibling Registry.

The registry is an online entity that allows the children of donor sperm or eggs to try to find half siblings, children of the same donor. The more ambitious can also try to track down the donors themselves, though those attempts tend to run into major roadblocks of anonymity and usually fail.

Of course, the moment we found the registry, we searched for California Cryobank Donor 8282, burning with curiosity about what might have been. It couldn't have been simpler to find him on the well-organized bulletin board. And there, the first thing we read was a posting from the mother of a 8282 child who was hoping to have another—and seeking extra vials from other women because he had stopped donating and declined contact.

Yet 8282 brought good fortune to many others: at least eight different women had borne nine children using his sperm. We checked the site for months, and, eventually, Donor 8282—going by the user name "Redbull"—posted a message agreeing to communicate by e-mail and provide sperm to mothers seeking half siblings for their (and his) offspring.

Our own vials failed to produce a child, but for us, perhaps they served their purpose. We're not saying that the sperm had the power to call in galloping princes. Clearly, it did not. But we do believe there is magic in the moment when a woman becomes convinced that she can reach her single-minded goal, to bear a child, by herself.

Carey Goldberg has been the Boston bureau chief of the *New York Times,* Moscow correspondent for the *Los Angeles Times,* and a health and science reporter at the *Boston Globe.* She now writes happily at home, where she is developing thewikioflove.com.

Beth Jones is a writer and educator who has contributed to the *Boston Globe,* the *New York Times,* and numerous academic journals; her next project is a novel. She plans to climb many more frozen waterfalls.

Pamela Ferdinand is an award-winning freelance journalist and former reporter for the *Washington Post, Boston Globe,* and *Miami Herald.* She remains an incorrigible romantic.

Carey and Beth live near Boston with their families; Pamela and her family live outside Chicago. Still close, the authors continue to believe in the power of good friends, love, and a little luck.

For more information:
threewishesthebook.com
bycareygoldberg.com
beth-jones.com
pamelaferdinand.com